D1601671

POLITICAL EXPRESSION
AND
ETHNICITY

To

J. Clyde Mitchell

'Race relations in New Zealand have never been, nor are they likely to be plagued by a colour problem, but rather by colourless ideas on how such problems exist and what needs to be done to ensure that they deteriorate no further' (Matiu Rata, 31 May 1981).

POLITICAL EXPRESSION AND ETHNICITY

Statecraft and Mobilisation in the Maori World

KAYLEEN M. HAZLEHURST

PRAEGER

Westport, Connecticut
London

Library of Congress Cataloging-in-Publication Data

Hazlehurst, Kayleen M.
    Political expression and ethnicity : statecraft and mobilisation
in the Maori world / Kayleen M. Hazlehurst.
      p.   cm.
    Includes bibliographical references and index.
    ISBN 0-275-94458-1 (alk. paper)
    1. Maori (New Zealand people)—Politics and government. 2. Maori
(New Zealand people)—Ethnic identity. 3. Self-determination,
National—New Zealand.   I. Title.
    DU423.P63H36 1993
    305.8'08994—dc20   92-35349

British Library Cataloguing in Publication Data is available.

Library of Congress Catalog Card Number: 92-35349
ISBN: 0-275-94458-1

First published in 1993

Praeger Publishers, 88 Post Road West, Westport, CT 06881
An imprint of Greenwood Publishing Group, Inc.

Printed in the United States of America

The paper used in this book complies with the
Permanent Paper Standard issued by the National
Information Standards Organization (Z39.48-1984).

10 9 8 7 6 5 4 3 2 1

CONTENTS

ILLUSTRATIONS

Photographs follow page 124.

ABBREVIATIONS

ADC   Auckland District [Maori] Council

MWA   Maori Warden's Association

MWWL   Maori Women's Welfare League

NZMC   New Zealand Maori Council

WCIP   World Council of Indigenous Peoples

Maori Usage

Many Maori words have gained common usage in New Zealand and have not been italicised throughout this book. For those who are not familiar with their meaning an explanation is given when they are first appear. A glossary at the back of the book is also available for quick reference. It is common not to pluralise Maori words with the addition of an 's'. The word 'Maori', for example, refers to both the individual and the people. This will always be clear from the context of the sentence. In order to facilitate the editing and typesetting process, macrons marking vowel length have not been included. Linguistics students may wish to consult *A Dictionary of the Maori Language*, by H.W. Williams, Government Printer, Wellington, for this information.

ACKNOWLEDGEMENTS

I am deeply grateful for the aroha and generosity of so many people in the Maori world who shared with me their knowledge, sentiments, and beliefs. In particular I have been inspired by hours of patient discourse with the following people, who are identified by the public positions they occupied at the time of my study in 1981: Hon. Matiu Rata, president, Mana Motuhake Party and candidate for the Northern Maori seat; Sir Graham Latimer, president, New Zealand Maori Council and chairman of the Tai Tokerau District Maori Council; Sir Henare Ngata, chairman, Tai Rawhiti District Council, Gisborne; Hon. Ben Couch, Minister for Police and Minister for Maori Affairs; Dr Ranginui Walker, chairman, Auckland District Maori Council and executive member of the Mana Motuhake Party; Dr Patrick Hohepa, secretary, Auckland District Maori Council and secretary of the Mana Motuhake Party; Professor Sid Mead, executive member of the Mana Motuhake Party; Arapeta Tahana, candidate for the Eastern Maori seat, Mana Motuhake Party; Amsterdam Reedy, candidate for the Southern Maori seat, Mana Motuhake Party; Eva Rickard, candidate for the Western Maori seat, Mana Motuhake Party; the Most Reverend Sir Paul Reeves, Anglican Archbishop of Auckland, Primate and Archbishop of New Zealand.

I am also grateful for the recollections and comments of former Prime Ministers Sir Robert Muldoon and Sir Wallace Rowling, and of the following members of the Kirk Labour Cabinet: Hon. Bob Tizard, Hon. Dr Martyn Finlay Q.C., Hon. Tom McGuigan, Hon. Henry May, and Hon. Warren Freer. For their professional guidance and assistance I wish to thank my teachers at the University of Toronto, Professors Gavin Smith, William Dunning, Shuichi Nagata, David Turner, Peter Carstens, Tom McFeat, Barry Wellman, Steve Berkowitz and other members of my advisory committee. I wish also to thank the Maori Studies Centres at both the University of Auckland and Victoria University for their assistance. And I owe a particular debt to those Maori leaders who read and commented on drafts of my manuscript: the Hon. Matiu Rata, Dr Ranginui Walker, Sir Graham Latimer, and Sir Henare Ngata. I have benefited greatly from the timely advice and criticism of Dr J. Clyde Mitchell, Fellow of Nuffield College, University of Oxford; Professor Robert Chapman, Department of Political Studies, University of Auckland; and Professor Erik Schwimmer, Department d'anthropologie, Université Laval.

For their cheerful and reliable supply of information, I am indebted to the staff of the National Library of New Zealand, the Alexander Turnbull Library, and the National Archives, Wellington; the Auckland Public Library; and particularly to Barry Hanfling, Department of Statistics, Auckland, and Robyn Schleiger, New Zealand High Commission, Canberra. Beverley Short and Melva Butterfield provided valuable information on the creation of the Alliance of opposition parties. I wish also to thank Maori linguist, Rhonda Paku, from the Maori Studies Department, Victoria University, for checking the manuscript for Maori vocabulary and usage, Dr Marion Stell for preparing the index and Hilary Kent for copy editing the final draft. Photographs for publication were generously provided by the National Art Gallery and Museum, Wellington; *New Zealand Herald*; *Auckland Star*; Anthropology Department, University of Auckland; and Parliament House.

Finally, I must thank my family for their patience. Without the continued interest and support of my late father Peter Morrison and my mother Una Morrison this research would never have been completed. My husband Professor Cameron Hazlehurst, who has been my steadfast critic, I especially thank for his sustained editorial advice and encouragement.

INTRODUCTION

In 1965 James E. Ritchie (1965: 80-6) argued that the concept of pan-Maori nationalism, entertained at that time by New Zealand scholars, was a myth, 'sustained by the appearance of co-operation on customary occasions and by a limited reciprocity between restricted sets of residents in local groups or kinship networks'. When I embarked on a study of Maori political expression in 1980 the importance of testing the question of pan-Maori nationalism once again was highlighted by current literature on ethnicity. I suspected that although there was no formal national political system, it was possible by the 1980s that an effective national Maori network had evolved. That is, that there could be a loosely knit but discernible grand network of associations and exchange between major and minor Maori interest groups throughout the country.

Modern discourse about 'the Maori world' suggested an awareness of a bounded ethno-political domain. Such an entity was too large to examine in its entirety. I expected, however, to be able to demonstrate through the study of recent history and contemporary socio-political action that substantial links between a number of major interest groups had been established and were presently being exercised. When one approached the phenomenon from the point of view of interaction, communication, and potential mobilisation, pan-Maori nationalism might take on a more tangible form.

During six weeks spent with him at Oxford prior to my entering the field, J. Clyde Mitchell encouraged me to apply the general concept of network analysis to my study of Maori political elites, rather than the more formalistic, mathematical network approach then used by sociologists. It would be more illuminating, he suggested, if I were to analyse Maori interaction in defined 'situations': for example, to study political strategy within the context of selected events, such as an election campaign. This 'situational' data, which Mitchell advised me to collect through traditional anthropological participant-observation techniques, should reveal the networking actions of the actors.[1]

My original fieldwork began in November 1980 and ended in December 1981. During that time I was based in Auckland city, the headquarters of the recently launched Mana Motuhake Party and the home of several leaders of the party. Mana Motuhake, the first Maori political party, had come into being some months before my arrival. Its emergence provided a unique opportunity to investigate the extent to which 'Maoriness' was dependent on, or determinative of, the rhetoric and ideological affirmations of a modern political movement. In addition to regular interviews and numerous daily communications with a dozen or so key Mana Motuhake figures and other Maori leaders, I attended political rallies, meetings, conferences, and social events around the countryside and in other major centres of the North Island.

On subsequent visits to New Zealand between 1982 and 1991 additional inquiries were made to clarify or check details of particular events, relationships, and the interpretation of documentary sources. Although most of what is presented here on Maori attitudes, beliefs, customs, and institutional arrangements remains valid as a description of the state of affairs a decade after my original fieldwork, I have generally written in the past tense so as to emphasise the particularities of time and place.

In Canada in the 1970s, I had seen something at first hand of the way in which the indigenous people in that country had been seeking greater self-determination. I had noted how, as Boldt (1981: 208) was to put it: `the pan-Indian political and cultural movement is forging networks of communication, participation and identification between tribal groupings'. In 1974 George Manuel and Michael Posluns had asserted that the descendants of the original inhabitants of Canada occupied a unique position of dependency and disadvantage. So powerfully different were the life experiences of the Indian from the European population that Manuel and Posluns called this phenomenon the 'Fourth World'. Native inhabitants, they argued, were never likely to gain independence in their own land and seemed powerless against the superstructures of the welfare state which administered their lives (Manuel and Posluns 1974).

During the 1970s there was a growing awareness among Canada's indigenous peoples that their common experience was a foundation for political action. Urban racial discrimination spurred the growth of 'a new expanded, more inclusive and generalized pan-Indian identity' (Boldt 1981: 208). Emerging regional and nationally based Indian, Inuit, and Metis organisations strove to draw their people together through the establishment of offices, the distribution of newsletters, the delegation of leadership, and the organisation of conferences in the Canadian and circumpolar regions.

Similar histories of land loss, population decline, and political subordination were seen to be shared with indigenous people in other countries. The World Council of Indigenous People (WCIP) founded by Manuel, then president of the Canadian Indian Brotherhood, at a conference held in British Columbia in October 1975, brought together nineteen delegates representing groups from Australia, New Zealand, Scandinavia, North America, and Central and South America. In North America, Australia, and New Zealand in particular, the indigenous experience was seen to have striking similarities. Following a period of disease, expropriation, and warfare, as immigrant Europeans settled in these territories, a period of recovery occurred. Government agencies were set up to protect and administer the impoverished and endangered remnants of the indigenous populations. These official bodies, often reflecting a genuine if paternalistic conscience, evolved into the formidable administrations of modern times.

Meanwhile, processes of detachment, deracination, and cultural reconstruction were occurring within the immigrant societies. Removed from the social structures, customs, and values of their homelands, often on the fringes of European society, dependent on trade, local knowledge, and local labour, they were susceptible to intercultural exchange and intermarriage with the indigenous inhabitants. In time the 'mother' cultures of the settlers lost some of their potency, and were clouded by the new identities and objectives of the colonies. Settler societies and governments were increasingly infused with nationalist sentiments.

Behind these similarities, however, are differences in the colonial/indigenous experience which are even more interesting to the scholar. In New Zealand the twentieth century consolidation of settler society produced its own myths, and an ideology of integration - 'One People' notions connoting religious, political, and racial harmony. But the containment, diversion, and dilution of the aspirations of the indigenous Maori population has never been complete. By the 1960s, increasing Maori access to higher levels of education, growing exposure to the hardships of a faltering economy, and the proliferation of political movements which challenged established political structures and attitudes, assimilationist welfare policies, exploitation of the environment, and denial of the rights of citizens began to undermine the stability and predictability of what had become a relatively tranquil society. The 'pathology of normality',[2] the serene superordination of the European or 'Pakeha',[3] was assailed by doubt and social dissonance. Emerging ethno-class consciousness and awareness of 'Fourth World' parallels marked the beginning of a new era in New Zealand history.

MODERN ETHNO-POLITICS

Contests over the meaning of 'ethnicity', its origins and preconditions, were commonplace in the anthropological literature of the 1970s. Was it primordially or circumstantially inspired? Was it fostered or extinguished by urbanisation? Was it involuntary or a consequence of elite manipulation?

One approach cut across much of the debate and provided a unifying perspective. 'Ethnicity', asserted Abner Cohen (1974a: 15), is 'essentially a political phenomenon'. Ethnic groups interact with each other in determining the distribution of power and resources in society:

> To the casual observer ethnicity is taken as a manifestation of conservatism, separatism and stagnation, when on careful analysis we discover that it is a dynamic organisational mechanism involving intensive interaction with other groups.

In his study *Custom and Politics in Urban Africa* (1969) Cohen had earlier concluded that there were two stages of 'political ethnicity'. The first was a process of 'detribalisation', where cultural differences between groups were eroded by 'various cleavages which cut across ethnic lines' creating new alignment and co-operation between these groups. The second was a process of 'retribalisation' where groups began to emphasise their ethnic identity, on the basis of some real and/or symbolic criteria for membership, in order to separate themselves into a distinct category of persons and to avoid assimilation with other groups. Both Cohen (1969) and Bailey (1977) would describe this latter process as strategic change.

Under certain conditions of competition for scarce resources or political power, new categories of ethnicity are thus seen to be created for socio-political purposes. Ethnicity can be redefined and can be used instrumentally to meet the changing economic, social, and political environment or in an attempt to gain greater access to avenues of power and resources hitherto closed off through regular channels. This new emphasis upon ethnicity (or 'retribalisation'), said Cohen (1969: 190-201), was not a display of traditionalism but was a means of organising vis-a-vis other groups in an attempt to protect the vital interests of the group which appeared to be threatened.

While Cohen was right to emphasise the oppositional and instrumental aspects of modern ethnic movements there were other elements to which subsequent writers have drawn attention. 'Ethnic redefinition in subordinate groups' may, Weinrich (1985: 507) argues, 'incorporate elements of identification with significant others, and their values, of the superordinate communities'. Moreover, traditional culture can continue to act as a guide and a reference point to self or group identity, even for some centuries. Spiritual, mythical, moral, and social aspects of traditionalism can be selected and employed to suit the present experience and needs of the minority group.

Primordial attachments may also maintain affective bonds that shape perceptions of common interest and of appropriate bases for mobilisation (McKay 1982). But, Burgess warns, 'many groups engaged in so-called primordial conflict are themselves recent historical creations' (1978: 267). While it may be true, as Geertz contends, that 'some attachments seem to flow more from a sense of natural - some would say spiritual - affinity than from social interaction' (1963: 110), such attachments are likely to remain passive sentiments in the absence of some animating impulse.[4]

Pioneer anthropologists like Evans-Pritchard, Radcliffe-Brown, and Malinowski tried to keep the intruding influence of outside governments and cultures at a respectable distance in their studies. Increasingly, however, these perceptible external influences could not be ignored. Not only because minorities were becoming 'encapsulated political structures' (Bailey 1977), or 'parapolitical structures' (Bailey 1968; Easton 1965b) - that is, 'partly regulated by, partly independent of, larger encapsulating structures' (Bailey 1977) - but because few traditional societies could avoid the necessity to organise or restructure themselves in relation to the wider social and political systems which surrounded them.

Studies in the United States and elsewhere of what have been described as 'persistent peoples' in 'cultural enclaves' (Castile and Kushner 1981) have illustrated a special case of what van den Berghe (1973: 961) describes as 'pluralism':

> a property, or set of properties, of societies wherein several distinct social and/or cultural groups co-exist within the boundaries of a single polity and share a common economic system that makes them interdependent, yet maintain a greater or lesser degree of autonomy and a set of discrete institutional structures in other spheres of social life, notably the family, recreation and religion.

In a refinement of the concept of pluralism, Keyes suggests that it is useful to distinguish between 'plural' societies in which ethnic groups occupy fixed social strata and have rigid boundaries, and 'pluralistic' societies in which groups and individuals choose freely whether or not to participate in ethnic group activity:

> If the members of a non-assimilating ethnic enclave are of sufficient number, they may seek to separate themselves from the society in which they are located to organise themselves into separate political entities. ... On the other hand, previously autonomous groups, such as certain American Indian groups, have exchanged enclave status for that of being an ethnic group within a plural or pluralistic society. (1981: 12-13)

Spicer's studies of 'persistent' peoples (1971: 797; 1980: 347,356) have emphasised the vital link between the maintenance of a common identity and the sense of separateness that is sustained by an 'oppositional process' of resistance to incorporation in an encompassing society. Green (1981), in reference to 'Black' communities in the United States, has argued that an enduring ethnic identity does not necessarily presuppose a single original ethnic or tribal entity. The African American identity is a modern construction derived from 'a generalized African ancestry, a shared history of bondage (if not actual enslavement), and public and private harassment'. Of these three factors, Green contends, the last is the most crucial element in the development of 'integrative symbols of identity' (1981: 77). Similarly, Trosper (1981: 247-8) contends that the transformation of American Indians 'from a diverse people with little common identity into an ethnic group' has resulted from a growing perception of shared experience. Indians have a common history of broken treaties which defines them as a group as well as providing them with a 'charter' for action.

The development of ethnic awareness into consciousness is not exclusively a function either of continuing enclave status or of the creation of new patterns of association through urban migration. Changes in residential patterns may undermine historic identities. But a number of studies have shown the inadequacy of the earlier 'community lost' model in which migrants were seen to be 'uprooted' from their homes and thrust into completely new environments, with the solidarity of the old community becoming increasingly threatened as more members leave.

On the contrary, it has been suggested that the sense of community is not determined by residential factors alone. There can continue to be a strong sense of belonging to a network of relatives and friends back home. The sense of belonging to a particular community thus may become 'liberated' from geo-physical considerations, so long as contact and interaction are maintained (Wellman and Leighton 1979; Craven and Wellman 1973; Mayer and Mayer 1974; Epstein 1969; Harries-Jones 1969; Cohen 1969; Mitchell 1969, 1987).

In a country in which they constitute almost twelve percent of a population that is racially unsegregated and substantially inter-married the Maori people are both a definably separate community and a major element of the society as a whole.[5] In New Zealand the terms 'Maoridom' and 'the Maori world' are common references. But by the 1980s the meanings of these familiar words had become encrusted with values, assumptions, and understood arrangements. Who could be said to belong to the Maori world? What were its boundaries? What constituted 'Maoriness'? A working delineation of Maori ethnicity was essential for any social or political study of this phenomenon.

There are three generally agreed defining elements of ethnicity: self-identification, identification by others, and shared activities. Racial difference alone does not differentiate ethnic groups (Yinger 1981: 250; 1983: 395). Physical characteristics (phenotypic criteria) are an uncertain foundation for ethnic identity in New Zealand. A person may 'look Maori' but may in fact be a Cook Islander, a Solomon Islander, or a Fijian. Then again some Maori 'look Pakeha' - displaying fair hair, fair skin, blue or green eyes in any imaginable combination with the Polynesian black hair, brown skin, and brown or black eyes.

The 'social' and 'cultural' dimensions of ethnicity, on the other hand, embody such factors as association and self-identity which require careful exploration. Maori people recognise as among their own those who assert some blood relation and who participate in Maori social life. Fluency in the Maori language is highly valued but not essential; passive bilingualism is common, especially among young people (St George 1980: 94). Maori consciousness establishes a claim; sharing central elements of traditional and contemporary Maori lifestyle sustains it.

The New Zealand anthropologist, Joan Metge, confirmed the continuation of the community after migration in her early studies of Maori rural and urban relations (1964). In addition to shared experiences, Metge stressed the crucial role of the marae - the communal meeting place and symbol of community life - in explaining this phenomenon. The contemporary wharenui, or large meeting house, which can seat one to three hundred people, is a post-colonial development. The term 'marae' had come to embrace the meeting house, dining hall, and other buildings, and surrounding grounds where the community may hold its social and political gatherings. Metge (1964: 231-2) explained:

Most Maoris in Auckland had a sentimental attachment to at least one rural community. This community was home to them, first because they or one or both of their parents had lived there long enough to develop real affection for it and for the people who lived there, and secondly, because their ancestors for at least three generations ... had lived and were buried there. They held on to interest in Maori land in the district so that they could claim the marae as their own and the privileges of tangata marae[6] during their visits home ...

It appeared that Maori people had been able to reconcile modern urban living with inherited social and political frameworks. This new mode of living might involve a strong sense of community with suburban Maori neighbours, reinforced by identification with a recently built urban marae or community centre. But it could co-exist comfortably with a continuing identification with ancestral rural communities. Indeed, Metge had observed in her fieldwork in the principal New Zealand city of Auckland in the 1950s (1970: 136) that 'Auckland Maoris found that they had to have a tribe: they were more conscious of tribal membership than in the country because of constant association with members of so many others'. Moreover, as Fitzgerald argued (1977: 150) in relation to Maori university graduates, Maori cultural identity transcended situational adjustments, giving 'common meaning, stability, and predictability to the individual's behaviour'.

SITUATION, CONTEXT, AND BEHAVIOURAL CHOICE

Anthropological interpretation cannot be divorced from time or place, from what is done and said, 'from the whole vast business of the world', asserted Clifford Geertz (1973: 18), without rendering it 'vacant'. J. Clyde Mitchell pointed out in studies of African urbanisation (1951, 1969, 1987) that the 'situational factors' of social and political life of formerly rural/tribal peoples had altered with urban migration. His work *The Kalela Dance*, originally published in 1956, became a classic study of these new experiences (Mitchell 1971). Studies of African townsmen (Banton 1957; Epstein 1969; Boswell 1969; Kapferer 1969; Harries-Jones 1969) which amplify Mitchell's insights are also consistent with Maori experience of urbanisation. While new social and political structures are identifiable, vestiges of older structures from the subjects' traditional culture are retained.

It has been shown that sentimental attachments to different areas can have more than a nostalgic significance. They may be activated and require commitment and action according to each individual's obligations, and the perceived relevance of particular situations. A multiplicity of ties can at times lead to personal dilemmas and conflict. What is often critical for effective political behaviour is the ability to make acceptable judgements about the priority of various obligations in specific social and political contexts.

Appropriate behaviour within the new social setting cannot be learned from traditional sources alone. Some must be devised or selected from a larger repertoire. Indeed, as Susan J. Smith (1984: 365-6) has argued in a study of urban ethnicity in Britain's north central Birmingham, 'the precise nature of ethnicity and the expectations made of its incumbents is conceived of as fluid and negotiable ... to be activated or minimised according to the situation with which its incumbents are confronted'.

The institutional arrangements and social practices of modern Maori society often serve to satisfy the dual purpose of maintaining cultural identity and communication with the rural homeland of the migrants, and of providing a familiar social framework for association within an unaccustomed milieu. 'Stranger' categories can be transformed into broad categories of ethnic 'brotherhood', classificatory 'kinship', and 'friends'. Thus ethnicity or 'Maoriness', devoid of its traditional tribal demarcations, can be invoked or denied, according to social and political convenience to serve both exclusionary and inclusionary purposes. As Paden noted in reference to urban Africa, 'situational ethnicity is organised on the observation that particular contexts may determine which of a person's communal identities or loyalties are appropriate at a point in time' (Okamura 1981: 452).

Writing in the mid-1970s, the Maori social scientist and educationist Dr Ranginui Walker concluded: 'The key to the successful adjustment of the Maori to urban life is voluntary association'. In this regard, Walker said, the Maori urban experience is little different from that outlined in the studies of urbanisation of tribal peoples in Africa undertaken by Little (1957), Banton (1957), Epstein (1969), and Mitchell (1969; 1987). The voluntary association which occurred within the multi-tribal context promoted the welfare of the Maori migrant, provided community cohesion, and enabled its members to maintain their 'Maori' identity in the face of an assimilating majority culture (Walker 1975: 167-71).

For a minority ethnic group that undergoes dual acculturation, the development and maintenance of Maori identity 'must involve a complicated process of decision-making in the face of multiple social situations and in the context of the total structure of New Zealand society' (Fitzgerald 1977: 19). By the beginning of the 1980s it was problematic, though not yet the subject of systematic scholarly inquiry whether, for many Maori, their Maori self-identity could co-exist with a 'New Zealander' self-identity. 'New Zealander' itself might have been in the process of transmutation from a 'national' to an ethnic identity (Garnier and Levine 1981: 130).

It has been established that neither shared racial, linguistic or cultural characteristics, nor common residence guarantee the production of an assertive ethnic identity. 'A collectivity of people without organisation is not a group', stressed Cohen. A collectivity becomes a political force only as it develops the 'mechanisms for the direct or indirect co-ordination of action'. The political potency of such groups also differs according to the 'significance of the interests which they articulate' (Cohen 1974a: 66), and their success in winning the commitment and support of members to chosen issues and interests. Thompson (1983: 129) cautioned, however, that shared interests do not necessarily impel political mobilisation: 'as with class interests the conception of the relationship between shared interests and action consistent with those interests must be a probabilistic one'.

Leadership is critical to the emergence of political ethnicity. What Rothschild (1981: 27) calls the 'ideologisation of ethnicity through the sacralisation of ethnic markers and the mobilization of the sharers of these markers' is a function of leaders and elites. Fox, Aull, and Cimino (1981: 207) stress:

> The common anthropological treatment of ethnic collectivities as basically unstratified or undifferentiated populations obscures that the leadership of ethnic nationalisms is often held by acculturated middle-class professionals who reconstitute their ethnicity and broadcast new symbols of identity and forms of organisation to an ethnic following.

Nevertheless, as Nagata (1981: 111-12) concludes, while the 'circumstantialist' approach to understanding ethnicity can be convincingly developed:

> the sole unique feature about the "ethnic" as a concept, category, or group, by which it can be distinguished from all other concepts (e.g. class) involves the nature of the charter membership, and in the ethnic case, this is primordial. Charters of identity that draw on a (putative) notion of common blood, origin, descent, or kinship connection as a reason for being or acting may be labelled ethnic. It matters little that such charters may be fabricated or manipulated, for as in the case of genealogies, it is the message that they carry that counts.

For some Maori, however, the fact that their 'charter' might be fabricated or manipulated does matter. An urban intellectual might be at ease with a Maori identity and with a 'shared cultural ethos' known as 'Maoritanga' (Hohepa 1978: 99). As Fitzgerald found (1977: 60) Maori graduates' perceptions of Maoritanga 'cannot really be measured as discrete cultural traits because it is an abstraction with no absolute boundaries (even the kinship tie is not finite)'. Hohepa (1978: 99) explained that the term 'Maoritanga':

> embraces a way of life, a way of acting, thinking and feeling; of attitudes to language, traditions and institutions; of shared values and attitudes to people, places and things, to time, the land and sea, the environment, life and death. It is a total way of life, a lifestyle which continues to survive despite the impact of the global village.

But, to Maori people whose identity is grounded in tribal descent and regional location, the very notion of Maoritanga may be seen as a dubious modern construct with undertones of Pakeha cultural imperialism (Fitzgerald 1977: 60). 'It seems to me', wrote John Rangihau (1977: 174), a prominent elder of the Tuhoe tribe, 'there is no such thing as Maoritanga because Maoritanga is an all-inclusive term that embraces all Maoris'. Rangihau's wry scepticism embodies a belief that would be a formidable barrier to any attempt to mobilise Maori political ethnicity:

> I have a faint suspicion that Maoritanga is a term coined by the Pakeha to bring the tribes together. Because if you cannot divide and rule, then for tribal people all you can do is unite them and rule. Because then they lose everything by losing their own tribal histories and traditions that give them their identity. (ibid: 174-5)

In exploring ethnicity and its political expression in a plural or pluralistic context, it is necessary therefore to be alert to a variety of symbols, processes, and structures: primordial identification (kinship, culture, religion) and its possibly ambiguous implications; shared history or experience; common opposition or resistance; socio-geographic considerations (tribal territory and residence); leadership, rhetoric and ideology; and modes of association. A satisfactory account of political ethnicity must deal with all of these features to the extent that they are disclosed in any specific context.

NOTES

1. In choosing to undertake research on Maori political action I was influenced by a growing tradition since the early 1950s of studies of social process and political organisation, particularly within urban industrialised society. Significant works in this genre include the pioneering research of Elizabeth Bott on family, neighbourhood, and class in Britain (1957); J. Clyde Mitchell on social networks in Central African towns (1969; 1987); John Barnes on kinship, religion and class as `partial networks' in a Norwegian fishing community (1977); M. Banton (1966, 1957) in his studies of complex societies in Western Africa; Adrian Mayer's study of a political candidate's `action set' during an election campaign in the Dewas District of Madhya Pradesh State in India (1977); Epstein's study of the social organisation of African townsmen (1969); R. J. Walker (1970) and J.S. Graham's (1972) thesis on voluntary association and social networks in urban and rural Maori society; H. Oxley's study of `mateship' (1973) and R.A. Wild's study of status, class and power (1974) and their effect on social organisation in small Australian towns; Gill Bottomley's description of a Greek community, and the restructuring process of Greek community life following migration to Australia (1979); and a number of studies examining the politics of social transaction, role choice, and behavioural decision-making (Barth 1966; Blau 1964; Lebra 1975; Mauss 1974; Paine 1974; Sahlins 1974). Studies by Canadian, American, and European sociologists on the network of associations between business, professional and

community elites are also of interest and relevance to anthropological pursuits (Boissevain 1979; Craven and Wellman 1973; Leinhardt 1977; Laumann and Pappi 1977; Coleman, Katz and Menzel 1977; Carroll, Fox and Ornstein 1977; Chrisman 1970; Wellman 1980; Berkowitz 1980; Capshew 1986; Wellman and Berkowitz 1990).

2. A 'pathology of normality' is a syndrome in which behaviour damaging to the social system is curtailed, and inequities are overlooked, in order to preserve opportunities for individual advancement and acceptance. The term was coined in reference to Brazil by Florestan Fernandes and the idea is developed in McFerson (1979).

3. The word 'Pakeha', which has been alternatively translated to mean 'colourless', 'fair skinned', or simply 'foreign', is a post-settlement term initially used to describe the first European immigrants and their descendants. Politically, 'Pakeha' is used in specific reference to the dominant white majority; and in Maori rhetoric the interests of 'the Maori' are juxtaposed with those of 'the Pakeha'. As this relationship is of primary concern to this book, this is the way in which I use it here. 'Pakeha' may also be used interchangeably with the terms 'European', 'non-Maori' or 'white' according to context.

4. For some recent attempts to capture the essence of ethnicity see Bentley 1983, 1987, 1991; Yelvington 1991; Nash 1989. On Cohen, Williams 1989 offers a useful critique.

5. By contrast Canadian Indians and Australian Aboriginals comprise about two percent of the population of those countries.

6. 'Tangata marae', meaning 'people of the marae', indicates a person's rightful 'belonging' to a place and a region. In traditional village society there was always a central meeting place or marae for community debate and speeches. Before European contact this was usually an open space, sometimes with a meeting house, which was used for secular, political, and religious gatherings.

POLITICAL EXPRESSION
AND
ETHNICITY

I

FROM RESISTANCE TO CO-EXISTENCE

Early Maori social organisation embraced the individual within an expanding trellis of rights and obligations from the primary family to the tribe. Social order and relationships were regulated within five main dimensions of 'belonging'. The whanau (family), the smallest social and economic unit, represented the primary household which sometimes extended beyond the biological family to include a patriarch, his wife, their single children and sometimes married children, and their families with the exception of affines. Today the whanau is the term used idiomatically in reference to the Maori 'family'. Immediate kinsmen (cognatic/affinial), or members of a whole community may refer to each other as 'whanau'. This latter usage usually signifies an affirmation of ideological solidarity and a shared collective identity.

In traditional society, whanau units which could trace blood ties to common ancestors, and which co-operated in the common use of land and defence, formed a hapu or sub-tribe. The hapu was a territorially and consanguinally defined corporate group, under the authority of a senior patriarch or chief. When a hapu grew too large the unit would divide. The new hapu would relocate to a neighbouring area.

A tribe, or iwi, consisted of several hapu villages which still recognised common ancestry through a founding ancestor, whether or not the actual links remained within genealogical memory. The tribe was the pre-eminent corporate body based upon the right to share a bounded territory and a mutual obligation to defend it. Members of the tribe attempted to trace their descent cognatically, to a common apexal ancestor even when connections with this person were vague. Establishing family or tribal connections with others, either through blood or by marriage, still plays an important part in Maori social relations and political strategy. Claims for co-operation by tribal federation (waka) were occasionally made, on the basis of a belief that the tribes concerned all had descended from ancestors of a common canoe in the days of the first great migrations across the

Pacific Ocean between 800 and 1200 AD. Knowledge of one's canoe, tribe, and sub-tribe is fundamental to Maori historical identity.

The term tangata whenua, 'people of the land', denotes territorial rights by prior occupation. In its original use tangata whenua referred to the first Maori settlers to an area, based upon traditional accounts of the landing and settlement points of the migrating canoes or customary occupation. Still in regular use today, it continues to encompass political authority and economic rights to the commonly recognised rural homelands of each major tribe, and more specifically, of each hapu. But it now is also used to highlight indigenous sovereignty by distinguishing the Maori people in general from later European and Pacific Island migrant populations.[1]

By the 1980s there were over 70 iwi runanga (major tribal groupings) in New Zealand - each claiming tangata whenua rights to generally recognised territorial regions, demarcated by rivers, mountains, hills, and other natural features. The integrity of the tribe remains the supreme principle of social organisation in Maoridom. Inter-tribal negotiation and collaboration generally proceed on an implicit understanding, and respect for, tribal sovereignty. Modern legislation acknowledges historic territorial arrangements as the basis for claims to rights of access and control over land and resources by Maori groups.

Social position in traditional times was mainly the result of birth. Rank and leadership was determined by the seniority of one's family line. Those who could trace their descent to an important ancestor (via either the male or female sides) through the eldest born in each family had claim to higher rank than the junior lines. The aristocratic class, the rangatira, carried high social status and performed leadership roles within the community. Those who were from the lowly (most junior) lines were regarded as noa, commoners. At the bottom of this class system were slaves, war captives who were considered the property of those they served.

The most senior chief of the region, the paramount chief, carried special mana[2] - power and authority - in negotiations and decision-making between hapu chiefs. Kawharu (1989: xix), speaking of the spiritual source of this special power, wrote:

> Mana is that power and authority that is endowed by the gods to human beings to enable them to achieve their potential, indeed to excel, and, where appropriate, to lead. It is in the nature of a spiritual contract mediated by the priests, chiefs, and elders of a tribal group between an individual member of the group and their deities. What is looked for, then, in a rangatira is evidence of a working out of a high order of spiritually sanctioned power and authority. Primogeniture, in so far as it refers to proximity by way of a line through the ancestors to the supernatural source of such power and authority, may thus be called the prescribed factor in rangatiratanga, and ability the achieved factor. Implicit in all of this is the matter of reciprocity: between the individual and his god, and between the individual and his tribal community. Both sets of relationships are specific and closed to the

community, both operate only within the laws and checks and balances of its political system. A rangatira is a trustee for his people, an entrepreneur in all their enterprises.

The primogeniture rights of senior families were guarded jealously and purity of descent was maintained by careful selection in marriage. The chief of a hapu was usually the most senior male of the most senior family in the hapu. The ariki, paramount chief or the chief of the tribe, was the hapu chief who bore the most senior descent line among the collective of hapu chiefs. In him was installed the power to call together the tribe. Decisions of importance were made by a body of elders formed by household or hapu heads. In community councils or public assemblies those with noted powers of oratory - with a deep knowledge of local history and lore - were particularly influential.

At modern marae gatherings public speech still represents the major tool of Maori political exchange. The community elders, men (and in some tribes women) of distinction and maturity, advised and guided their chief in his decision-making on behalf of the hapu. The will of the people, and particularly of the kaumatua (elders), had to be taken into account.

The protection and maintenance of personal or group mana - honour, authority, and power - were of primary concern in pre-European times, and many battles were fought in response to perceived insult or slight. It was not necessary for the instigator of the insult to be killed in such battle, as long as utu (revenge, payment) was procured by the shedding of the blood of one or more of his tribe. Thus, many tribes were caught in an endless cycle of feud. 'War is a devouring fire kindled by a spark' (Maori proverb).

Traditional Maori religion entailed a belief in a spirit world from which powerful forces could intervene in everyday life. Underlying even the most mundane tasks was a philosophical and spiritual approach to the material environment. There was considerable reverence for ancestral gods, and respect for the disembodied spirits of the dead who were believed to permeate human action and interaction and the physical world around them. Fear of supernatural retribution and sorcery (reinforced by fear of legal plundering or personal revenge, public admonition or loss of status) was an important instrument of social control. Offended gods or neglected ancestors could be pacified by ritual cleansing ceremonies and offerings, or by the removal of the polluting or dangerous condition of tapu by a tohunga (traditional priest and spirit medium). In traditional Maori society religious, social, and political life were so firmly dove-tailed as to form a comprehensive and indivisible whole.

The preservation of tribal identity is still closely linked to the Maori sense of continuity with the past: the correct use of the traditions and kawa (customs) of the tribe, the acknowledgement and reiteration of tribal history and physical location, the celebration in debate of the feats of tribal ancestors, the vision and wisdom of the kaumatua (elders), and the nobility of spirit in great leaders.[3]

THE PAKEHA PRESENCE

With the coming of the European, Maori 'residential patterns and organisation underwent a radical change during the early nineteenth century' maintained the Maori scholar Michael Jackson (1975: 29). The development of Maori agricultural production and trade which resulted from European intrusion into New Zealand was no less than revolutionary. It required 'large co-operation on a permanent basis', he wrote. The spread of literacy among the Maori (McKenzie 1985; Binney 1986), their adoption of time-efficient technology, and their pride of industry during the first years of contact are attributed by Jackson (1975: 32) as much to 'traditional bases of rank and status' and to their quickly learned skills of bicultural manipulation, as to the permeating influences of the immigrant culture.

Conquest, population loss through inter-tribal warfare, tribal migration, and the resulting chaos and confusion over title to land bred despair (Sinclair 1980: 41). Historians have attributed the apparent mass conversion of the Maori to Christianity during this period partly to the disillusionment with their tohunga, who had been unable to turn the tide of death and disease. By the mid-1830s a halt was called to inter-tribal warfare and many customs abominable to Christianity. But missionary Christianity was not totally successful in extirpating Maori spiritual and naturalistic beliefs. Certain traditional perceptions of the supernatural infused Christian beliefs and practices.[4] Contemporary Maori social and political life continues to be carried upon spiritual undercurrents and meanings which often are not explicit but which form a part of a shared understanding between the people concerned. This separates them in mind and in culture from the outlooks of European New Zealanders, the 'Pakeha', who they believe are more materialistic and less spiritually inclined. A sense of 'belonging' - to the whanau, to the culture, to the history, and to the land of their people - is an inseparable qualification of 'Maoriness'.

In 1839, following pressure on the British government from humanitarian societies, William Hobson was sent to negotiate with 'the chiefs of the confederated tribes' a treaty which would place the country under British sovereignty. Under the English version of the Treaty of Waitangi the Maori chiefs ceded 'all the rights and powers of sovereignty' which they possessed 'over their respective territories' to the Crown (First Article). Queen Victoria confirmed and guaranteed to the chiefs and tribes of New Zealand 'the full exclusive and undisputed possession of their Lands and Estates Forests Fisheries and other properties, which they may collectively or individually possess' (Second Article). In the Third Article the Queen, on her part, extended 'to the natives of New Zealand Her royal protection' and imparted to them 'all the rights and privileges of British subjects' (Buick 1934; 1976; Cleave 1989; Ross 1972; Sorrenson 1989; Williams 1989: 78-80).

The signing of the treaty began at a gathering of chiefs at Waitangi on 6 February 1840. It was then taken throughout the country in order to gather the signatures of other chiefs. Five hundred and twelve signatures were secured in all. The mixed feelings of Maori leaders towards British governance were clearly recorded in the Waitangi debates of 5 February 1840, in the speeches of Te Kemara, Tamati, Pukututu, Kawiti, Hone Heke (Caselberg 1975: 44-6; Orange 1987; Kawharu 1989). Translations of the original Maori text of the treaty revealed significant discrepancies between the Maori and English versions. Precisely what it was that the Maori were ceding and being granted was confused from the beginning. An attempted distinction between Tino Rangatiratanga (full chieftainship) retained by the Maori, and Kawanatanga (government) given up to the Queen, sowed the seeds for a century and a half of contention over the nature and location of sovereignty (Cleave 1989).

In response to the growing domination of the European settler and its facilitation by land sellers (hoko whenua), the non-sellers (pupuri whenua) increasingly asserted their independence and used tribal federation as a means of protecting common interests. Between 1840 and 1850 resistance of the tribes to Europeans was sporadic, usually in the form of revolt under the leadership of strong chiefs in response to disputed sales of Maori land under multiple ownership (Sinclair 1980: 95; Graham 1981: 112). In the following decade leaders were able to organise a more effective resistance to land sales by common consent. As Maori resentment of land loss spread throughout the country so the foundation for organised effort was laid.

A remarkable young chief, Tamihana Te Rauparaha, on his return from a trip to England where he was presented to Queen Victoria in 1851, conceived the idea of forming a Maori kingdom. In 1858 a powerful paramount Waikato chief, Te Wherowhero, who had ties of allegiance by kinship and political affiliation with many sub-tribes and tribes of the central and upper North Island district, was elected as the first Maori King. After his election Te Wherowhero was given the title Potatau I. The European institutions which the King movement adopted - such as the king's code of laws, his council of state, his resident magistrate and police - were grafted upon the indigenous institutions of the tribal runanga (assembly). The king followed the pattern of the tribal chief by guiding rather than ruling his subjects. The movement brought under its umbrella a loose federation of tribes of the Waikato, Taupo, Hawkes Bay, and some East Coast regions. After its establishment the Kingitanga introduced rigid restrictions on land sales among its member tribes and hapu (Jones 1975: 132-3; Sinclair 1980: 115).

Tribal federation was also used in another way. Scarcely a month before the first Parliament met in Auckland, in April 1854, about a thousand Maori from the southern Taranaki tribes gathered at Manawapou to discuss an inter-tribal agreement to resist the sale of Maori land. The concept of 'kotahitanga' (unity movement) was used to promote a series of large inter-tribal gatherings. Settlers became nervous as larger numbers of Maori joined the anti-land selling movement. They feared that a 'land league', or worse, a 'war league' was being formed. As early as 1847, wrote Sinclair (1980: 113-4), Grey, then Governor of New Zealand: 'remarking on the decline of the "mutual jealousies and animosities" between the tribes and on the rise of a "feeling of class or race", observed that many of the younger chiefs "entertained the design ... to set up some national government" '.

Skirmishes broke out periodically between settlers and local tribes in Taranaki, and on the East Coast of the North Island. These foreshadowed the Land Wars between the anti-land selling Maori and the Crown which erupted in the North, Taranaki, and Waikato. Between 1844 and 1872 there were four waves of war between the European and the Maori, conducted primarily over questions of land. Under the leadership of renowned warrior chiefs, their fighting prowess, aptitude for political coalition, and their knowledge of the terrain, made the Maori formidable opponents to the small and inexperienced parties of soldiers dispensed by the Crown. These uprisings were not easy to put down.[5]

The latter part of the nineteenth century was a dismal period for the Maori. The resistance movements led by the Maori warlords and prophets had failed to stop the flow of European settlers. By the turn of the century most of the remaining Maori population (some 45,500) were scattered throughout the country's rural regions, concentrating mainly in the North Island. The tribes were still largely separated from each other, as were Maori separated from Pakeha. Family elders and hapu heads continued to speak on behalf of the community on the occasions of marae debate. Those with a hereditary claim to leadership, the rangatira, still depended upon the support and confidence of their community's elders - their kaumatua. Like the settler government, Christianity was a force which was going to remain. The Maori people adopted Christianity through the orthodox Catholic and Protestant churches, the new Mormon faith, or the independent Maori churches which arose from the ministerings of the late nineteenth century prophets (de Bres 1985). On evidence of widespread ill health, social decline, and loss of hope the government adopted an assimilationist policy towards the Maori, in the expressed hope of being able to 'smooth the pillow' of a dying race. They believed that those who remained would be soon absorbed into the larger population by education and intermarriage.

By the early 1890s a series of large inter-tribal conferences was uniting the tribes in the Northland, the East Coast, and Hawkes Bay region. In a petition to the New Zealand government in 1893 a loose federation calling itself the 'Kotahitanga' (Maori parliament) requested 'that power to govern the Maoris be delegated to a Federated Maori Assembly of New Zealand' (Pocock 1965: 48). Spearheading the thrust to retain tribal sovereignty, and resources of land and sea, were the new institutions which emerged during this period: the Kauhanganui (Great Council) of the Maori King movement; the Kotahitanga or Maori parliament movement; and a handful of messianic prophets who founded their own political forms of resistance or religious creeds.[6] Increasingly, leaders came to share the view that the heart of the problem lay not in the surveyor's peg but in the content and structure of European law. The only way to deal with the European was to learn how to influence the system which governed them.

The necessity to subdue old rivalries was understood. But the concept of 'Maori' or 'Maoriness' had as yet little cultural or political meaning. Maori identity still derived essentially from the hapu and tribal territory. Maori ethnicity, at the twilight of consciousness in the 1890s, was to dawn on the political horizon over the next three decades.

PARTICIPATION IN NATIONAL POLITICS

A new frontier for political action had opened in 1867 when four parliamentary seats were reserved for the Maori people. The colonial government located three of these in the North Island and one in the South Island. Maori leaders took hold of this opportunity and began to make their own way in Parliament. But the Maori did not abandon for some years their attempts to establish a separate Maori parliament through the Kauhanganui - the Great Council of the King movement, and its rival Kotahitanga parliament movement which had emerged from inter-tribal meetings in the 1880s. In 1892 leaders of the Kotahitanga movement formally established their parliament at Waitangi. They continued to meet annually until 1902 to discuss problems and issues of concern - mostly to do with Maori and Pakeha relations. In the 1890s the Kotahitanga made three unsuccessful petitions to the New Zealand government through their elected Member of Parliament for Northern Maori, Hone Heke Rankin, to have the Maori parliament recognised in legislation.

The twentieth century saw the rise of a new kind of leadership. A 'Maori Renaissance' was led by a handful of Maori intellectuals who founded, and became known for a time as, the 'Young Maori Party'. Systematic reforms were made in the areas of Maori health, land management, employment, and housing under the determined lobbying of James Carroll, Maui Pomare, Apirana Ngata, Peter Buck, and several others - some of whom received knighthoods for their service to the Maori people (Pool 1977:27; Schwimmer 1975: 333; Metge 1964: 12).

At the turn of the century there was strong Maori pressure to place the remaining Maori land into the hands of a Maori-governed organisation. James Carroll, Minister of Native Affairs in the Liberal Government from 1899 to 1912, attempted to delay land sales and encouraged instead the leasing of Maori land to Europeans. Influenced by Carroll, a young East Coast lawyer Apirana Ngata, and the lobbying of the Kotahitanga movement, the Liberal government passed two acts in 1900 and 1905 for this purpose. Maori-dominated land councils and boards were established under the Maori Lands Administration Act of 1900. Land councils were to manage Maori land and to provide a limited form of Maori self-government. The council act also sought to provide, as an alternative to the Kotahitanga, a common forum for the tribes to come together to discuss Maori problems.

Maori councils led to the formation of district health councils - established to improve sanitation and living conditions in Maori communities. The work of Ngata as organising secretary for these councils from 1902 to 1904, and of the two doctors, Pomare and Buck, was significant in reversing the trend of disease and decline in the Maori population. The 'primary problem in the Maori revival', noted one historian, 'was the conquest of disease' (Oliver 1960: 260).

Carroll, however, came under considerable criticism from his Pakeha colleagues and electorate for his Maori land policy. The practice of leasing was distasteful - not only because of the objection to white dependence on a brown race but because the very idea of landlordism was anathema to people who had so recently fled its injustices in the British Isles. In 1905 the government yielded to pressure, placing Maori land councils and boards under tighter European control. 'An increased volume of Maori land', King wrote (1981: 285), 'passed through the boards into Pakeha occupancy and use' following this change in policy.

It became clear to Maori leaders of foresight that land issues and the question of future Maori economic prosperity could only be resolved by the Maori people developing their own land. While they had the material and human resources, what they lacked was capital. In 1920 loans to individual farmers became available from the accumulation of Maori funds through the Maori Trustee. But this was not enough. Large tracts of rough land needed to be broken in, developed into usable farms, and managed more efficiently. In the mid-1920s Apirana Ngata, Liberal MP for Eastern Maori from 1905, devised a way of joining smaller land-holdings by 'consolidation' - the exchange of land interests to enable the uniting of several family plots (Butterworth 1972). Later, by 'incorporation', land held in multiple ownership could be run under a committee of management in blocks large enough to prove economically viable. The first area where these schemes were applied was among his own people - the Ngati Porou on the East Coast.

Under the influence of Ngata, who became Minister of Native Affairs in 1928, the government was eventually persuaded to provide for Maori farmers the state credit needed in order for them to develop their land into pastoral properties. In his first year as Minister, a period when the government was in need of the support of the Maori MPs, Ngata established the Maori Purposes Fund Board and government financed Maori land schemes. These state development schemes, administered under the Department of Native Affairs, incorporated hundreds of small Maori farms. There were 76 schemes operating by 1934, covering 650,000 acres mostly in the eastern and central parts of the North Island. Three years later 18,000 people were finding a livelihood mostly in what King described (1981: 286) as 'revitalised communities'. Economic prosperity from the use and development of their own resources was not the only feature of these schemes. A central focus of Ngata's legislation was the preservation of the Maori rural, communal way of life, so that traditional activities centred around the marae could continue. A renaissance in art, craft, carving, and music - with government support - helped to sharpen Maori ethnic identity by emphasising common elements of a culture not shared by the dominant Pakeha. New marae, with larger and more decorative wharenui (meeting houses) than the earlier varieties, were built in the rural areas.

The Maori resistance movements of the nineteenth century had foreshadowed the cultural and political revival to come. On the whole the Kingitanga and Kotahitanga political movements, and the Ringatu, Te Whiti, and Rua Kenana messianic resistance movements, were regionally based (Binney, Chaplin and Wallace 1979). Early attempts to develop a system of district runanga or Maori councils with quasi-legislative and judicial powers had enjoyed only limited success in securing lasting co-operation between hapu and tribal chiefs. But the necessities of dealing with the inexorably expanding power of the Pakeha - whether by armed resistance, negotiation, or participation in the functions of the state - fostered a more widespread appreciation of common Maori interest. The Maori, moreover, were not immune to the nationalist sentiments and developing New Zealand identity of the European settlers.

It is clear that tolerance of the Pakeha was being preached by some Maori leaders even during the Land War period and certainly by many afterwards. The official ideology of 'amalgamation' (assimilation), if pursued with genuine conviction, could be seen to offer real benefits to a people who might otherwise be exposed to a far less restrained, ever growing settler invasion (Ward 1978: 309). A generation later a sense of shared nationhood was symbolised by the substantial number of Maori who volunteered to serve in World War One. The Taranaki and Waikato tribes stood aloof, and the messianic Tuhoe leader Rua Kenana dissuaded his people from volunteering. But the active presence of Maori soldiers at Gallipoli and in France fostered pride among the Pakeha about the fighting skills and bravery of 'their Maoris'.[7] The well-publicised wartime contribution made by Maori servicemen and their communities, as well as the efforts of the Maori MPs, created a more responsive atmosphere in government towards Maori needs. The gains won by their MPs were widely appreciated by the Maori people who sought their help on an increasing range of community and personal concerns (Oliver with Williams 1981; Sutherland 1940; Hancock 1946; Sinclair 1980; Metge 1976).

Figures like Carroll, Ngata, Buck, and Pomare were respected in Pakeha society as exemplars of a policy and ideology of assimilation. Themselves of mixed parentage, these men were able to move freely between Pakeha and Maori worlds but, as Winiata suggested (1967: 150), 'better able to gain a recognised position in the minority group than in the majority'. These essentially conservative leaders felt that Maori people had to win acceptance as individuals by the display of personal diligence and accomplishment - qualities highly prized by the Pakeha. 'The majority of the Maori people' had also, as Ward concludes (1978: 311), chosen 'to pursue advancement and reform through the framework of state institutions rather than intensifying the separatist tendencies of the Kotahitanga'.[8]

With the increasing participation of the Maori in general New Zealand social and political life, there came greater responsiveness to Maori interests by New Zealand governments. In the meantime, however, the group of intellectual politicians, who had once 'embodied elements of protest in their position'

(Winiata 1967: 155) were being by-passed by a new Maori movement that stood completely apart from the Pakeha establishment.

THE RATANA/LABOUR ALLIANCE

One day in 1918, so the story goes, Tahupotiki Wiremu Ratana of Orakeinui (near Wanganui), while sitting upon his porch gazing towards the Tasman Sea, was struck unconscious by the Holy Spirit. In a vision he was commanded to unite and cleanse the Maori people and turn them to Jehovah. In the vision Ratana was appointed as 'mangai' - 'the mouthpiece of God' (Henderson 1972: 253; Sinclair 1980: 274).

Ratana's mission and person took on extraordinary charisma and drive. He travelled extensively throughout New Zealand. His preaching and use of faith-healing attracted a large following. Like past Maori spiritual leaders, Ratana offered his people an Old Testament explanation for their loss and suffering and his message identified strongly with Christianity. His followers felt themselves to be, like the Israelites, the chosen people of God, and Ratana their chosen deliverer. Drawing on both biblical sources and Maori thought, Ratana introduced a new ministry of apostles, angels, prophets, and Io, the supreme God from Maori tradition. Although regarded at first as heretical, Ratana gradually gained acceptance from conventional Christian groups. He had moulded his congregations upon 'simple Wesleyan lines', removed many traditional fears of sorcery, tapu, evil spirits and the tohunga, and added a Maori flavour of ritual, music, colour, symbolism, and ceremony.

Early in his mission Ratana identified himself with the working-class and downtrodden: 'My friends are the shoemaker, the blacksmith, the watch-maker, carpenters, orphans and widows ...' (Henderson 1972: 57-8). Ratana also opposed rangatiratanga - the emphasis upon inherited power and chiefly authority by order of birth and nobility. His message was for the humble folk. It had great appeal to those who could not relate to the sophisticated leadership of Ngata, Buck, Pomare, and Carroll.

Ratana urged his people to submerge their tribal differences in favour of higher and more spiritual considerations. Like some of his predecessors, Ratana divided New Zealand into 'the four winds' or the 'four quarters'.[9] The departure from tribal affiliations - so deeply rooted in tradition - could only indicate the strength of the prophet's influence. In fact, Ratana's most fundamental challenge was not to Christian orthodoxy but to the Maori social order. He had created 'a detribalised unit, devoid of tribal affiliations ... a strange and completely new departure for a people steeped in tribal tradition' (Raureti 1978: 50). By the mid-1920s Ratana had succeeded in 'defeating the tohunga', Henderson wrote (1972: 55), and he united the 'mutually hostile tribes' in the Christian faith.

In 1924 Ratana made a world tour visiting England, Japan, Switzerland, and the United States seeking support for the restoration of mana Maori by the incorporation of the Treaty of Waitangi into legislation. In the early stage of his mission he had said: 'In one of my hands is the Bible; in the other is the Treaty of Waitangi. If the spiritual side is attended to all will be well on the physical side' (ibid.). But the Pakeha population did not give ear to his spiritual teachings and all was not 'well' with secular life for the Maori. When in England Ratana requested the opportunity to place Maori grievances and distress before the King, which he felt to be a direct result of the dishonouring of the Treaty of Waitangi by the Crown. His request was denied.

On his return from overseas, having established his church and auxiliary organisations under the management of a retinue of apostles and clergy, he decided to address the material needs of his people. In the 1922 general election Ratana's eldest son, Tokouru, came within 800 votes of unseating Maui Pomare in the Western Maori seat. The Ratana movement collected over 30,000 signatures on a national petition demanding the ratification of the Treaty of Waitangi. In 1928 Ratana declared that the era for his spiritual works was over, that his mission was now a temporal one. In 1943 he achieved his goal, filling all four Maori seats in Parliament - the four quarters - with Ratana candidates.

During the 1930s a pact was forged between the Labour Party and the Ratana Church. It was an alliance which was to last for over 50 years. In 1935 Labour triumphed over the conservative government. From this time onward the four Maori seats were filled by Labour candidates - almost all of them being nominees of the political arm of the Ratana Church. The seats became known not only as Maori seats, but also as Labour seats. While Ratana support was always for Labour candidates - and was at times delivered *en bloc* - the relative significance of religious, party, and class impulses in this form of political expression remained unclear. But in the parliamentary arena the rise of Labour to power, with an entrenched Maori presence in its ranks, meant a new era for Maori leadership and the 'Maori cause'.

COMMUNITY, POLITY AND URBAN TRANSFORMATION

The sweeping reforms introduced by the Savage Labour government from 1935 onwards established a welfare system which dramatically affected the social and economic well-being of the Maori people and improved relations between the two cultures. Between 1946 and 1949 Maori MPs held the balance of power. But a 'National' Party, born in 1935 as a fusion of the Liberal Party and other anti-Labour Party groups, took again the reins of power from Labour in 1949. Apart from two terms, one between 1957 and 1960, and the other between 1972 and 1975, the National government kept a firm grip on office until 1984.

In the post-war years, an expanding urban economy was able to absorb the rising tide of rural migrants into the labour market. After the 1950s small-scale family farms become less and less viable. As workers began to seek employment in the towns and cities, settling into jobs well-paid by rural standards, urban migration became increasingly attractive to younger siblings and relatives. A disproportionate number of Maori filled skilled and semi-skilled labouring occupations during the 1950s and 1960s (Forster 1969: 198-232). With improved health, a higher fertility rate, and to some extent an increased willingness to acknowledge 'Maoriness', a steady acceleration in Maori population figures was seen. In the 1945 census the 'New Zealand Maori' (persons of half or more Maori blood) were reported as being 5.7 percent (100,044 Maori persons) of the total New Zealand population. This increased to 6.9 percent (167,086) in 1961; 7.9 percent (227,414) in 1971, and 8.9 percent (279,252) in 1981.[10]

Within a fifty-year period the Maori people had undergone massive demographic change. They were fundamentally rural folk until after World War Two. In 1936, 82.7 percent of the Maori population resided in the country. By 1966 this had dropped to 38.4 percent, with more than a third of all Maori living in the Auckland region. By 1981, 78.5 percent were living in cities and towns. Nine out of ten lived in the North Island, with 61.2 percent of them concentrating in the local government regions of Auckland, Wellington, the Northland, Bay of Plenty, and Waikato.[11] However, as the historian Michael King observed (1981: 287), the process of urbanisation created a new environment for inter-racial tension in New Zealand. Stress was also placed upon migrant families as kinship obligations were expanded to accommodate the new situation. With more than half of the Maori population in 1971 being under 15 years of age (compared with less than a third of the non-Maori), urban concentration placed enormous strains on family viability and cohesion (Pomare 1980: 1; Koopman-Boyden and Scott 1984: 35). Writing in December 1972 Butterworth emphasised (1974: 33) the marginality of the Maori in the New Zealand economy and lamented the absence of 'definitive research work' on the urban Maori community. He commented on a 'notably pessimistic attitude about race relations fed by press attention on crime and juvenile delinquency, family breakdown, and racial discrimination'. Butterworth saw hope in the 'resilience' of the Maori social structure and the emergence of a new leadership, particularly with a new generation of Maori MPs (ibid.: 6, 33).

Probably the most influential document in reflecting on the implications of post-war change, and directing Maori policy in the 1960s, was the *Report on the Department of Maori Affairs* prepared by J.K. Hunn between 1960 and 1961. While misunderstood at the time, and criticised later for emphasising racial integration, Hunn's recommendations on ways to cope with mass migration were generously conceived and politically astute. There were fears of racial disquiet and possible conflict as a result of the changing population distribution. Europeans needed to learn to live beside and with Maori people. The Maori needed to be equipped with skills which would ensure they competed more effectively in the new environment. Hunn recommended the establishment of a Maori Education Foundation, subsidised pound for pound by the government; the promotion of Maori education from pre-school level upwards, with a particular emphasis upon apprenticeships in skilled trades; substantially expanded government housing and home ownership mortgage programs; the arrest of further Maori land title fragmentation; and the consolidation, retention, and utilisation of unproductive Maori land where possible.

Some expert commentators felt that early paternalistic policies had actually worked to the advantage of the Maori at a time when migration was at its peak, particularly in the area of welfare and housing needs. The Department of Maori Affairs had become increasingly focused on Maori welfare, housing, employment, and land development. A vast number of unskilled Maori migrants were absorbed into the economy of New Zealand's industrial towns and cities. The changes brought improvements to the migrants' standards of living and to the occupational chances of their children. 'The remarkable increase in the Department's scope, size, and complexity in the period 1930-60 is interesting', observed Schwimmer (1975: 336), 'since it seems to run counter to the policy to do away with separate Government agencies for the Maori'.

On the future relationship between the two major cultural groups of the country, Hunn stated: 'Full integration of the Maori people into the main stream of New Zealand life is coming to be recognised as just about the most important objective ahead of the country today' (Hunn 1961: 78-9). By 'integration', Hunn said he meant a combination, rather than fusion of 'the Maori and Pakeha elements to form one nation wherein Maori culture remains distinct' (Trlin 1979: 203). The Hunn report, recognising that much remained to be done, introduced the principle of special facilities for special needs ('positive discrimination', as it was later called) as a means of overcoming some of the socio-economic handicaps which faced the migrating Maori. The creation of the New Zealand Maori Council and the Maori Education Foundation can be attributed to this newly introduced principle in Maori affairs. By 1970 a 'marked improvement' in Maori living standards was noted; but continuing Pakeha prejudice, stereotyping, and discrimination remained to be tackled in the unfavourable economic climate of the next decade (Trlin 1979: 203; Schwimmer 1975: 336-7).

NATIONAL ORGANISATION

The Second World War had brought a turning point in Maori political perceptions. Apirana Ngata and other leaders rallied Maori people for the war effort. Ngata travelled throughout the country calling for the Maori people to provide human and material resources. His campaign had a special effect upon the tribal regions, linking community with community in a loosely knit fabric of communication and organisation where it had not previously existed (Ngata 1940; Hazlehurst 1988a).

The benefits of a national Maori organisation became apparent to Maori leaders, MPs, and the Labour government during the war. This awareness led to the Maori Social and Economic Advancement Act (1945), which made 'provision for the social and economic advancement and the promotion and maintenance of the health and general well-being of the Maori community'. The responsibility of implementing the new act was assumed by a second generation of leaders, many of whom had gained experience through the Maori Battalion and the Maori War Effort Organisation. Along with other soldiers on their return, Maori ex-servicemen were retrained in the professions or trades, and repatriated into positions of status appropriate to their service and training. Some returned to their home districts to help in local land management or community welfare. Others took positions within the government. 'They accepted that western education and administrative skills were necessary in order to function within the bureaucracy', King explained (1981: 296-7). Larger in number than the last, this generation of leaders was deeply committed to implementing sweeping social policy reform and to establishing racial equality. Over the next forty years, intelligently and diplomatically rejecting assimilation, they promoted the idea of two major cultures living side by side. The Maori war effort had had a profound effect upon race relations. 'It became more difficult for Pakeha leaders to discriminate against Maoris' (ibid.).

By the late 1950s Maori leaders active in district welfare councils were urging the creation of a national Maori council. Sensing that such a national advisory body might be a useful counterweight to the Labour-dominated Maori parliamentary seats, the National government legislated in 1962, replacing the Maori Social and Economic Advancement Act with the Maori Welfare Act. The new act (renamed the Maori Community Development Act in 1981) established the New Zealand Maori Council - a national body to act as the principal advocate of Maori interests. The New Zealand Maori Council (NZMC) was empowered to deal with the full gamut of Maori concerns and was structured to provide administrative machinery and policy forums at local, regional, and national levels (Fleras 1986; Hazlehurst 1988a). In its form and objectives it was what Jeffrey Ross has called (1982: 453) a 'consociational structure', bringing together ethnic elites into 'a set of specific administrative structures that function as a cartel of elites'.

Although the recipient of a small amount of government funding for its administration ($50,000 in 1981), the NZMC primarily relied on the voluntary services of elected Maori leaders. In 1981 the national body, or the 'Council', met four times a year in a sitting of some thirty delegates from ten districts. Affiliated district Maori councils and local Maori committees met, at a much greater frequency, as business required. But each level of the organisation continued to act as an autonomous community-focused agency. The New Zealand Maori Council's local and regional boundaries were carefully drawn so as to be in harmony with tribal domains, thereby creating a blend of traditional and modern political structures. In NZMC politics it became paramount that tribal sovereignty and integrity should remain intact.

At its national and regional levels, in particular, the New Zealand Maori Council evolved into the most influential articulator of Maori interests throughout the country - both within the Maori world itself, and between the Maori people and wider society. As well as distributing government funding for community development and performing a major role in Maori welfare administration, the NZMC acted as a primary channel of communication to government, industry, and commerce. In addressing economic, social, cultural, and inter-racial issues, it sought to protect Maori interests through legislative reform, political representation, submissions, and public lobbying.

Other organisations, such as the women's counterpart of the NZMC, the Maori Women's Welfare League (MWWL), the associated Maori Wardens' Association (MWA), and Maori Trust Boards also functioned on the national level. The Maori Women's Welfare League was the earliest such organisation. Deriving from the Maori Women's Health League which dated from the late 1930s, it was set up in 1951 with the aim of improving Maori health, child-care, and home-making, and of promoting Maori values, arts, and crafts (James 1977). Like the NZMC, and often in close collaboration with it, the MWWL made policy proposals to government on all levels of Maori welfare, including housing, education, employment, land issues, and cultural preservation.

Connected with the NZMC and administered under its same act was the Maori Wardens' Association (Fleras 1980a, 1980b). Maori wardens were appointed by the Maori committee and acted in a quasi police/security officer role. This enabled wardens to police Maori functions and to assist and control Maori people in those environments - such as public bars and on the streets - which might otherwise lead them into trouble with the police. Maori Trust Boards administered Maori funds for marae activities, education, and community needs. By the end of the 1970s the effectiveness of nationally based Maori organisations had been established. But their achievements tended to be overshadowed by the publicity and controversy associated with a series of protest movements which took the challenge to discriminatory and inequitable land and other social policies to the streets and to the courts (Hazlehurst 1988b).

VOLUNTARY ASSOCIATION

The movement of Maori migrants and immigrant Pacific Islanders to peripheral suburbs, facilitated by government provision of low-rental housing and favourable purchase schemes, was 'totally unpredicted by existing theory' wrote the geographer, J.S. Whitelaw (1971: 70). Auckland did not develop the inner city ghetto that American textbooks generally assumed would be created by disadvantaged visible minorities. Observing the dispersal of Maori and Islander populations to outer suburbs in 1969, Whitelaw (1971: 74) expressed concern in that:

the absence of community organisations such as the Pacific Islanders' Congregational Church and the Maori Community Centre, and the lack of close physical proximity to kin may result in new migrants to such areas experiencing greater difficulty in adjusting to urban life than in the acknowledged problem area of the central city. (see also Rowland 1974: 37)

Separated from the ambience of tribal custom, elder authority, and kinship obligation, the urban Maori constructed communities from affiliatory ties of kinship, friendship and 'belonging'. 'Kinship now becomes a principle of inclusion', observed Walker in his study of an Auckland city suburb, 'rather than exclusion from rights in the tribal and family estate' (1970: 22-3, also Walker 1972b: 399-410; Walker 1975: 167-85; Walker 1979a: 31-42; Wheeldon 1969: 128-80; Lopata 1967: 117-37; Epstein 1969: 77-116).

Social relationships, created and renewed through attendance at marae social events, Maori committee and Maori Women's Welfare League branch meetings, church functions, Maori welfare or Maori wardens' committee meetings, and educational and community development activities, replaced inherited identity in the urban Maori community by a system of belonging by association. Affiliatory ties - and, more importantly, the holding of office and the exercise of power - required a sustained commitment to membership. However, with just 9,300 Maori men aged 45 and over in 1966, and nearly 60 percent of them living in rural areas, the male leadership in the mid-1960s was, as Franklin (1978: 15) observed with concern, 'drawn from an incredibly small cohort'.

In the generationally fragmented, multi-tribal situation, shared ethnicity was to take on greater importance as a bonding agent. A younger leadership cohort, adept in pan-Maori rhetoric, began to flourish on the factory floor, on Maori committees, and at the urban community centre in the 1970s. Among most of this emerging group, rural ties and tribal origins were not rejected, but were frequently confirmed and reinforced. Social visits, conferences, and festivities provided opportunities for urban Maori to speak with their elders, to exchange gifts, and to 'recharge' their Maoritanga in the rural homelands. Rural and urban interests also converged at regional and national levels of Maori organisation and politics.

For the Maori urban existence was characterised by many pitfalls and temptations - overcrowding, unemployment, loneliness, racial tension, higher crime rates, and more zealous policing. Traditional child raising practices, which allowed children the freedom to explore their environment, produced special problems in the city. Many Maori children became street-wise and primary targets for gang recruitment and police suspicion. Parents also experienced the temptations of alcohol, gambling, and easy credit (Lane and Hamer 1973: 14; McEwen 1967).

The establishment of Maori committees, marae complexes, and community centres created a new form of community life for the urban Maori. Networks of support took shape by regular interaction, the creation of formal organisations, the transmission of moral codes and values, and the exercise of collective sanctions. 'The Maori way' - Maori sharing and caring - was articulated, idealised, and given reality where traditional filaments of tribal or hapu obligation could not sustain those who were far from home. While maintaining their separate identity, local interest nets were inevitably linked into the extended authenticating network of the 'Maori world'. In the process of exchange in the wider arena the political loyalties, affiliations, and interests of each community were defined and affirmed. A cohesive sector of interest emerged, built upon ties of interaction and common goals, and consolidated by a perceived sense of position in a larger context of identity.

EVOLVING LEADERSHIP

While a new social infrastructure was being created, the touchstone of Maoritanga remained in the rural homelands. Traditional knowledge, marae etiquette, songs, and chants were carried by the people to the marae and centres which sprang up in the cities. Although urban communities were typically composed of Maori from different regions and had a distinctly multi-tribal flavour, it was not unusual to find that chain migration had resulted in extended families clustering in, and dominating, certain localities. 'This marae', I was told in 1981, when visiting a centre in the heart of Auckland city, 'is Waikato'. It was right and proper that those welcoming us on to the marae should make mention of the Maori Queen. 'That is an old Waikato chant'.

Contact with one's own tribal homeland, one's parents' homeland, or one's ancestors' homeland was maintained by regular telephone calls, letters, and visits. For 'big hui' - such as a wedding, church festival, tangi or tribal conference - whole delegations of urban people would travel 'home' by car or hired bus.[12] Continuing links with rural communities meant that Maori social interaction was now being conducted over long distances, often hundreds of miles. Maori leaders and those who were active in 'Maori things' developed a stamina for travel which would have exhausted many a devoted European politician. Many younger leaders, whose mana might be derived from service or office-holding in a suburban setting, continued to seek advice from their kaumatua in the homelands, giving added authority to their leadership in the modern political context.

In addition to the new patterns of social activity arising from urbanisation, the development of national Maori organisations greatly increased the movement of Maori leaders across the country. Avenues for men and women with leadership qualities and aspirations multiplied rapidly in the 1960s and 1970s. The consolidation of Maori politics at the national level resulted in increasing demands and requirements for leaders to attend functions throughout the country - particularly within the North Island. The New Zealand Maori Council, in particular, provided a ladder of opportunity for service in the national political arena.

But there were many ways in which Maori leaders could come to be recognised. The historian Michael King (1986: 202-3), perhaps the most sympathetic and astute Pakeha student of modern Maori political culture in the 1970s, distilled his understanding of the bases of contemporary Maori leadership in this way:

Some have inherited and acquired mana that make them universally regarded as national Maori figures (Sir James Henare, Dame Whina Cooper); some achieved recognition by virtue of their office (Race Relations Conciliator, Secretary of Maori Affairs, Director of Maori Education); some became leaders by virtue of elected office (Chairman of the New Zealand Maori Council, Member of Parliament); some, such as Mira Szaszy (former president of the Maori Women's Welfare League) remain powerful long after they have relinquished elected office; some have the mana of unchallenged tribal leadership (John Rangihau of Tuhoe); some secure leadership of a group concerned with a particular project (Eva Rickard and the Raglan golf course dispute); some have the mana of acquired expertise on a particular subject (Professor Hugh Kawharu on Maori land tenure); and some are leaders, by-election or consensus, of a particular marae or community.

Men with traditional authority, perhaps reinforced by experience of command in war and values of enterprise and efficiency assimilated in business or army life, tended to bring to the political domain a cooperative style of negotiating with government. Their primary objective was to take full advantage of existing opportunities rather than seek significant gains through confrontation. Although their radical critics portrayed them as conservative or compliant, many of these leaders were assertive in the expression of Maori opinion. They identified and nurtured political allies for the Maori cause. The most effective of them (men like James Henare, Henry Ngata, and Graham Latimer) became renowned in both Maori and Pakeha worlds for their skills in advocating the interests of their people in a political environment preoccupied with other claims and expectations.

With the exception of those few who openly rejected and confronted the Pakeha way of life and Pakeha dominance, the most successful leaders from the 1960s onwards were comfortable with the values and customs of both the Maori and the Pakeha. They generally enjoyed middle-class professional, or 'respectable' working-class lifestyles. Though compelled by economic necessity (and perhaps more by choice than it would be prudent to admit) to live and work outside traditionally oriented communities, 'their rangatiraship and leadership is acknowledged in the community, even though they are absent for much of the year' (Mahuika 1977: 82). Api Mahuika attested in the mid-1970s that among the Ngati Porou, and probably more widely, the rangatira had not yielded their responsibility to the tribal kaumatua. Nor had achievement displaced ascription in establishing credentials for leadership. Maori leaders who combined rangatira status with political support from a tribal or regional area could be formidable indeed (Oliver with Williams 1981; Schwimmer 1975; Sutherland 1940; Metge 1964; 1976; Chapman 1975; Sinclair 1980; Sorrenson 1986).

THE PROTEST MOMENTUM

As issues arose in the 1970s that generated alliances and continuing action in urban areas distant from historic loci of authority, it was inevitable that militancy and media attention would be conducive to the development of new leadership styles. For all the support that Maori organisations were able to give, it seemed to an increasingly vocal, comparatively youthful, and better educated Maori cadre emerging in the urban sector in the 1970s that the assimilationist tendencies of government policy, and the economic disadvantage of the Maori generally, needed to be fundamentally challenged rather than merely ameliorated. As they made their views public, growing support was forthcoming among Pakeha liberal, academic, and church sectors. The public campaigning and confrontationist tactics employed by this third cohort of modern liberal leaders gave them the character of a 'radical' vanguard. They typically played leading roles in Maori organisations and were often active in party politics, particularly in the Labour Party. While they worked closely with the ascendant conservative national leaders, the younger group appealed particularly to a less affluent and more urbanised constituency.

With the declining fortunes of the national economy from the mid-1970s, rising unemployment affected those in the lower socio-economic sectors most dramatically. By the 1981 census 14.1 percent of the Maori labour force, compared to 3.7 percent of the non-Maori labour force, were unemployed (*New Zealand Official Yearbook 1984*; *Census of Population and Housing*, Department of Statistics; Pearson and Thorns 1983: 206-9; Carmichael 1979; Rosenberg 1977; Brosnan 1984; Hill and Brosnan 1984). Common disadvantage served to strengthen Maori identity along ethno-class lines. During the 1960s there had been a measurable strengthening of Maori identity among young school children. Data on inter-group preferences revealed 'a clear shift away from out-group preference among Maoris'. A decade later Graham Vaughan noted (1978: 302-12) that there was 'a groping for a new Maori identity, mediated particularly by knowledge that other minority groups are mounting a worldwide clamour for social equality'. Both among Pakeha and Maori young people there were many 'questioning the status arrangements which previously regulated the relationships between Maoris and Europeans and ... demanding change' (Thompson 1977: 155).

Influenced by Marxist/Socialist, trade union, feminist, Black American, and other civil rights ideologies of that period - 'Brown proletariat' rhetoric achieved wide currency in an emergent protest movement in the late 1970s. These different influences, combined with increasingly assertive expressions of anger over the loss of Maori land, drew together a broad coalition of activists. Central to their political strategy was an attempt to create an ethnic identity that would unite bearers of traditional grievance with alienated urban youth, working families, and the unemployed. Nga Tamatoa (Young Warriors), which was formed following a Young Maori Leaders' Conference in 1970, amalgamated a group of young intellectuals and an urban street gang. Among the concerns of this initially *ad hoc* organisation were opposition to all forms of racism, promotion of equal rights in employment, and preservation of culture, language, and land. Nga Tamatoa also agitated for the introduction of improved Maori studies programs in school curricula (Walker 1990: 210-12).

In recognition of growing cultural and linguistic losses, young Maori reformers in the early 1970s were able to elicit aid from the Departments of Maori Affairs and Education.[13] By 1979 Maori language was being taught in 171 secondary schools to 1500 students, only half of whom were Maori; and Maori studies were available in 250 primary schools. Even so, the supply of qualified teachers of the Maori language was not equal to the demand (Kaai-Oldman 1988: 24-6; James 1986: 51; Walker 1990: 240-41).

Prime Minister Norman Kirk had done much between 1972 and 1974 'to bring back the feeling of optimism among the Maori people that multiculturalism was government policy and not an election promise' (Hohepa 1978: 101). Kirk's successor, Bill Rowling, also encouraged New Zealanders to regard cultural difference as a part of their enriched national heritage. This ideology, however, was more a sentiment of the seventies than it was a monopoly of the Labour Party. Moreover, it was a sentiment that had to compete with the powerful disintegrative forces of the urban environment. A measure of the magnitude of Maori cultural loss was the estimate that, in spite of the recent expansion of Maori teaching, by the end of the decade less than half, and possibly only a third, of the Maori population was fluent in the Maori language (Benton 1979).

In the face of these developments the Maori Affairs Department was itself experimenting with its role. Through the 1970s there was a steady progression in Maori affairs policy towards greater community participation and autonomy. There was also increased Maori employment within the Department of Maori Affairs administration and a heightened demand for more equitable recruitment of Maori staff at all levels of government. In 1977 the department, under a National Government, began a review which was to lead to its Tu Tangata policies. The objective was to involve the Maori community more actively in departmental decision-making. Tu Tangata - meaning 'Stand Tall' - emphasised the need for the community to initiate government aided-development programs and to take the lead in their management (Fleras 1985b: 27). With the re-evaluation of its welfare function, the philosophy and administration of the department underwent a major shift. Direction of social and economic development was seen to be the prerogative and responsibility of Maori leadership and their communities. The role of the Department of Maori Affairs was to be responsive and supportive, not to direct the way. Community goals and departmental resources were evaluated by Maori leaders in consultation with departmental officials, community leaders, and their elders. Because of their close working relationship with the department, negotiations were invariably facilitated by local Maori committees, and developments were communicated at regional and national gatherings of the NZMC, or through other Maori organisations.

'Kokiri units', first set up in the active Wellington region in 1980, were established for the management of community development. These projects ranged broadly from the promotion of skills-training in youth, the teaching of Maoritanga and Maori language, the running of pre-school programs and homework centres for school children, to local economic enterprises. The opportunity to design and run these programs was welcomed and grasped by rural and urban Maori communities alike. Enthusiasts spoke of these changes as a second Maori 'renaissance' (Spoonley 1988: 1, 70; 1984; Walker 1981b; 1984a; 1985). But it was a renaissance which could not immediately shake what an Auckland sociologist described in 1977 as 'an inescapable correlation between membership of a Polynesian minority and low socioeconomic status' (Macpherson 1977: 99). Nor did it touch the ingrained prejudices of the Pakeha majority whose strategic control of employment opportunities appeared unlikely to yield quickly even to a rising generation of better-educated Maori youth (ibid.: 107-11). In the face of continuing evidence of discrimination reinforcing historical inequalities, Maori activists - especially those choosing unconventional forums such as marches, sit-ins, and demonstrations for political expression - had helped to stimulate a pan-Maori consciousness of immense potential. Briefly harnessed in support of well-publicised causes, this new sense of ethnic solidarity transcended the ideological impulses of its principal promoters.

Meanwhile, by the late 1970s there were signs that the major political parties were disposed to settle on a tacit consensus that fell far short of the radical public agenda. While older generations of politically active Maori were accustomed to pursuing Maori interests through the established parliamentary parties and Maori statutory organisations, examples of extra-parliamentary pressure group mobilisation testified to the effectiveness of alternative political strategies. Influenced by the freedom movement in the United States and the ideas of radical trade unionist and socialist organisations, 'Brown Power' and Maori liberation rhetoric began to circulate in the newsletters and manifestos of small Maori protest groups. Organisations such as Nga Tamatoa, Te Matakite, and He Taua shaped protest action in the form of litigation, public petitions, sit-ins, and large-scale land marches. The physical occupation by protesters of disputed Auckland prime real estate at Bastion Point culminated after several months in a massive confrontation with police and the army in May 1978 (Hazlehurst 1988b; Walker 1990).

Among Maori leaders secure in traditional authority there was a mixture of irritation and paternal indulgence towards outspoken younger people. But there was also a shrewd appreciation that Maori causes could be well served by the frisson of apprehension which unruly dissident youth could provoke among complacent Pakeha. If some radical demands and behaviour were thought to be needlessly provocative, there was also admiration for their persistence, and a growing, if sometimes wavering, belief that even their apparently unrealistic goals were legitimate. It was arguable that some notable gains - including the official inclusion of Maori language and culture into the New Zealand education system and the favourable settlement of several land rights issues - could be attributed to protest action. When radical activists fell foul of the law, the community was quick to stand by them, with elders ready to speak in extenuation. If a campaign was launched to seek redress of an ancient grievance, the prominent participation of respected figures would confer mana on what might otherwise be portrayed as ill-considered and perniciously motivated agitation.

The variety of temporary alliances and coalitions, the momentum of protest movements, and the erosion of commitment to existing parliamentary parties were harbingers of a significant discontinuity in Maori political loyalties. A handful of perceptive observers had begun by the late 1970s to reflect on the morphology of the Maori world and the prospects for re-orientation and re-structuring of political action in the national arena. Those who best understood the linkages and tensions in existing forms and processes held the keys to purposeful change.

NOTES

1. This simplified account of Maori social organisation and custom draws on Best 1924; Buck 1977; Firth 1959; Schwimmer 1977; Metge 1976; Caselberg 1975; Salmond 1985, 1980; King 1977b, 1978; Pearce 1980; Mitcalfe 1981; Oliver with Williams 1981.

2. 'Mana' and 'tapu' are two of the most important concepts in Maori lore and social action. Mana ranges in meaning from the description of the status, dignity, and honour of a person or group in secular life to the spiritually imbued power and authority of superior leadership. Its twin concept, tapu, also alludes to supernatural power. It can connote the spiritual potency of powerful rank or sacred objects, as well as prohibition and the danger of defilement resulting from human interference with things under religious restriction. Mana and tapu pervade all levels of human interaction (Bowden 1979; Metge 1986: 61-79; Douglas 1979).

3. See Buck 1977; Winiata 1956-1957, 1967; Metge 1964, 1970, 1976; Kawharu 1977; King 1977b, 1978; Karetu 1977; Mahuika 1977; Dansey 1977; Marsden 1977; Bowden 1979; Sinclair 1980; Oliver with Williams 1981; Mitcalfe 1981.

4. In the Ringatu Church, founded by Te Kooti, and the Ratana Church, founded by Wiremu Ratana, there was a potent blending of Christian teaching and Maori custom (Tarei 1978; Henderson 1965).

5. For further accounts of Maori resistance to European domination and massive land loss, and of the economic, social, and political arrangements which developed during the nineteenth and early twentieth centuries, see Firth 1959; Wright 1967; Winiata 1967; Miller 1973; Caselberg 1975; Kawharu 1975a, 1977, 1989; Adams 1977; Pool 1977; Simpson 1979; Sinclair 1980; Schwimmer 1975; Metge 1964, 1976; King 1977a; Williams 1977; Oliver with Williams 1981; Lyons 1979; McKenzie 1985; Belich 1986; Orange 1987.

6. See Buddle 1979 (lst edition 1860); Gorst 1959 (lst edition 1864); King 1977a; Webster 1979.

7. About 2,200 Maori, 20 percent of those aged 20 to 44, served overseas in World War One (Butterworth 1972: 166), and 5,300 'were accepted for overseas service' in World War Two (Hancock 1946: 10). Among the Pakeha fighting men themselves there is evidence of some ambivalent feelings about their Maori fellow combatants (Phillips 1987: 287).

8. While the Kotahitanga movement was no longer an overt political force after it disbanded in 1902, the flame of its beliefs in Maori self-government was kept alive and shrouded with secrecy, by elders and devotees, until the movement's revival in the 1970s and 1980s.

9. References to the 'four winds' (South, West, North and East), have been, and continue to be, common to speeches of welcome on marae. For an archival record, see the speech of welcome at the Kotahitanga meeting, held at Waipatu 14 June 1892 (Maori Parliament of New Zealand, Governor Grey Collection, Auckland Public Library).

10. Prior to 1976, 'New Zealand Maori' figures in the New Zealand Censuses of Population and Housing referred to those persons who specified themselves to be of 'half or more Maori blood'. In the 1976 census figures those who stated that they were Maori, but did not specify degree, were also included in the 'New Zealand Maori' figures. In the 1981 census a new category, 'of Maori Descent', was introduced. Thus, in 1981 while 8.9 percent (279,252) of the total New Zealand population claimed to be 'New Zealand Maori' (half or more Maori blood), 12.1 percent (385,524) claimed to be of Maori Descent (*Census of Population and Dwellings,* Department of Statistics, 1960-1981).

11. On Maori population and demography see Pool 1977: 20; Rowland 1971; Gould 1982: 179; Hunn 1961; *New Zealand Official Yearbooks 1974-1989.*

12. 'Hui' ('huihuinga') are social functions staged by local people at a marae or local centre, frequently involving hundreds and even thousands of visitors. Hui incorporate all ceremonial, social or political gatherings. 'Tangi' ('tangihanga') are funerals or wakes. See *Hui* by Anne Salmond (1985).

13. See Walker 1979c, 1979d, 1979e, 1981b, 1984a; Sharples 1980; Wood 1978; Kawharu 1979; Oliver with Williams 1981; King 1983; Greenland 1984.

II

THE STRUCTURE OF MAORI POLITICAL LIFE

ORGANISATION AND AUTHORITY

In August 1981, Matiu Rata, a former Labour Minister and now leader of the newly created Maori political party, Mana Motuhake, announced that he had appointed one of his colleagues as spokesman on 'Pakeha affairs'. With pungent irony Rata drew attention to a rarely questioned assumption about the political order in New Zealand. By proposing a Maori spokesman on Pakeha affairs, from the point of view of his supporters at least, 'he had turned that system on its ear!' (Minutes of the Mana Motuhake Secretariat monthly meeting 28 August 1981; *New Zealand Herald*, 19 September 1981).

After over a century of confinement within European perceptions and institutions, a growing body of Maori opinion in the 1970s was challenging the established framework of New Zealand law and government. There were by the beginning of the 1980s both understandable Maori disillusionment with the major political parties and emphatic voices proclaiming the need for greater autonomy, elimination of persisting social and economic injustice, and even the recognition of Maori sovereignty. But there was also a very significant element in the Maori world that was conscious of the notable extension that had occurred in the years since the end of the Second World War in the domain of Maori influence and authority.

Media preoccupation with protest over land and other inequities tended to obscure - for both Maori and Pakeha alike - the extent to which there had already been achieved a substantial devolution of power and responsibility to exclusively Maori organisations. Academic political studies had largely ignored the role and activities of Maori organisations as well as the broader political dimension of the modern Maori experience. As Levine and Vasil later pointed out (1985: 16), the concentration of political scientists on voting behaviour and party fortunes in the four parliamentary seats reserved for Maori representation was accompanied by neglect of 'the much wider scope of Maori politics and ... the other institutions of government orientated towards Maori needs and interests'.

In addition to having full access to the national electoral system of the country, and the rights and benefits conferred by it, Maori people had two kinds of statutory organisations designed explicitly for Maori needs. As part of the central government machinery, organisations were created, staffed, and controlled by what Schwimmer described (1975: 31) as 'Officers paid by the Crown'. The best examples of this first category are the Department of Maori Affairs, the Maori Land Courts, the Maori Education Foundation, and the Maori Purposes Fund Board. Although these organisations were sometimes seen to personify 'the government' and therefore an imposed order, they manifestly catered to the welfare of the Maori community - housing, community improvement, education, skills training, the protection and development of land, and so forth. They also acted as important lines of access for the Maori people to the government.

As they were set up specifically to administer areas of Maori affairs, and as they had from the 1960s a growing policy of hiring Maori staff (though progress was slow at top managerial levels), they were increasingly seen to 'belong' to the Maori world. The encouragement of direct community involvement in the planning and administration of Department of Maori Affairs' programs over the late 1970s was to transform the relationship between the Department and the Maori people. The government was widely seen to have friendlier intent, to be relatively approachable, and to no longer occupy an other-world, distant from the Maori. 'There is optimism and hope in the minds of many that development on Maori terms is still possible', Hohepa had written in 1978 (1978: 104). But at the beginning of the 1980s this belief was only germinating.

The second category of national organisation consisted of those officered by elected and appointed Maori representatives. These were autonomous organisations - run by Maori, for Maori. The elite in such organisations as the New Zealand Maori Council, the Maori Women's Welfare League, Maori Trust Boards, and the Maori Wardens' Association were men and women with considerable status and authority in the community. They were often people of consequence in European society as well as in strictly Maori spheres. Some had acquired fame or notoriety, certainly in their own regions, and sometimes in the country as a whole. They usually had valuable affiliations with people in power, necessarily including key Pakeha in Parliament and the public service.

To these two realms of administration, a third institution was added in 1975: the Waitangi Tribunal, established as a forum to examine Maori grievances in the context of the Treaty of Waitangi and to make recommendations to government. Its existence, and the potential to extend its ambit retrospectively by a simple legislative amendment, created both an avenue for expressing current discontent and a highly visible target for continuing activism and protest. In Schwimmer's taxonomy, the Waitangi Tribunal might be regarded as being part of the government machinery officered by paid servants of the Crown. But this would be to confuse form with substance. For the tribunal, by its very existence, acknowledged the legitimacy of much that had previously been repudiated by the Crown.

In the 1950s Firth (1951:114) followed by Winiata (1967:136) had posited the existence of a 'dual frame of organisation'. Winiata described Maori leaders as living in two worlds and operating 'within two distinct, and often conflicting, systems of value'. A decade and a half later it was possible to perceive a degree of convergence, blurring the boundaries between Pakeha and Maori values and political practice.

By 1980 - and throughout the next decade - one could characterise contemporary Maori political life as occupying three inter-penetrating domains:

a) **The micro-political system:** local Maori organisations and traditional decision-making practices. Indigenous politics operated in an autonomous fashion through continuing tribal structures, the marae, and a range of neighbourhood and local Maori committees and other community-based organisations which dealt primarily with community welfare and the distribution and protection of specific resources. Because of the existence of their own long-established institutions, and the creation of separate systems of resource allocation and land administration, the Maori played a relatively minor part in local government. In Keyes' terms (1981: 12-13), therefore, many rural communities continued to function as enclaves.

b) **The macro-political system:** the party political and bureaucratic arena of wider society. At this level Maori political action had been integrated into the national political system through parliamentary representation and participation in government and national party politics. Maori supporters were present in all political parties and, while sometimes pursuing separate Maori interests, they also could engage fully in support of, or opposition to, any political objective.

c) **The bridging political system:** regional and national Maori organisations operated on behalf of the Maori community, striving to protect the interests of the Maori people at higher political levels. As watchdog and facilitating organisations they made representations to government, commerce, and industry on issues of concern to all Maori, or to Maori in a particular region. Acting as both focal points and arteries of communication, negotiation, and distribution, the bridging institutions played a dynamic interactional and brokerage role both within the Maori world, and in Maori relations with the national political system.

The existence and vitality of the bridging domain differentiated the New Zealand experience from both plural and enclave models of indigenous political expression. As defined by Keyes, New Zealand had a pluralistic polity. The continuance of rurally based traditional structures and practice (and the burgeoning of Maoritanga in urban community life) sustained enclaves of Maori culture and identity. But Maori participation in the public service and parliamentary government of the country was substantial and effective. The pluralistic character of New Zealand was further reinforced by Maori national organisations which channelled strength and authority from one domain to another. Maori ethnicity, therefore, was much more complex than the 'essentially political phenomenon' described by Cohen (1974a:14). Neither was it merely a subordinate and encapsulated entity (Bailey 1977), but one which maintained parallel and interacting systems as well.

THE DIVERSITY OF MODERN LEADERSHIP

In the mid-1960s Bhagabati (1967) observed that modern Maori leadership was moving away from traditional modes of authority and becoming increasingly more preoccupied with wider political issues. Maori 'politicians' (as opposed to traditional elders), she said, functioned primarily through Maori organisations and derived their power from the positions which they held on these organisations. There was also evidence, said Bhagabati (1967: 401-4), that leaders consolidated their positions and power 'by working through formal agencies outside the community, including the church and the government'. Maori leaders, therefore, had to be skilled in approaching and negotiating with outside agencies on their community's behalf.

In 1968 Schwimmer suggested (1975: 331) that 'the Maori political system of today has a significant range well beyond the village'. But, whereas village politics saw fierce contests over concrete local issues, at the national level there was 'a dense cloud of ideology', a preoccupation with general issues related to Maori identity which were less problematic in rural communities. Deepening ideological and party political divisions, crystallising in the 1970s and early 1980s into different modes of political ideology and leadership, were coming into play at all levels of Maori political action. This was particularly pronounced in the cut and thrust of business conducted in national organisations.

These varying styles of leadership had grown out of different historical and social experiences. In the nineteenth and early twentieth centuries the warrior-chiefs, sage/prophets, and royal heads of the Kingitanga movement exemplified a form of leadership that had vanished by the Second World War. They were charismatic and militant - deriving their authority from both divinity and antiquity, resisting European penetration and challenging exploitation. Their style of leadership and mission inspired a recognition by their followers of a special quality, transcending ordinary power and authority. They had the vision to offer a certain future to their people, and to shape that future by their direction. In doing so they exhibited their possession of a high level of 'mana' which, as Kawharu (1989: xix) has explained, 'is that power and authority that is endowed by the gods to human beings to enable them to achieve their potential, indeed to excel, and, where appropriate, to lead'.

While there are ambiguities and multiple meanings embodied in the concept of 'charisma', in the sense adopted by Tucker (1968: 737) it may properly be used in reference to the great resistance leaders of the past: 'The charismatic leader is not simply any leader who is idolised and freely followed for his extraordinary leadership qualities, but one who demonstrates such qualities in the process of summoning people to join in a movement for change and in leading such a movement' (see also Rejai and Phillips 1983, Part 1). In this sense most modern Maori leaders exhibited elements of charisma but, in the absence of a single cause or movement, to a lesser degree than their legendary predecessors.

What Bhagabati and Schwimmer were discerning was the effect on traditional structures of the growing differentiation of the three political domains. While some elements of enclave politics had survived a century and a half of national integration, the increasingly dominant arenas were the bridging and macro-political domains. Operating within and across the domains, working for different causes and from different bases of support (King 1986: 202-3), several different Maori modes or styles of leadership could be loosely distinguished at the beginning of the 1980s:[1]

a) **The 'traditional':** the kaumatua, or community elder who was knowledgeable in, and was the custodian of, tribal lore and custom; derived authority primarily by seniority of descent and exercised it mainly in relation to the maintenance of customary values and practices.

b) **The 'conservative':** these leaders employed conciliatory and brokerage techniques (initially at the national political level and later in local and regional politics).[2] Operating as brokers in all political domains, they might be known to have close associations with major political parties but their eminence in the Maori world gave them a standing in national affairs not available to Pakeha.

c) **The 'liberal':** typically members of the educated elite who emerged in the urban setting in the mid-1960s and early 1970s. Theirs was a confrontationist and crusading style of politics for Maori rights; they worked most significantly in the bridging and macro-political domains but allied themselves with the causes of protest groups. Like the conservative leaders, they might have inherited rangatira status, but they were frequently urbanised, well educated and less likely than conservatives to have a rural power base. They placed great reliance on the potency of ideas and made extensive use of the media.

d) **The 'radical':** leaders of the mid-1970s and early 1980s generation of protesters who employed direct, and often physical, methods of confrontation and civil disobedience. Shock techniques designed to grasp media attention were used for the first time by this generation. They were not afraid to risk imprisonment in challenging what they proclaimed to be an unjust State. Impatient, sometimes scornful of traditional and conservative leaders, they were characteristically uncompromising in pursuit of particular goals. The ideal models of the protesters were the great warrior-chiefs and resistance leaders of the past.

Within living memory in 1980, national Maori leadership had been the province of a handful of men who linked traditional communities and Pakeha institutions. The rise and multiplication of Maori organisations, accompanied by the penetration of radio and television into all quarters of the country, had transformed the Maori political landscape. In the late 1960s it was easy to understand why it was 'extremely difficult to find a person who can speak for the

"Maori" and expound a coherent policy behind which all Maori will stand'
(Forster 1975: 112). Maori Labour MPs had minimal influence with National
Party governments which worked comfortably through the New Zealand Maori
Council and the Maori Women's Welfare League. But the 1970s saw increasing
tensions as conciliatory Maori leaders, and cautious governments, were less able
to satisfy demands based not only on needs but on rights.

For modern leaders, their proclaimed ideology, their chosen realms of action,
and perceived effectiveness of political strategy all contributed to their public
image. While radical leaders relied essentially on their vehemence and
pertinacity, with occasional gains punctuated by minor martyrdom, other Maori
leaders continued to enhance their mana by the use of oratorical profundity,
invocation of the supernatural, and allusions to regional history and custom. In
acting as cultural brokers and interpreters of systems and codes between New
Zealand's two largest ethnic groups, most Maori leaders derived their authority
from strong local and regional associations. The radical activists were unusual in
asserting a pan-Maori ideology which emphasised ethno-class solidarity through
a common history of deprivation, rather than affiliation by homeland or region.

The leadership styles that may be delineated in this way are not necessarily
mutually exclusive. But they are useful in identifying the origins and
characteristics of successive waves of challenge and brokerage in Maori/Pakeha
relations, and in explaining the impulses towards opposition and coalition
between political interests in the Maori world.

The orientations of modern Maori leadership spanned the full range of
political action. Traditional elders concerned themselves principally with the
etiquette and kawa of their ancestors and regions. They sought to preserve Maori
identity by expounding and conserving its store of 'traditional knowledge'.
Conservative leaders were 'establishment' oriented. They used moral persuasion
and participation as a means of monitoring and effecting change. Liberal leaders
did not disclaim the value of conservative techniques, but they were more 'cause'
oriented. They made greater use of pressure politics and were less concerned
with maintaining good relations with those who were the object of their
chastisement.

Radical activists functioned with a small but committed core, and a shifting
periphery of support. They were 'issue' oriented, and used protest to address
these issues. Radicals depended more upon the shared ideology and passions of
their participants than upon the support of a particular community or region.
They organised as needs arose, and sought to extract official compliance with
their demands by the threat or display of social unrest.

Charismatic leadership historically provided both a spiritual and political
expression of Maori sovereignty. Those charismatically inspired movements
which survived, such as the Kingitanga movement and the Ratana Church, were
the most successful in establishing a lasting organisational foundation to these
ideals. A modern charismatic politician, by presenting his aims as a continuation
and latter-day manifestation of the historic Maori struggle, might tap the same

collective energy - a people's belief in their divine mandate - that once propelled the Maori prophets and warrior-chiefs.

The rise of the first Maori political party, Mana Motuhake, owed much of its early success in acquiring a following and an authoritative place in the Maori political cosmology to the ingenuity of its first theoreticians in linking their new movement to its 'past' - to the nineteenth and twentieth century tradition of political resistance. As for the personal qualities that would command respect in the Maori world, those who inquired about attitudes to parties and leaders in 1980 thought they found a 'uniformity of perspectives'. 'Maoriness, commitment to the Maori community, and personal integrity mean more than fidelity to political principles', observed Levine and Vasil. 'Ideology takes a second place. Sincerity - or its appearance - and honesty are more important than party labels. Even humility has a role' (Levine and Vasil 1985: 89).

While these were the values that might be endorsed to an inquisitive social scientist there were tests soon to be encountered in the real world of political choices that would reveal actual trade-offs between sincerity, humility, and party allegiance.

A DYNAMIC AND DEMOCRATIC NETWORK

Emerging ethno-politics saw the development of strategies and new socio-political constructs to impede and compete with the encroaching influences of the European. New institutional palisades were erected to protect the inner organs of Maoridom - the tribes and hapu, customs and language, history and integrity in which its primary identity was lodged. These secondary institutions - Maori organisations which served local needs, which upheld the tradition of regional sovereignty, and which increasingly collaborated on a national basis for the common good - gave the impression of a pan-Maori political system (Ritchie 1965: 80-6). But it was a system, more latent than actual, whose acceptability was dependent upon a consciously respectful co-existence with older political forms.

The organisation and leadership of modern Maori society remained rooted in traditional political conventions. 'One of the basic sources of social strain between Maori and Pakeha is the different concepts of social structure', wrote Walker. In contrast to the stratification and functional separation of powers in the Pakeha-dominated macro-political domain, the Maori are a 'segmented society', he explained, 'where each segment or hapu is an independent political unit'. On the other hand, Pakeha society 'is based on a highly centralised political authority, an attendant bureaucracy, legal system, judiciary and law enforcement arm' (1987: 155; see also Walker 1979b: 115).

The hierarchical or pyramidal nature of Pakeha social and political culture was not replicated by the Maori. A search for hierarchy as 'evidence' of a national political system would have obscured important realities. For example, although its act prescribes that the New Zealand Maori Council should have authority over its regional and local branches this was not, in fact, how the Council functioned. Each District Maori Council was a politically discrete and autonomous unit. In the rural areas old tribal demarcations were honoured. In large urban areas, such as Auckland or Wellington, regional interests represented new residential patterns and loyalties.

The macro-system of the national Maori network reflected the form and dynamics of the smaller 'worlds' of the micro-system. Even in its most prominent and broad-ranging manifestation, the New Zealand Maori Council, the segmentary nature of the power arrangements was clear and it dominated interaction. For instance, at all levels of the NZMC decisions were generally taken by a process of debate and consensus-building at committee and council meetings. Decisions of concern to all Maori would be forwarded, by means of remits and recommendations, to the wider-based organisation. But the traditional philosophy of tribal sovereignty demanded that the ultimate responsibility for each community (or region) remained in the hands of its members, committees, and elected leadership. In their regular activities, local Maori committees and district councils maintained a remarkable degree of autonomy and did not require the blessings of the wider bodies concerning their operations.

Joint action might be taken on matters of common concern, but between quarterly national meetings, district councils of the NZMC got on with managing their own affairs, and likewise at the local level between district council meetings. Neither was subject to the dictates of the wider body. Rather, the influence of opinion came from the other direction - radiating from the community outwards.[3] Indeed the full Council could not make decisions without consulting all its district councils. The NZMC quarterly meetings therefore had a primary function of co-ordinating and harmonising regional interests by mutual consent.

Maori leadership on the national body of the NZMC was frequently distracted from the pursuit of common goals by regionally based disputes. In conducting business the organisation had to accommodate waves of district lobbying, and to contend with the ideological differences and periodic jockeying of its members for power and influence upon the Council. At its national level, therefore, the NZMC represented a collection of determinedly independent district councils which, on any given agenda, had to negotiate their position, manoeuvre their alliances, and trade their votes in order to accomplish national action. The contracting of NZMC business was a lengthy and difficult process. But it was a process which had, over time, generated effective mechanisms for orchestration and control (Hazlehurst 1988a).

The stability of the national Maori network was enhanced by this segmented democracy of its various units. It could not be undermined easily by the dismantling of the Council at its so-called 'pinnacle', or by the withdrawing of government funds. If the NZMC were to be abolished and another institution put in its place, one could predict that any new system would strongly reflect existing regional and local loyalties.[4] The 'network' would continue to exist on the basis of voluntary association, kinship, tribe, and whatever overlay of instrumental decision-making or resource allocation was placed upon it. Thus, particular elements of the Maori world network were overtly and consciously tied together by factors such as regular interaction of leaders in the exchange of business, by inter-group conferences on common issues, and by the mobility of relatively scarce decision-making talent - either between different organisations or between the different levels of action or influence within those organisation.

Pat Hohepa, a Maori linguist, lecturer in Maori Studies at Auckland University, and an outspoken and liberal minded campaigner with strong Northland ties, asserted in 1978 that there was 'one unifying theme' among those who identified as Maori: 'the desire that the destiny of the Maori people must be one with which they agree and this agreement must be by real consultation' (Hohepa 1978: 100). In Hohepa's view, political processes were as important to the Maori as political outcomes.

One of the questions raised at the outset of my research was whether Maori socio-political activity represented a web of associations and meanings which could be understood as a pan-Maori political system. The answer, according to my findings, is both 'yes' and 'no'. The 'Maori world', as it had become fondly known, could be described as a gregarious, heterogeneous, self-conscious, and self-regulating network of 'actually existing relations' (Radcliffe-Brown 1968: 190). As a network of relations it could function as an informative, supportive, competitive, responsive, and even coercive system.

But the relationship between the various major and minor segments, or interest nets, of the Maori world was not so formally arranged as to warrant the description of a 'national political system' in the hierarchical European tradition. In the late 1960s Schwimmer (1975: 332) could not perceive any 'centralised authority even in the rudimentary form' above the 'village' or community level of the Maori political system. 'We find various councils and other figureheads which can be invoked as symbols of unity, and we find concepts which assert symbolic unity', he said. However, the reality underlying the symbolic unity had been tested and strengthened during the 1970s. The New Zealand Maori Council acquired greater status. Protest movements drew larger numbers into political action. But neither the NZMC nor Maori parliamentarians, still less the radicals, were 'representative of the grass-roots' (Kernot 1975: 229). No grand design or unifying theory apportioned responsibilities or determined relationships between the patchwork of traditional and modern institutions. Undeniably, greater coherence continued to exist within the different interest nets and localities than between them.

The linkages between the interest nets, which comprised the Maori world network, varied in intensity. Some were strong and drew upon many years, or even an ancient tradition, of collaboration. Others were weak, spontaneous, or based upon most recent political alignments. Collaboration proceeded through customary processes of invitation, debate, and consensus formation between the groups' members, sometimes followed by formal agreement. Leaders could not make unilateral decisions for alliance on behalf of their groups. Support between interest sectors - whether between tribal regions or districts, or between specific organisations - fluctuated according to the issue, the group's accumulated obligations, and the degree of conflict or confirmation which the alliance might pose to group autonomy and present alliances.

The New Zealand Maori Council, though its scope and aspirations gave it a uniquely extensive and authoritative unifying role, nevertheless remained essentially a mechanism of co-ordination rather than a focus of loyalty. It was a forum for debate and a channel for influence. It was a symbol of a will towards unity and it formalised habits of co-operation. But it had neither the power to command nor the appeal to stir the heart.

While by the 1980s Maori nationalism had no single institutional embodiment it had certainly become manifest in the Maori political vocabulary and in the realm of political expression. Informal inter-organisational exchange had revealed a latent framework for the co-ordination and integration of political action: groups or clusters of interest (several 'interest nets') working together in a loose knit 'network'[5] of associations linking Maori people over the country's length and breadth, providing a vital link between the micro and macro levels of Maori society, on one hand, and between Maori society and that of the European, on the other.

The Maori world network consisted in 1980 of a large number of loosely linked pockets of interest. These interest nets came in two main forms: socio-geographically located communities or regions, and geo-politically located organisations. In rare instances, an individual prominent in the judiciary, the bureaucracy, or the professions might enjoy a status that was independent of other affiliations. Such a person would be part of the network without necessarily representing any specific 'interest'.

Ties of administration, mutual aid, and even political competitiveness bound together the fortunes and welfare of thousands of Maori people. In each interest net factors of tribe and territory, party and group affiliation, and organisational specialties came into play. The particularities of jurisdiction, purpose, ideology, and strategy, and the manner in which these cross-cut other factors, gave interest nets their distinctive identity. Common interest and voluntary association between interest nets, even if changeable and infrequent, created clusters of interest - and ultimately the 'Maori world' network (Lopata 1967; Mitchell 1969; Leinhardt 1977; Friedkin 1980; Walker 1972b, 1975, 1979a).

In the face of the dominant European population many Maori liked to think of themselves as a united force, rather than a set of competing interests. In reality the sovereign nature of these interests had frustrated their evolution into any permanent and cohesive political entity. Thus the Waitangi Tribunal, for example, acted both to assess claims of Maori people against government departments and agencies, and also at times to adjudicate on rival Maori claims to land or fishing rights. The New Zealand Maori Council could speak for all Maori only so long as it managed to avoid significant damage or offence to any of the interests it encompassed and had secured consensus between them on that issue.

Typically, after the event of a land rights march, a major business deal with an industrial corporation, or the passing of legislation, the focus of activity would segment again to the more manageable organisational concerns of the interest nets. A common ideology and a history of political collaboration might lead to further co-operation at a later date. But effective alliances between groups whose beliefs and practices varied widely were difficult to mobilise and unlikely to last.

THE ELECTORAL CLIMATE

The historical involvement of Maori leadership in party politics, the augmentation of their influence through parliamentary representation, and the infusion of leadership styles with party ideology permeated all levels of Maori political action.

From their establishment in 1867, the number of reserved Maori seats under the Maori roll was fixed at four - notwithstanding substantial increases in the total number of seats in Parliament, increases in the Maori population, and an attempt by the Labour government in 1975 to expand their representation. Before 1975 Maori people, of more than half Maori blood, were not qualified to register on the 'European' roll (later known as the 'general' roll). The 1956 Electoral Act required adult Maoris to register on the Maori roll. 'Half-caste' electors were given the choice of registering on either the Maori or the general roll. Those who were less than half Maori had only the general roll option available to them. Following the passage of the Electoral Amendment Act of 1975 all adult Maori, irrespective of their degree of Maori blood, were granted every five years the option of registering on the roll of their choice. 'Maori' was henceforth defined in the act as 'a person of the Maori race of New Zealand; and includes any descendant of such a person who elects to be considered as a Maori' (Electoral Amendment Act 1975: 206).

In theory, from 1967, any person of any ethnic background could stand as a candidate in any seat. In practice, most general seats continued to be contested exclusively by candidates from the dominant Pakeha sector. But Maori candidates had been known to stand for general seats; a few had been elected to those seats, and some had achieved ministerial rank. Maori voters on the general roll, however, had rarely had significant influence as they were greatly outweighed by non-Maori voters. Little is known even now about Maori voting behaviour in general seats. New Zealand political scientists and pollsters, anthropologists, and sociologists have been uniformly incurious about the number, characteristics, and motivations of those Maori who have chosen to express themselves politically in the predominantly Pakeha arena.[6]

As for Maori candidates in general electorates, they have been in most respects indistinguishable from other representatives of their party. For the electors it has usually been a case of 'voting for the party, not the man'. Maori

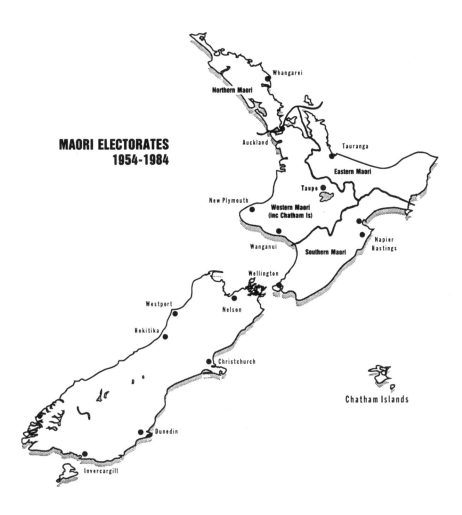

Maori Electorates 1954-1984
Source: *New Zealand Electoral Atlas* (McRobie 1989).

MPs elected to general seats typically placed greater emphasis on party policies other than Maori affairs. Thus, they were more likely to maintain Pakeha confidence and, in the expressed judgement of some of them, be granted the power to do more good for their people in the long run (Ben Couch, interview 9 June 1981).

Many Maori have long contended that they were greatly under-represented in Parliament. The effectiveness of the Maori MPs in influencing government policy is hampered by the sheer size of their constituencies. The fact that the number of Maori seats has not been increased since they were introduced is seen as a gross injustice. One common argument against increasing the Maori seats was that, as many Maori had chosen to go on the general electoral roll, the work of the Maori MP was not as great as it once was.[7] The NZMC responded: 'Regardless of whether Maoris vote on the general roll or not they tend to refer matters of concern to themselves as Maoris to Maori Members. They do not cease to be Maori when they vote on the general roll' ('Maori Representation in Parliament', NZMC 9 June 1981: 2).

In a small Parliament, with relatively evenly balanced support for the major parties, there were understandable expressions of alarm when Maori lobbies claimed that, under the same formula used to calculate the number of non-Maori electorates, the Maori people should be entitled to between seven and nine seats. While it seemed that Maori seats were the inviolable preserve of the Labour Party, the Nationals seized the opportunity to reverse moves that were certain to favour their opponents.

Where the size of the Maori population was itself of political significance, it was predictable that the shift in 1975 from arbitrary fractions of genetic inheritance to an essentially subjective definition of ethnicity would be accompanied by controversy over Maori political representation and the administration of enrolment choices.[8] A new requirement, under the 1981 census, to divulge *degree* of ethnicity sparked Maori outrage. There was suspicion that the manipulation of census definitions constituted a Pakeha manoeuvre to undermine the intent of the Electoral Amendment Act (1975), and to discredit demands for more Maori seats.[9]

While registration of an elector is compulsory in New Zealand, voting is not. Maori people were frequently accused of displaying greater political apathy than the Pakeha. In 1978 the Labour candidate, Matiu Rata, won the Northern Maori seat with 71.47 percent of the votes cast, defeating Social Credit (14.44 percent) and National Party (12.35 percent) candidates. But Rata won with the support of only 26.47 percent of the qualified vote. Only 43.20 percent of the qualified electors for the Northern seat actually turned out to vote. Of these, a remarkable 14.25 percent cast invalid votes. The proportion of spoiled or incorrectly completed ballot papers was puzzlingly high when compared to informal votes in the other Maori seats that year (Eastern Maori 1.87 percent, Southern Maori 1.34 percent, and Western Maori 2.07 percent). The turnout rate on the general roll for the same year was 69.5 percent and the average number of informal votes recorded on the general roll was 0.52 percent (*New Zealand General Elections,*

Journals of the House of Representatives of New Zealand 1977-1981; *New Zealand Official Yearbooks, 1978-1984*; Chapman 1986; Sorrenson 1986).

Despite the 'continuing Maori plea for separate representation', Sorrenson notes (1986: B-62), 'there has not been a corresponding grass-roots support for the Maori seats in terms of registration and voting on the Maori roll':

> In 1949 77.7 percent of the eligible Maori population were registered, but by 1975, when the basis of registration was changed from half or more to anyone descended from a Maori, the percentage had fallen to 58.3. There has been an even larger fall-off in valid votes as a percentage of the total eligible population - from 84 percent in 1940 to 27 percent in 1975. Though the change in 1975 increased the potential Maori electorate very considerably - from some 118,180 persons of half or more Maori descent in 1975 to some 154,400 who were descended from a Maori - there was no corresponding increase in the number of registrations in the Maori rolls. (Sorrenson 1986: B-62; see also 1980 Parliamentary Electoral Roll Revision, Department of Justice, 1981)

Many Maori eligible to vote, possibly 'as high as one-third', Sorrenson pointed out, were registered on neither roll. They could be young people 'unschooled in their rights as citizens', or those who remained unpoliticised by the marae, the political parties, or even by the radical sectors of the Maori world (Sorrenson 1986: B-64). Some presumably chose to remain outside an electoral system that returned few tangible rewards. Some could see no point in participating in contests whose outcome (in the Maori seats) seemed a foregone conclusion or (in general seats) was likely to be unaffected by their vote. Others registered protest by non-participation.

Registration on the Maori roll required a positive assertion of this preference at the appointed time. Those who did not make their choice in the correct manner were automatically included on the general roll and could only correct this position every five years. Inaccurate completion of registration cards or political drowsiness, at a time when elections were a distant concern, resulted in many errors. High mobility of population would inevitably have serious consequences upon electoral roll stability. Accurate address keeping of a transient population, particularly those who were single, unemployed, or seeking seasonal work, was no simple task.

Maori observers had only partial explanations for these phenomena, and academic inquiries into election results were uniformly unsatisfactory (Mahuta 1981a: 22-3). Matiu Rata rejected the diagnosis that the low electoral participation of the Maori was proof of political apathy. He asserted that a fundamentally unsympathetic system was the cause of these baffling figures. The greater complications which confronted Maori voters in registering and casting votes, the further disadvantages of poorer education, geographical isolation, lack of transport to polling booths, and what seemed to be excessively stringent scrutinising of Maori ballot papers, could account for poor Maori voting patterns (Tabacoff 1972: 51-52).

The muddled state of the Maori roll was a deeply contentious issue during the 1981 general election. The opportunity to correct errors on the roll was not afforded Maori voters until the next census - which would occur after the election. Maori leaders reasoned that it would be more logical for people to be given a choice just prior to elections, rather than directly after them. Certainly, this would provide greater incentive and attention to enrolment. A possible solution, that Maori communities be involved in managing enrolment to help overcome these problems, was not seriously canvassed during this period. But Maori leaders were demonstrably eager to seek remedies to what amounted to entrenched impediments to the democratic rights of their people in national elections.

Unresolved issues regarding the Maori roll inevitably continued to affect Maori and Pakeha party political relations. For years there was a widespread expectation that the Maori people would elect to have the Maori seats abolished and would join the rest of the country on the general roll. Electoral integration, like other forms of integration, was seen by many Europeans as an enlightened goal that would be achieved in the fullness of time. Although it was a heatedly debated topic within the Maori community - in 1976 Nga Tamatoa had advocated more Maori seats but another protest group, Te Matakite, had been in favour of abolition - by far the majority of Maori voters still voted for Labour on the Maori roll (McRobie 1981: 13).

While seven out of ten 'Europeans' agreed with the proposition that separate Maori representation should end, the question, wrote McRobie, was 'largely ignored by both the House and the country' (1978: 272; Levine and Robinson 1976: 99). It was not until 1981 that a thorough study of the likely outcome of abolishing the Maori seats was published. Alan Simpson demonstrated that only the National Party had anything to gain from such a change. The recent proposals for the development of a Maori party based on separate representation held, in Simpson's view (1981: 43, 51), 'rather more promise for increased Maori participation and influence in the Parliament, politics and administration of New Zealand than is offered by a continuation of present arrangements ...'

For many years, prior to the 1980s, Maori political preferences had been as much expressions of class interest as they had been for the Pakeha, with the working-class giving most of its support to the Labour Party.[10] For more than five decades, however, real benefits in Maori welfare policy flowed under both Labour and National governments. Although they were not aloof from questioning the fairness of outcomes - particularly over the sharing of land and resources - conservative leaders saw activist public protest as a threat to their hard-won congenial relations with the Pakeha establishment. It was feared that open attack upon the system would impede the steady progress to greater concessions from government (Walker 1979d; 1979e; 1981b; 1984a; 1984; Kawharu 1979; King 1983; Awatere 1984; Spoonley 1988: 35; Hazlehurst 1988b).

On the other hand, the value of common action, the growing habit and expectation of co-operation, and the recent history of organisations that were better led and financed with an ideology of mutual support, were hard to deny. Modes of open expression of grievance by way of land rights marches, sit-ins, public petition, and civil disobedience were salient features of contemporary Maori action. Whether approved of or not, conservative Maori politics to some extent accommodated these new tactics and demands arising from the urban deculturated and disaffected.[11] But the adaptation was neither enthusiastic nor complete.

By 1980 Maori ethnic identity was expressed in a kaleidoscope of socio-geographic interest sectors, a range of formal and informal pressure groups and protest organisations, and a distinct set of leadership styles, strongly influenced by party political and ideological affiliations. While it may still have been true in the late 1960s, as Schwimmer had contended (1975: 11), that 'the Maori tends to be little concerned with general political issues and to limit his interests almost entirely to Maori affairs', participation in national party politics had become a well established fact of Maori political life and loyalties. Maori candidates were regularly being put forward for parliamentary election, through party branches. There was, however, no independent Maori machinery for the running of Maori candidates. Although the Ratana Church itself continued to put forward its own Ratana Labour candidates, no Maori group or leader with sufficient renown had attempted to mobilise a parliamentary party on a purely ethnic basis, to cross-cut existing Maori interests to create a pan-Maori party. All this was about to change.

NOTES

1. For a review of modern theories of leadership see Blondel (1987). The survey of the literature on African American leadership in the United States by Davis (1982) is also instructive.

2. Conciliatory and brokerage techniques were pioneered by the 'Young Maori Party' leaders in national political arenas. This was the style of leadership which Bhagabati (1967) observed emerging in the early 1960s in a formative stage at the community level.

3. Any level of the NZMC was free to contact any government agency at any time, and at any level if it so wished. However, it was generally understood that representations from the district or national levels would carry more weight.

4. In 1988 the government was known to be considering dismantling the Department of Maori Affairs and replacing the management of government funds for Maori development entirely through a runanga system - that is, a system of autonomous and self-determining local and regional councils, based on traditional iwi or tribal units. It was not clear what role, if any, was envisaged for the New Zealand Maori Council if the runanga system was adopted. The issue remained unresolved when the Labour

government was voted out of office in 1990 but, as a policy, was shortly after abandoned by the National government.

5. In its broadest sense a local 'interest net' may consist of a community collective, its organisations, institutions, and leadership. A regional 'interest net' may consist of several collaborating communities, their organisations, institutions, and leadership. The 'Maori world network' refers to the loosely connected and occasionally collaborating consortium of interest nets. The structure of the network will appear to vary according to the emphasis given to its political and socio-geographical dimensions.

6. In *The New Zealand voter*, Levine and Robinson (1976: 9,15,99) admitted: 1) that their postal survey had a response rate of 38 percent; 2) 'some lack of participation by persons designating themselves as "Maori"' (3.3 percent compared with 7.9 percent in the population); and 3) that they were unable to distinguish between Maori on the general roll and those on the Maori roll. They did tabulate Maori party preferences: 19.6 percent National Party, 58.8 percent Labour Party; 5.9 percent Social Credit; 0 percent Values Party.

7. The 44 percent of Maori respondents in the 1975 Levine and Robinson (1976: 99) survey who did not support the retention of the Maori seats were a good indication of the unrepresentativeness of the sample from which they came.

8. For 1981 population figures, see Chapter III, footnote 2.

9. The 1981 census provided examples of how these calculations could be given: Example 3 represented someone who was 9/16ths Maori:

Mother = 5/8 N.Z Maori + 1/2 European

Father = 1/2 N.Z Maori + 1/4 European + 1/4 Samoan.

Not surprisingly, this fractionation of ethnicity for the census aroused criticism - particularly where the required calculations were so complicated that people could conclude that their fractions added up to 115 percent or more. Europeans, however, were not required to declare Scottish, Irish, Welsh, or English ancestry. The arithmetical exercise seemed only to apply to those with 'brown' skin.

10. Clive Bean (1988: 303) shows that since the 1960s 'the level of class voting has declined considerably, as it has in many other countries', brought about by 'new age cohorts with weaker class-party alignments', but that 'occupation remains the central social structural determinant of the vote in New Zealand'. It is of course difficult to fit the long-term unemployed into an occupational framework.

11. The Haka Party incident and its aftermath, involving a clash between urban Maori youth and Pakeha university students in 1979, illustrates the processes of this accommodation (Hazlehurst 1988b).

III

FROM LABOUR TO INDEPENDENT

Matiu Rata was born a member of the Te Aupouri tribe on 26 March 1934 in the far north settlement of Te Hapua. After the death of his father - a gumdigger and farm labourer - he moved with his mother to Auckland in 1944 where he completed his primary education. Following a brief secondary school career Matiu left to make his living.

From 1950 to 1954 Rata journeyed between South America, Australia, the Pacific Islands, and New Zealand as a merchant seaman. He gained his Able Seaman's certificate and became a member of the Seamen's Union. Between 1954 and 1963 'Mat' worked as a truck driver, storeman, farm and forestry labourer, and spray painter. During a period of employment with the New Zealand Railways between 1960 and 1963 he became well-known as a trade union organiser acting on the executive of the Amalgamated Society of Railway Servants at the Otahuhu Railway workshops. It was through his involvement in the New Zealand railway union that he entered the national political arena.

Rata also became strongly committed to the Ratana Church during his years in Auckland, becoming an active leader and president of the Ratana Youth movement. Later he became the Chairman of the Auckland Branch of the Ratana Church and a registered 'Apostle' and Minister of the Church. In an article on Rata, journalist Peter Isaac pointed out (*Te Maori* May 1973: 3) that: 'Traditionally, Ministers of the Ratana faith are strong-minded individualists who believe a hard day's work is the closest thing to Godliness'. Rata was no exception. His family background and his involvement in the trade union movement had a lasting effect upon his politics. His strong identity with the working-class was reinforced by the fact that most employed Maori earned their living by the 'sweat of their backs'. Professional men were still very rare in the Maori world in the 1950s and 1960s. Just as the Labour Party was seen as the proper home of the Maori voter, strong affiliations between the union movement and the Maori people were also considered 'natural'.

Rata was partly motivated to enter politics because of the social and economic inequities which he saw between the Maori and the Pakeha. When growing up he had observed differences of privilege and status between local farmers' children and Maori children in the same area. 'It annoyed me that my people had to work so hard, and yet put up with such poor conditions' (ibid.).

In his later political life Rata was to become adamant in his expressed beliefs in the social importance of the Maori family, in the right of Maori to retain their communal ownership over land, and in the maintenance of the traditions and values of Maori life. Married with three children himself, he translated this commitment, as many Maori leaders did, into a heavy involvement with numerous community enterprises and committees. He acted as a Labour area organiser in support of T.P. Paikea, a man who had greatly inspired him in his early years, in the latter's candidacy for the Northern Maori seat. Following the passing of his respected friend and leader, Rata himself won the northern seat in 1963, beginning a seventeen year parliamentary career.

RATA AS LABOUR POLITICIAN

After his election Rata sat on the back benches of the Opposition for almost ten years, 1963-1972. This, he said, never discouraged him as, to his constituents, he was still 'their man in Parliament'. As a leading authority on Maori leadership had said (Winiata 1967:137), 'membership in Parliament has been the main leadership position available to the Maori in the wider New Zealand society'. Simply by being a Member of Parliament Rata was a person of considerable consequence.

During this time Rata became involved in many parliamentary committees such as Fisheries, Maori Affairs, Defence, Public Petitions, and Island Affairs. On occasion he chaired Labour Party Caucus committees on Maori affairs, forestry, and fisheries. He also combined his experience in Maori oratory with a personal study of international methods of debate. It was said that he read what he could on the techniques of some of the world's great orators (*Te Maori* May 1973: 33).

As a Member of Parliament Matiu Rata was regarded in the Maori community as an idealist and a man of unwavering principles. He took an early stand against the role of the press in negative stereotyping by the invidious labelling of 'Maori' offenders in court reporting (Ballara 1986: 144), and he was active in the campaigns against sporting contacts with South Africa (Chapple 1984: 8-9):

Some people believe that he overemphasises the division between Maori and Pakeha ... He has been criticised for building his political fortunes by constantly underlining issues of race. Yet he never flinches at vigorously drawing attention to an issue if he detects something wrong about it. Right from the start he never lost an opportunity to denounce apartheid and all that went with it. There was no room in his make-up for half-denials, or mealy-mouthed platitudes. His criticism was total, and his opposition so great that even some of his Labour colleagues in the House wished that Rata would shut up. (*Te Maori* May 1973: 30)

Among less charitably inclined Pakeha, Rata was characterised as 'clumsy, inarticulate ... not well read ... repetitious ... consistently inconsistent' (Garnier and Levine 1981: 131). Even his friends would admit that he had a tendency to speak at excessive length and too abrasively. One front-bench colleague, who met him first in January 1963, recalled 'unpunctuated gushes - the words just poured out and the listener usually got lost long before he ran out of breath' (Hon. Bob Tizard to the author, 7 October 1991). But Rata was also well-known for his occasional quick-witted and poignant statements. He received recognition for his optimism and his 'undoubted powers of persuasion' (*Te Maori* Dec./Jan. 1979/80: 30).

By the early 1970s Rata recognised that the emergence of the urban street gang was a symptom of what he called 'a general urban crisis which Maori and Island people face' (Tabacoff 1972: 84). He criticised the government for its slowness in dealing with urgent housing, educational, and employment needs in the urban areas and for its lack of financial support for community services offered by the churches. Rata felt that the National Party government still paid little heed to the opinions of the largest minority in the country. He charged them with making little effort to consult the Maori people and with legislating against Maori interests.

Apart from a brief period in the 1960s when he saw virtue in the 'One New Zealand' philosophy of the Hunn era, Rata strongly urged an increase of Maori representation in Parliament. Maori seats, he said, should be apportioned according to the percentage of the national population which the Maori represented. Because of the complicated procedure of Maori registration on the Maori roll, and the format for the special (absentee) vote, thousands of Maori votes were declared invalid on the grounds that they were either unregistered, improperly filled out, or had not been placed as a special vote. Rata contended that the statistics gave a false impression of Maori voting patterns.

On Maori matters Rata had the ear of both parties in Parliament. He chaired the Labour Maori Policy Committee. The three other Maori MPs, other Maori delegates including the well-known Maori academic Dr Patrick Hohepa, and the Labour leader Norman Kirk himself, also served on this committee. From first-hand experience the Maori members of the Maori Policy Committee were able to play a decisive role in examining the needs of the Maori, and in helping to set Labour policy priorities. When he presented the Maori Policy Committee report to the May 1972 Annual Labour Party Conference Rata stated that 'some 62 specific remits have been and are under consideration by your committee' (Maori Policy Committee Report to the 56th Annual Labour Party Conference presented by Matiu Rata, 11 May 1972: 3). Tabacoff observed (1972: 58) that the Maori

Policy Committee acted as 'the most important organ by which Maori problems are brought to the attention of the Labour Party'.

In the later 1960s Maori anger exploded in the public and political arenas, greatly sharpened by what was perceived as a deliberate attempt by the government to facilitate further land loss to the Pakeha through legislation. The 1967 Maori Affairs Bill, observed Tabacoff (1972: 95), resulted in a direct confrontation between government and Maori leaders. This bill acted as a 'turning point whereby Maori opinion began to form a more articulate position on issues that directly affect Maoridom'. The National government was accused of being 'actively hostile to Maori interests' and it was this which spurred on the higher and lower ranks of Maori leadership alike to 'actively protest against inequities in society' (ibid.).

In the House and on the Parliamentary Maori Affairs Committee Rata strongly supported the opposition to the bill registered by the NZMC following its conference. Multiplicity of ownership, which the new bill was resolute in undermining, he said, merely reflected the Maori tradition of tribal ownership and association with a specific area of land. It guaranteed the continuation of tribal identity and location. Individualisation or Europeanisation of title, on the other hand, would break down this tradition. People should have the right to maintain communal forms of ownership if they wished, he said. In defence of this position Rata quoted the NZMC: 'That the strong ties between people and their land persist and the preservation of kin-groups as proprietor of land is an important principle' (Tabacoff 1972: 102).

Rata asserted that the recommendations on Maori land development, made in the Hunn Report six years earlier, had never been seriously pursued by the National government. The Labour Party, on the other hand, he said, would promote Maori land development and would do it without taking the land or the initiative away from its rightful owners. The proposed bill merely guaranteed further sale of Maori land, and the leakage of incorporation shares, into the hands of Europeans. By the time the bill returned to Parliament for its final reading a number of clauses had been amended by the Maori Affairs Committee. Altered status of Maori land was redefined as having 'ceased to be Maori land' instead of being declared 'European land'. Safeguards were included concerning land sales and development which provided for greater consultation and rights of appeal for owners. Incorporations were given the option, hitherto denied, to allow their shareholders to trade in shares; unclaimed dividends could be retained by incorporations for the benefit of the owners rather than being handed over to the Maori Trustee; the conversion of uneconomic shares was fixed at 50 pounds instead of the proposed 100 pounds; and a few other small concessions which provided some maintenance of special protection were allowed to remain intact (Kawharu 1977: 291).

To the Maori people the amended version of the bill was, however, a case of the lesser of two evils. To the very last the 1967 Maori Affairs Amendment Bill was resolutely opposed by Maori leaders, intellectuals and Members of Parliament throughout the country, with the support of their Pakeha friends and sympathisers. 'It is doubtful', wrote Kawharu, 'if any other piece of legislation concerning the Maori has been attended by so much publicity and heated debate'. Following the death of the Eastern Maori Member, P.T. Watene, the task of leading the opposition to the bill was taken up in the House by Rata. Kawharu observed that:

> he [Rata] led with considerable resource, disclosing a firm grasp both of the legal-economic implications of the bill itself and of the hard realities of the political arena. Under banner headlines the *Auckland Star* depicted him as a real parliamentary leader of his people: "He spearheaded the Opposition and marshalled his forces and arguments skillfully and vigorously. He displayed a knowledge of parliamentary tactics that kept the fight going fiercely to the end. Nor did he sink into the intemperate language that some of his European colleagues used so lavishly and pointlessly" (19 Nov 1967). It was perhaps worthy of comment too, that the Opposition as a whole was willing to accept Maori direction - something Maori members of the National Party were seemingly not able to achieve with the government ... Outside Parliament, Sir Turi Carroll said on behalf of the New Zealand Maori Council that despite the removal of most of its objectionable features the bill continued to allow self-interest to dominate group interest. (Kawharu 1977: 291-2)

When the 1972 general election swept Labour into power the caucus elected two Maori MPs into the ministry. The new Prime Minister, Norman Kirk, made Rata Minister of Maori Affairs and Minister of Lands. His colleague Whetu Tirikatene-Sullivan, who succeeded her father in the Southern Maori seat, became Minister of Tourism. The Maori people were elated with these appointments. At only 38, Matiu Rata was described as having 'already soared like a meteor across the New Zealand political scene' (*Te Maori* May 1973: 29). Soaring with him was his campaign manager and confidant, Dr Patrick Hohepa, who was appointed as joint adviser to the Minister of Maori Affairs and the Minister of Education.

The Minister of Maori Affairs and his advisers immediately set to work to produce a White Paper and a number of draft bills which would undo the paternalistic Maori Affairs Act (1953) and its 1967 amendments. Rata's White Paper, and his subsequent legislative achievements, the Maori Affairs Amendment Act (1974), the Maori Purposes Act (1974), and the Treaty of Waitangi Act (1975), represented a major philosophical shift in the administration of Maori affairs in New Zealand. On language, he called for a statutory recognition of Maori, encouraging its use among staff members of the Maori Affairs Department. He proposed that a 'Maori Language Service' be established to provided assistance to government bodies. As it is the 'principal obligation' of the department to aid and assist the Maori race, Rata said the department 'must foster, promote and provide for the retention of Maori culture'. While it was conceded that a way of life could not be enforced by law it was the duty of the officers and policy-makers of the department to develop their aroha (caring and empathy) towards things Maori.

Perhaps the most significant objective of Rata and his associates was to change the earlier policy towards Maori land from one of enforced Europeanisation to one which gave greater protection to Maori interests. The Labour government's amendments to the Maori Affairs Act provided for a greater involvement of Maori owners in all matters concerning the use and development of their land. Among the many objectionable provisions in the act Rata repealed was the use of land for the payment of debts. He proposed new ways in which uneconomic or fragmented land interests could be utilised more efficiently without loss of Maori ownership, and introduced a protective quorum system for the sale of multiple-owned Maori land. These changes during his ministry were lauded by conservative and liberal Maori leaders alike. 'Without them', stated Latimer, 'we would have had a lot less land than we have today (interview 2 July 1981). The 'first six months', after the act came into force, wrote Walker, 'the sale of Maori land amounted to only 1700 acres compared to 10,000 acres at a comparable period in 1979' (1980: 3).

In addition to slowing the alienation of Maori land, Rata promoted a trend in government to listen to major tribal land claims, and to offer compensation by the return of Crown land to its original owners when State injustice or error could be demonstrated. He succeeded in opening up negotiations for settlement of 50,000 acres confiscated in 1867 under the Ngaiterangi land claim and the return of Mt Taranaki (Mt Egmont) to the Taranaki tribes. He also established a Commission of Inquiry into Maori Reserved Land.

In 1975 Rata was the driving force behind the setting up of the Waitangi Tribunal. The function of this quasi-judicial body was to hear and deliberate on a wide range of social, legal, and economic injustices which were perceived as direct breaches of the Treaty of Waitangi. The tribunal, however, was seen to be a 'toothless tiger'. Many Maori grievances were rooted in the large land confiscations which had occurred during the latter part of the nineteenth and early twentieth centuries. The tribunal was not empowered to act retrospectively. Although its few deliberations up to 1981 had brought little result, many Maori waited in hope that the tribunal would one day provide an effective avenue of appeal against earlier injustices.

This period marked the passing of a substantial body of legislation which corrected, to a considerable extent, earlier legislation which had disadvantaged Maori people. It inaugurated a more tolerant attitude towards Maori social and cultural integrity in Maori affairs policy. It made way for greater employment of Maori personnel at higher levels in the Department of Maori Affairs and for direct community participation in the planning and management of departmental programs. Although many of these changes had been called for by his predecessors in earlier years, the political climate and the personality of Rata converged to produce a major breakthrough for Maori influence over government policy and legislation. 'When Labour was in power 1972-5', Metge observed (1976: 206), the Maori people 'commanded more political weight than they had for a very long time'.

Some of the ground gained on behalf of the Maori during Rata's term in office was won against a backdrop of public disapproval and personal criticism. The introduction of a national holiday in 1973, when New Zealanders celebrate the day when Maori and Pakeha contracted the country's nationhood, was an innovation that owed much to Rata's influence.

Since the early 1960s there had been a Northland area holiday on February 6 known as Waitangi Day. Rata shared with Norman Kirk a desire to develop a sense of 'New Zealandness'. To complement the practical action envisaged for the Waitangi Tribunal they and their colleagues in the Labour Party's Maori Policy Committee had conceived of transforming the provincial Waitangi Day into a national public holiday to be called New Zealand Day. Attempts to effect this change by a private member's bill which Rata introduced while in Opposition were rebuffed by the National government (Rata to the author, 12 October 1991). Celebrating a national holiday of this kind, the National government objected, would cost an estimated eleven million dollars.

The Labour Party went into the 1972 election with the creation of 'New Zealand Day' as a relatively inconspicuous part of its manifesto. In the new Cabinet the Minister of Internal Affairs and Local Government, Henry May, was promptly charged by Kirk with responsibility for bringing in the New Zealand Day legislation early in 1973 (Hon. Henry May to the author, 10 October 1991; Hon. Tom McGuigan to the author, 2 October 1991).

Rata and his colleagues thus won the holiday, but at a high price in symbolic manipulation. 'Waitangi Day' had commemorated the unique pact by invoking the Maori name of the place at which the treaty was first signed. 'New Zealand Day', well-meant as a recognition that there could be one nation with two people, had overtones of Pakeha dominance. Ironically, this gave the conservative New Zealand Maori Council, together with the radicals of Nga Tamatoa (Walker 1990: 211), an opening to criticise the change as offensive to the Maori. A subsequent National government preserved the national holiday, restoring the name 'Waitangi Day', the name which has endured since 1976.

In evaluating Rata's achievements during the 1970s as a Cabinet Minister it is possible to depict him as the most influential Maori politician of his generation. In the two decades after the end of the Second World War, Maori politicians operating at the national level had seemed to provide less effective leadership than the giants of the past (Winiata 1967: 161-2). This was as much a consequence of the influence exerted by the growing number of post-war voluntary associations and Maori organisations as it was a reflection on the quality of particular MPs.

Just before he died at the end of August 1974 Kirk apparently contemplated a ministerial reshuffle in which he would have taken the painful step of dropping his friend and ally (confidential information, member of the Kirk ministry, 4 October 1991). Some supporters, suspecting inadequacies in Rata's executive capacity, wondered why he did not press their cause even further. Others believed that Rata was restrained neither by his own abilities, nor by his inclinations, but by the determination of his Labour colleagues to step forward in Maori affairs only with the utmost delicacy and circumspection (Garnier and Levine 1981: 131).

In fleeting references to Matiu Rata throughout her controversial book, *Diary of the Kirk Years*, Norman Kirk's private secretary Margaret Hayward indicated (1981: 139-40) that under stress, in ill health, and with his unpredictable and eccentric personality, Rata had at times caused concern to Kirk and to his parliamentary colleagues. In July 1973 Rata had been hospitalised with a heart condition. According to Hayward it was Matiu's 'high living' and his periodic appearance of 'not being able to cope' with the fullness of his responsibilities which had most concerned the Prime Minister. 'Mr K', she said, 'is fond of Mat and doesn't like taking him to task ...' Kirk was quick, however, to point out to Mat when he felt he was 'letting his people down'.

In February 1974 Kirk was very displeased with Rata for not attending a dinner given by Queen Elizabeth II aboard the royal yacht, *Britannia*, when it was anchored at Lyttleton. Kirk was said to have told his private secretary later that he had 'really blasted Mat, demanding that he write a personal note of apology to the Queen' (ibid.: 212). Three days later, Rata made amends by arranging that he and Kirk board the *Britannia* in lavish pageantry: 'he and Mat Rata clambered into the ornately carved 80-man canoe and were paddled out. Photographers flocked to picture a beaming Mr K almost obscured by the delighted paddlers' (ibid.: 312). Rata later explained that he had turned down the initial invitation from the Queen in order to register his disapproval of the dishonouring by the Crown of the Treaty of Waitangi, particularly Article Two, in regard to Maori land.

At a hospital bedside meeting between Rata and the Prime Minister, Kirk reminded his Minister of the dreams he had had for the Maori people and that if he would 'put the machinery into gear ... Great things could be done'. This little talk, Rata's wife was later to confide, had 'made a tremendous difference - all the difference' to Mat (Hayward 1981: 152). Much of his despondency passed. In June 1974, after Rata's doctor gave him a 'clean bill of health', Kirk returned Rata's Lands portfolio, which he had earlier withdrawn (ibid.: 259).

The untimely death of Norman Kirk was a tremendous emotional and political blow to both Matiu Rata and the Maori world (*Te Maori* Dec./Jan. 1979-80: 29). In a tribute to the late Prime Minister delivered in Parliament, Rata called him a 'friend of the multitude, a colleague, a worthy New Zealander and a personality who spoke in direct and passionate terms':

No-one I believe had a better grasp of the value of cultural diversity such as New Zealand enjoys ... Doubtless, he provided to the minority comfort, confidence and inspiration ... He will be sadly missed on every Marae in New Zealand. For them he was a prime source of their hopes and dreams in a sensitive and challenging period of their history. (*Te Maori* October 1974: 6-7)

As a result of his affinity with the Maori world Kirk had been a protector as well as a friend to Rata. After the National Party reclaimed power from Labour in the 1975 election, this privileged position was not sustained. The new leader of the Labour Party, Wallace ('Bill') Rowling was less tolerant of what he perceived to be Rata's managerial incompetence, both as Minister and in developing policy through the party apparatus. Although there was no real animosity between them, Rowling felt impelled to take a tough stand:

Two problems emerged during Mat's time as Minister. The first, which upset me as Minister of Finance, was the degree of financial irresponsibility evidenced in his handling of his portfolios. He tended to do things for the right reasons but without regard for the financial consequences. The second problem arose when on one occasion one of his colleagues acted for him with the Lands portfolio and found when taking over that Mat's desk was piled high with unactioned files. That kind of situation did not endear him to any of his Cabinet colleagues. (Rowling to the author, 20 August 1991)[1]

At first Rowling reduced Rata's status within the shadow ministry. Then he stripped Rata of his rank as shadow minister and as committee chairman and spokesman on Maori affairs. Thereafter Rowling carried the shadow portfolio of Maori Affairs himself. 'I finally relieved him of his responsibilities as Maori Affairs Spokesman because, in my view, he was simply failing to perform in the best interests of his people', said Rowling (ibid.).[2] From this time Rata felt he was given the back seat in Opposition on Maori affairs.

The impact of Rata's loss of status within the Labour Party resounded throughout the Maori world in a way which Rowling clearly had neither anticipated nor understood. Without their own parliamentary Maori spokesman many Maori people felt more vulnerable than they had for years, wrote Walker (1980: 3):

This was one of the most volatile periods in modern Maori history. In that time there was gang violence, the He Taua raid on the Engineers at Auckland University, the disco-kids attack on police at Whangarei and Te Atatu, and the bloody confrontation between the Stormtroopers and police at Moerewa. During these traumatic events there was a thunderous silence from the Opposition benches.

From his position of isolation Rata observed what appeared to him a marked loss of interest and responsibility towards Maori issues being displayed by the Labour Party. Eight years after his triumphant journey around the country as the newly appointed Minister of Maori Affairs he was left with only the embers of his, and his people's, earlier enthusiasm. By the end of 1979 a disheartened and ignored Rata had been pushed aside, far from the centre of political influence. The loss of his shadow portfolio and his physical removal from the front bench were a severe public humiliation. What accentuated Rata's disillusion was the realisation that under the National government an energetic and determined public servant, the secretary of Maori Affairs Kara Puketapu, was launching the Tu Tangata program of Maori self-reliance - a philosophy and policy of community advancement that had not hitherto been fully embraced by Rata's own party (Levine and Vasil 1985: 39).

In the ebb and flow of political life Rata's loss of favour with the Labour Party should not have been such a surprise to him. It could be expected that he would patiently wait out this dance, as he had done on the back benches in the past, until his tune was played once again. Perhaps the loss was too great. Perhaps he suspected that the opportunity to gain such ground would never come again. Although Rata would not himself admit it, many others in the Maori world felt that this demotion was an unbearable slight to his mana, and the mana of the people whom he had striven for seventeen years to protect. To ignore such a slight might well have dangerous consequences.

RATA 'DEFECTS' FROM LABOUR

Without warning, or even prior consultation with his elders, Rata announced on 6 November 1979 that he was going to resign from the Labour Party. Overnight he was once again a celebrity. The public registration of astonishment soon turned to puzzlement. The mystery of Mat's 'defection', people said, was how he thought he could better serve the Maori cause outside the halls of power. The abruptness of his action was criticised by many of his Northland electorate. Other Maori MPs and politicians felt that he had made a serious error of judgement. Some time later Sir Graham Latimer (well-known as a National Party sympathiser) reflected:

> I think there are ways and means of showing your disapproval without defecting from the Party. I think that Mat Rata's contributions while he was Minister have gone unrecognised. Some day when he's dead and gone they'll probably say what a hero he was. Having worked closely with the man and knowing his desire to do well as Minister of Maori Affairs I can understand his frustration. But I still feel that there was no real excuse to defect from the Labour Party. The result of Mat's defection from the Labour Party was the total political confusion of the Maori people. (Latimer, interview 2 July 1981)

The media speculated that Rata may have been under considerable pressure for some time from the Maori academics Patrick Hohepa, Ranginui Walker, and Sid Mead, and that it was they who encouraged him to take an independent stand. Others surmised that Rata's greatest frustration was seeing the National government initiate programs and policies in Maori Affairs which he had originally proposed, but for which he had been sharply criticised in his earlier years as Minister. Rata himself adamantly denied these suggestions, reasserting that his decision to leave the Labour Party had been both personal and a matter of principle. It had been taken, he said, because the party had become 'insensitive' to and 'neglectful' of the interests of the Maori people (*Auckland Star* 10 November 1979; Rata, interview 8 January 1981).

For the first few days after his resignation the Labour Party attempted to woo Rata back into the fold. It became clear, however, that Rata had no intention of returning to the party and was, in fact, setting himself up as a competing independent. Words of reconciliation turned quickly to bitter public recriminations. He was blamed by Rowling and some of his former Maori colleagues for having 'blocked up' Labour's policy pipeline on Maori issues by his personal 'inaction'.

The conflict which arose between the Southern Maori MP, Mrs Whetu Tirikatene-Sullivan, and Rata was described as nothing more than a 'family quarrel'.[3] As one of Labour's 'most fiery advocates', she was 'stung most' by Rata's resignation on the grounds of Labour's 'insensitivity' (*Te Maori* June/July 1980: 14-6). Still aglow from her newly appointed chairmanship of Labour's Maori Policy Committee, Tirikatene-Sullivan accused Rata of a 'dereliction of duty'. She said that Rata, as chairman of Labour's Maori Affairs Committee, was personally accountable for impeding a substantial number of policy proposals. She claimed, on the other hand, that she 'had now unblocked the clogged pipeline and presented a total package "wholeheartedly endorsed" by Mr Rowling'. Both Tirikatene-Sullivan and Rowling told Rata that he 'should look squarely in the mirror' at himself if he wished an explanation for Labour's lack of concern for Maori affairs (ibid.; *Auckland Star* 7 November 1979).

In refutation of these accusations Rata's supporters pointed to the comprehensive policy paper which he had delivered at the Labour Maori Policy Committee Convention at Rotorua only two months earlier. This, they said, detailed 'many of the Maori proposals that have just been released' (*Te Maori* June/July 1980: 14). Rowling, it was said, had attended only long enough to deliver a short speech, leaving the conference before the policy paper was delivered.

There appeared to be some dispute between Rata and Rowling over Rata presenting this paper at the Annual Labour Party Conference on behalf of the Maori Policy Committee. According to several sources the document had been 'hammered out' by the Maori Policy Committee. Its policy proposals were formed on the basis of remits received from branches across the country. The paper, outlining directions for Maori people, had been approved by the convention as the committee's current policy. As Rata's confidant, Patrick Hohepa, later explained:

This was going to be taken back to the Annual Conference, but meanwhile this Government [National] had started a whole series of Royal Commissions. So the Maori people then said that this [document] shall be the Labour Party Maori Policy submission to the [Maori Land Court] Royal Commission. That was vetoed. Bill Rowling demanded that that be presented as Mat Rata's private opinion rather than from the conference. Finally it was presented, but memory of that left a lot of bitterness. Then there were shuffles which were going on in the Labour Party hierarchy which gradually saw the ousting of Maori people who had been there a lot longer, who were more senior, and in many cases a lot brighter than those they were promoting. By this time a lot of us had withdrawn without resigning - waiting for a better time to get back in again. (Hohepa, interview 10 December 1980)

There was considerable suspicion among some Maori leaders that Rowling vetoed the suggestion to use the policy paper as a submission to the commission on advice he received from Mrs Tirikatene-Sullivan. This 'cavalier treatment' of Maori opinion was the 'last straw' that led to Rata's resignation, said Walker. 'It was the strongest message he could deliver to Labour that the Maori vote should not be taken for granted'.

Although Rata's dissatisfaction with the Labour Party was clear, in a personal conversation between Tirikatene-Sullivan and Rata where, she said, they had spoken 'as brothers', she had asked him to explain his reasons for leaving:

I said: "Mat, it is important that you tell me what policies the Labour Party knocked you back on. Depending on your answer, I will make my stand". Rata, she claimed, had replied: "Whet, it would be fair to say the Labour Party didn't knock back anything I put up. I believe that they would have agreed to anything that I put up to them". (*Te Maori* June/July 1980: 14)

In private interviews Rata declined to place direct blame on the Labour Party for his resignation. In fact, he became angered at the suggestion. His reasons were far more complicated. His admission to Tirikatene-Sullivan was a recognition that there were inhibitions, deficiencies of will, which had prevented him from pursuing his goals as forcibly as he might have done. The tragic paradox, to which severance from the Labour Party seemed the only answer, was that even if his sense of potency had been vindicated Rata had lost faith in the entire system of Maori political expression through Pakeha organisations.

The fact that he had felt it was time to leave a situation of unbearable personal conflict, and later to offer his people a political alternative to the Labour/Maori arrangement, did not mean that Rata was prepared to be openly ungrateful or dismissive of the years which had been shared with Labour. That the time was right, in his view, for a political coming-of-age of the Maori people, did not mean that he felt no sorrow at the parting.

This was expressed in the first public meeting he held following his resignation. 'Mr Rata began by paying tribute to the many Labour Party people who had helped him over the years. He also pointed out that the Maori people have loyally backed the Labour Party for 40 years and hoped that Labour people would now support his movement' reported the press. Continued affiliation of the Maori people with any national political party would mean that their interests would always be a minor pre-occupation of such a broadly based organisation. His withdrawal from the Labour Party 'was only related to Maori affairs', he told the meeting, 'he could well support Labour in other fields' (*Auckland Star* 8 November 1979).

To Robert Mahuta, arguing for a fundamental political restructuring that would dissolve the power bases of 'Maori members and traditional leaders' and the networks of 'consultation and participation in the decision-making process' which had been constructed by the 'Ratana Church, Kingitanga, and other traditional organisations', Rata's move was understandable. But Rata had not gone far enough for Mahuta, a leading Kingite and Director of the Centre for Maori Studies and Research at the University of Waikato: 'If he had set out on a course of political martyrdom, then he should not only have severed his ties with the Labour Party, but also encouraged the Maori people to denounce a political system which leaves them with little effective power (Mahuta 1981a: 23, 25).

Rata admitted that his own involvement with the Labour Party had made him 'a victim of constant compromise'. The political interest and enthusiasm of the Maori had been weakened and drained by divided loyalties to the existing party political system. As an example of this he referred to his earlier promotion of the Hunn Report recommendation that separate Maori organisations and the four Maori seats in Parliament be abolished in favour of a 'One-New Zealand' philosophy. He confessed to his own error in adopting this as Labour policy, and in also attempting for a time to financially starve the New Zealand Maori Council out of existence. Ultimately, reported *Te Maori* (Dec./Jan. 1979-80: 28-30), he felt he had been 'gagged and chained' into 'powerlessness' by virtue of his involvement in the party machinery. In the end his own energies had waned:

So we find that Rata was immediately trapped between two powerful conflicting causes: Labour's stated policy to integrate the races, along with Rata's own proclaimed fairly radical Maori rights program. Rata gradually merged further and further into the background and became a spent force. He seemed to have exhausted all his political capital.

Rata's problem, as Mahuta (1981a: 23) diagnosed it, was that he had not 'brought into focus the real question which is the effectiveness of maintaining separate ethnic representation'. In disclaiming his youthful espousal of the abolition of the Maori seats, Rata had missed the opportunity to force the political parties to be more sensitive to Maori needs. Or had he? The validity of Mahuta's contention was undermined by a battery of psephological analyses and speculations in 1980. Rata was to heed these calculations.

One development, not reported at the time, which may have influenced Rata's thinking about his future was discussion amongst some protest movement leaders about the possibility of forming a broader-based Maori political organisation. In November 1979 Syd Jackson, secretary of the Clerical Workers'

Union (and a founding member of the protest group Nga Tamatoa in the early 1970s) revealed that, for the last six to nine months, he and other activists had been considering the formation of a body, perhaps even a party, which would 'take direct action over issues' (*Auckland Star* 9 November 1979). A 'radical' initiative of this kind, if it were to take shape, would inevitably attract support from some of those whom Rata would consider part of his own potential constituency. But Jackson and his associates had not drawn Rata into these early deliberations. Neither did Rata actively seek involvement (Rata to the author, 12 October 1991). Because its appeal would be too narrow to draw active support from those who had hitherto stood apart from Maori militancy, a new protest group was more likely to be a divisive than a unifying force.

The announcement by Rata of his intention to resign from the Labour Party on 6 November 1979 was not treated by the Maori world merely as the act of an individual parliamentarian. Nor did its symbolic significance entirely escape the press. To many Maori its 'meaning' could be interpreted within the spiritual and historical framework of the Labour/Ratana pact:

> It is very significant to us what happened the day that Ratana went down to Michael Savage [then Labour Leader]. He presented him with four objects. The potato to show that the land on which we grow our crops was disappearing. A broken watch, to signify that there was a break-down going on due to Westernisation. A huia feather, to symbolise the mana of the Maori people that has to be maintained. The greenstone [New Zealand jade], to show the continuity of Maori thinking. He said: "Now you can accept these until such time as they no longer apply. When you don't want them, give them back". Every part of this pact has somehow failed. Gradually Maori policies were no longer important to the Labour hierarchy. The Maori people have been taken for granted by Labour. They were important in terms of the election, but once they're in power, then they get pushed back. (Hohepa, interview 10 December 1980)

The proposition that Rata might lead an exodus of Maori voters away from their Labour loyalties reflected on Rowling as the Labour Party's first leader to have lost the confidence of the Maori people in four decades. Rowling appealed to the Maori world to stand firm and united against the 'defection' of the 'rebel' MP. But there was an emptiness about these words addressed to Maori party faithful poorly organised at branch level and rare in the upper echelons - a situation that was at best a sign of indifference by the party leadership (James 1986: 155-6). The failure to appoint a Maori spokesman on Maori affairs was more than tactically inept; it was an affront. Insulted by this action a number of Maori leaders publicly denounced Rowling, laying blame on him for Rata's resignation. Some resigned from the Labour Party to reinforce their objection: 'How can you move without a voice?', they asked (*Auckland Star* 10 November 1979).

By encouraging the Maori people to follow his example and remove themselves from the position of compromise which the Labour/Maori relationship now represented; by calling on them to 'take command of their own destinies' (*Auckland Star* 8 Nov 1979); Rata, it was argued, was reclaiming the mana of his people. This was in accordance with the original agreement between Ratana and Savage.[4] There was great excitement in the Maori world - the like of which, it was said, had not been seen since Kirk's victory. There was ardent marae debate on the spiritual correctness and political timeliness of Rata's move; on the personal sacrifice which his resignation represented; and on his lack of consultation with the elders in making his decision. In a surge of emotion many threw in their lot with Rata. Many others remained unconvinced or resentful. But few were without curiosity or opinion about what his action would 'mean' for the Maori people.

Matiu Rata had resigned from the Labour Party in a climate of expectation and change. On 29 September 1978 the National Party Minister of Maori Affairs, Ben Couch, had authorised the New Zealand Maori Council to redraft the 1978 Maori Affairs Bill. Earlier that year the NZMC had made extensive submissions to the Select Committee of the House of Representatives on the bill. The objective of the bill was to consolidate existing legislation on Maori affairs. Because of multiple amendments and redraftings of the act over the years, and its complex nature, the NZMC strongly recommended that the old legislation be completely abandoned and a new act be drafted in its place. Couch decided to place this difficult task in the hands of the Council, allowing them to conduct consultations and to receive submissions from the Maori world, and to submit their results in the form of draft legislation.

During 1981, Maori Affairs Bill conferences and their related land conferences were still being organised throughout the country to deal, in great detail, with each item of the bill. Although Couch expressed impatience with the Council over the time it was taking, the honouring of the NZMC with this responsibility was acclaimed as a major break-through in Maori/government relations by conservative and liberal Maori leaders alike.

Just before Rata's 'defection' a well-known Maori intellectual, Sid Mead, Professor of Maori Studies at Victoria University in Wellington, presented a controversial paper at the Labour Party Maori Policy Convention held in Rotorua in September 1979. Mead called for the creation of an independent Maori Parliament. The country, he said, should not be partitioned, but a twelve-member Parliament should control all Maori land, marae, and businesses registered as Maori-owned. Mead said he was concerned about the increasing signs of street gang and other violence. Until the Maori were prepared 'to fight for political freedom and for the survival and dignity of their cultural heritage', he said, this violence would clearly lead to 'trouble'. Although the convention agreed with Mead that there were signs of serious problems, many did not agree with his idea of forming an autonomous Maori Parliament. The Eastern Maori candidate, Dr Peter Tapsell, argued that there was no future in this line of thought.[5] The Maori, he said, received greatest protection under Labour Party policies and special educational and job-creating provisions (*New Zealand Herald* 3 September 1979). Graham Latimer, a National supporter, announced that he was 'puzzled' by Mead's idea of a Maori Parliament. He pointed out the gains already won, in particular the decision taken by the government to authorise the NZMC to redraft the Maori Affairs Bill. Any dispute over legislation could be overcome, Latimer said, by Maori people working together. 'We just need to put ourselves together to capitalise our case. We have a lot going for us' (*New Zealand Herald* 4 September 1979).

The flaw in the reasoning of Tapsell and Latimer was that it ignored the palpable evidence of Maori discontent and division. As Walker pointed out in the *New Zealand Listener* on 29 September 1979 events such as the Maori Land March, land protests at Raglan and Bastion Point, the 'haka party' incident at Auckland University, and the activities of Maori gangs were 'manifestations of the stifled desire of the Maori people for self-determination in the suffocating atmosphere of political domination and Pakeha paternalism'. Walker suggested that a Maori Parliament, parallel to the existing Parliament, had successful precedents in the King Movement, the Maori War Effort Organisation, the Maori Battalion, and even the Maori rugby competition. A Maori Parliament could do no worse, and might do better, for the Maori than had been done so far by the Pakeha.

Two months later a cluster of press articles reported that Mat Rata 'quit' the Labour Party and had decided to 'go it alone' in his attempt to form a new Maori political movement (*New Zealand Herald, Auckland Star* 7 November 1979). His 'quest', reported the *Herald*, did not have the support of the other three Maori Labour MPs, but Rata claimed that the full electorate committee of the Labour Party in his Northern constituency had declared that they would resign *en bloc* in his support. Walker was quoted as saying he was personally 'stunned' by Rata's resignation. Few had warning of his plan. His resignation had the effect of a 'bomb-shell' upon the Maori world (*New Zealand Herald* 7 November 1979).

When Rata entered the chamber following the announcement of his resignation from the Labour Opposition, he received an ovation from the members of the National Government (*New Zealand Herald* 7 November 1979). His Labour colleagues were less appreciative. The Western Maori Labour MP, K.T. Wetere, was reported to have said that Rata's move 'was not in the interests of the Maori people'. 'I believe the Labour Party', he said, 'is the right vehicle with the right policies to achieve those ends'. Whetu Tirikatene-Sullivan acidly commented that she was 'far less concerned about perception of personal prestige than the flow of well-researched, well-thought-out social policies for our people'.

Rata, journalists and colleagues reasoned, was surely aware of the history of the independent MP in New Zealand politics. People voted for the party, not the man. Why, then, did he wish to risk the security of salary and position to launch out alone? 'Most people, whatever their political inclinations', reported the *Star*, 'will find it hard to see what Mr Matiu Rata is driving at':

He is resigning from the Labour Party, he says, to symbolise the plight of the Maori people. He thinks the best way to revive what he sees as diminished Maori interest in the Labour movement is for him to be an independent MP. On the face of it, this scarcely seems a logical reason to try to buck the tradition that politicians without party ties don't accomplish much. (*Auckland Star* 7 November 1979)

Such is the power of the modern party system that Mr Rata's resignation from the Labour Party looks very much like the first step towards political suicide. (*New Zealand Herald* 7 November 1979)

Many of his supporters, however, felt that Matiu Rata would be no ordinary independent. His flair for bold experimentation had once been described on the front cover of *Te Maori* (May 1973) as 'Idealism as an Adventure'. Rata's personal strength was founded upon the belief that he was only part of a far deeper spiritual, historical, and social drama which related back to the formation of the Ratana Church and the earlier Maori political movements. He felt swept forward on a wave of social change which would ultimately direct his course; and that his support would come from the broadly based national political network of the modern Maori world, to which he felt firmly tied. If the cause was right, timely, just, and confirmed by God, he could mobilise also the aspirations and frustrations of all sections of Maoridom.

This political philosophy, which takes its origins from traditional Maori thought, was clearly still an integral part of both kaumatua and modern Maori leadership. It was strengthened by the sense of spiritual foreboding and sustenance and of the expectation that, sooner or later, divine justice would be done. For Rata there had been a choice of either a drastic political move or a slow, suffocating death by compromise. Either way, political suicide appeared almost certain. In choosing the former, with the slim margin of chance it offered, he demonstrated a faith and a willingness to put his own future at risk. It was a faith which had a contagious attraction in even the most unlikely quarters.

NOTES

1. When questioned some years later, Rowling denied that their relationship had been anything but congenial. He attested that 'at no time have I ever had a personal dislike for Mat Rata. He was always friendly and, as far as I am concerned, a person without malice. Nor were our differences philosophical. It was entirely a question of performance' (Rowling to the author, 20 August 1991).

2. Until 1979 the Labour Caucus did not elect a shadow cabinet, although it did elect a Labour ministry. It was the leader's prerogative to select and dismiss front bench spokesmen in the Opposition.

3. The rivalry between Rata and Tirikatene-Sullivan was fanned by a remark made by Rata that a woman should not be made 'spokesman' for the Maori people as this created difficulty with marae etiquette. On more than one occasion Mrs Tirikatene-Sullivan had been refused the right to speak on certain marae which still upheld the custom of excluding women in marae debate - thus she was seen to be handicapped as a politician.

4. In the following two years Rowling's career took a serious down-turn. He lost considerable mana, not only with large sections of the Maori world, but also with other Labour interests. He resigned as Labour Party leader at the end of 1982, having lost the 1981 general election.

5. Tapsell was later to win the Eastern Maori seat for Labour in the 1981 election.

IV

THE FOUNDATION OF MANA MOTUHAKE

The break with the Labour Party released a new charge of energy and commitment in Rata. Over the ensuing months, according to followers and friends, he became a 'clearer spokesman' and a 'better politician'. Freed from the burdens of office, which so often circumscribed the grass-roots activity of Maori MPs, Rata launched a campaign of tours and meetings, beginning in his own electorate, to promote his new-found cause. For political counsel, he immediately called upon the support of his close former governmental adviser, Dr Patrick Hohepa. Through him he also solicited the aid of Hohepa's long-term friend and Auckland University colleague, Dr Ranginui Walker. These two men were to act as key theorists and organisers in moulding the philosophy and structure of his 'movement' (*Auckland Star* 8 November 1979).

Walker, a prominent political columnist, educator, and activist, claimed that he was extremely cautious about becoming involved in the new movement. But eventually, he explained, his personal and political loyalties drew him in. Rata announced his invitation to Walker to come and chair the movement's first public meeting during a radio talk-back show. Privately, Hohepa also urged Walker to attend (Walker, interview 10 December 1980). Rata's public request for Walker's demonstrated political support nevertheless followed proper etiquette. It gave recognition to Walker's position as the chairman of the powerful Auckland District Maori Council (ADC) - a district representing just under a quarter of the Maori population in the country. Walker and Hohepa, as chairman and secretary of the ADC, were significant power brokers in the Auckland region. Their association with Rata gave him access to the formidable New Zealand Maori Council national network.

The first 'mana motuhake' meeting was to be held at the Te Unga Waka Community Centre, in the Auckland District, on 7 November 1979. A heterogeneous collection of about 300 people turned up at the meeting. Walker was 'impressed by the variety' of attendance. In two separate interviews he described this first meeting. 'All the existing networks were there - young, old, grass-roots, gang members some of them. There were workers. There were clerics and youth. All Maoris, a few Pakeha':

> It was almost like a religious curtain - people came out of the woodwork - people that I have never seen at a public meeting before. I felt that seeing as my own people were there, who was I not to put in my contribution? (Walker, interviews 10 December 1980; 9 July 1981)

At this first gathering Rata made it clear that he had been disturbed over the growing urban discontent of his people. Labour in Opposition appeared to have lost interest in pressing the needs of the Maori which had arisen out of escalating problems of unemployment, inadequate housing, and lower health and educational standards. Unemployment in the rural areas was also chronic. In his own northern electorate five in every seven Maori were unemployed. The rancour of Maori protest groups was becoming louder each day in their opposition to incidents of discrimination.

Rata explained at this meeting that he wished to establish a 'mana Maori motuhake' movement (Maori self-determination) which would make the protection of Maori interests its major if not sole objective. He wished to offer himself as a 'rallying point', around which the Maori people could focus their aspirations for social and political autonomy:

> He said his decision had not been taken lightly and was final ... "we demand the absolute right to command our own destiny" ... For too long Maoris had apologised for what they are. "Too many New Zealanders will not accept that there is a distinctive Maori way of life" ... "We should not have to explain or justify to our fellow countrymen what we want". (*Auckland Star* 8 November 1979)

The 'young activists and radicals' in attendance, Walker related later (Walker, interview 9 July 1981), urged the meeting to launch a Maori political party that evening. But the 'more level-headed' who were present cautioned against this, stating that their 'political enemies' could easily 'destroy' such a party which had been established without first laying the appropriate 'ground work'. At this time Rata also argued against this, saying that his 'movement' was 'more than a political party' (*Auckland Star* 8 November 1979).

An unusual incident occurred towards the end of the meeting. At the back of the hall a leading National Party activist, Dennis Hansen, stood to deliver a speech. Hansen has been described by Walker as a 'rough diamond Kiwi' who was almost always 'on the wrong side of the political argument' with Pat Hohepa and himself. He was said to be 'conservative, pro-rugby, and pro-Springbok' in his attitudes. As he thought Hansen's speech would provoke argument, Walker said he considered using his prerogative as chairman to cut him short. But he decided against this: 'I knew he was not Labour and pro-National. I thought "no, it's a democratic place, let him run" ' (ibid.). Hansen told the gathering that:

he had turned down the job of National Party chairman for Northern Maori when he heard of Mr Rata's decision to become an independent ... he had been a National supporter for 25 years but "I support Mat in this brave, bold move. I will work with Mat". (*Auckland Star* 8 November 1979)

This unexpected declaration of support brought an excited round of applause. Hansen approached the stage with the clapping, Walker recounted. When he reached the head table he turned on the people and said:

"I don't want your applause, I want your money". And so he put out a ten or twenty dollar note in a grand gesture on the stage, and he got a kit [bag] from someone and then went around and collected 400 dollars just like that ... Thus was established the first fund of the new movement. (Walker, interview 9 July 1981)

While the character and trajectory of Rata's nascent 'movement' were evidently unpremeditated, his emancipation from the Labour Party was an implicit challenge to all Maori political loyalties. By speaking of 'mana motuhake' Rata was invoking the memory of self-determination asserted by Tawhiao, the second Maori King, with whom the expression seems to have originated, and of Ratana, who had revived it. If he could meld the Kingite and Ratana followers under a new banner, his movement would have a formidable base of support.

With his Auckland coadjutors Walker and Hohepa in place, Rata turned his attention first to the national machinery of the New Zealand Maori Council. At the next Auckland district council meeting the subject of Mat's resignation was placed on the agenda. There was considerable debate on the matter. Some of the members, as strong National Party supporters, were opposed to Rata for party political reasons. In the past the NZMC had avoided functioning along party political lines. To have done so would have turned it into yet another forum for Pakeha ideological conflict (Hazlehurst 1988a). Eventually the Auckland District Maori Council agreed to endorse Rata's action. A motion was passed to support, in principle, his move to bring about Maori self-determination. No other Maori district council openly endorsed Rata's movement. However, over the following year recognition was given to him in less direct ways. Just before the 1981 general election Rata was invited, as other party leaders had been, to address the national body of the NZMC. If pressed, claimed Walker, none of the district councils could deny the 'principle of Maori identity' as 'a discrete power entity in its own right'. But, in the context of other political alliances, it was quite another matter for them to openly declare support for the new movement as the ADC had done (Walker, interview 9 July 1981).

Because of the complex network of political ties and interests, some support had to be given to Rata more discreetly. As chairman of the Northland Tai

Tokerau District Maori Council and president of the NZMC, Graham Latimer was a case in point. Much of Latimer's success in influencing the National government rested upon his strong political and personal affiliations with highly placed members of the ruling party, particularly Maori Affairs Minister Ben Couch and Prime Minister Muldoon. Latimer could not be seen to endorse Rata's new cause. But he indicated on several occasions his respect for Rata and tried not to interfere with the development of his movement. Privately he said that he might have joined Rata, had the movement not appeared to him to be 'dominated' by his old adversary, Ranginui Walker.

Latimer's loyalties to the National Party, on the other hand, clearly reflected the conservative sentiments of his supporters in the Tai Tokerau district. Other conservative enclaves of the Maori world, such as the land-rich East and West Coast tribes and the Kingitanga regions, would also prove to be major barriers to new political alignments. A Maori organisation as widely flung and as politically potent as Rata and his followers hoped to establish required careful planning and diligent nurturing. Rata's own people and his closest allies would be the first to be approached. Support in principle or even benevolent neutrality, if not a major realignment of loyalties, needed next to be solicited from more politically distant interests. If this organisation was to attract a diversified Maori membership, mobilisation required universalising the philosophy of 'mana motuhake', so that it appealed to all sectors of interest in the Maori world. The 'cause' of self-determination had to be articulated - uninhibited by past regional, tribal, or party affiliations. This ideal, obviously, was no small undertaking, and it was bound to be fraught with pitfalls.

Rata recognised that the Maori world was already an effective, self-conscious entity. It was possible to think of it, with some degree of imagination and optimism, as a communicating, operating network merely waiting to be shaped into a new political form. Rata's ethnic, territorial, political, and religious connections entitled him to a continued place in the national Maori political scene. The questions which most perplexed his people, following his abandonment of a major element in the accustomed structure of Maori/government relations, embodied a mixture of concerns about identity and power. Where would he now belong? How would Rata plan to make approaches to the government on their behalf outside the major party power structures - the channels which had been used by Maori people for over 40 years?

Matiu Rata was acting on instinct about the mood of his people when he left the Labour Party. He had clearly not thought through all of these questions. His departure from Labour was not the outcome of protracted dialogue or clandestine plotting. He left what he felt was an enfeebled party; a party without commitment or capacity to satisfy Maori aspirations. He had a vision but not a program. Political events would carry Rata forward, as they had Ratana, from spearheading a social movement, to confronting the harder realities of building an independent organisation. Unlike the prophet, however, Rata did not claim a divine mandate. He was, and would remain, a politician. But, if prophets were no longer in vogue, a century and a half of Maori resistance had bequeathed both a tradition and a challenge to a renewed mission.

The structure of the Mana Motuhake Party emerged in stages over several months. The day after Rata had announced his resignation from the Labour Party he declared that he would immediately start a five day tour of his electorate as an independent member of Parliament, to 'explain to his electors the reasons for his resignation from the Labour Party' (*New Zealand Herald* 7 November 1979; *Auckland Star* 7 November 1979). Following his first public meeting at the Te Unga Waka Community Centre in the Auckland suburb of Epsom, on the evening of November 7, Rata was to travel to the Northland centres of Whangarei, Matawaia, Kaikohe, and Kaitaia to give similar addresses. At his first meeting it was clear that Rata wished to receive the endorsement of his people for the launching of a 'mana motuhake' (self-determination) movement (*Auckland Star* 8 November 1979).

The Labour Party, still somewhat in shock, gave the press a confused and contradictory response. While they assured Rata that it was not too late for him to change his mind, stern criticism was also levelled against him by his Maori parliamentary colleagues. The president of the Labour Party, J.P. Anderton, said that he was unhappy about the resignation, but that the 'door is still ajar' if the former Cabinet minister wished to return to the Labour Party. Party leader Bill Rowling, however, indicated that he could not see any justification for the accusation of Labour 'insensitivity' made by Rata. He did not think that anyone else in caucus shared Rata's view. The 'main view' in caucus was the hope that Rata would realise he had 'gone off on a tangent', Rowling said. As 'nobody could be in a more direct position to influence the situation' for Maori people, he contended, Rata might well look to himself for an explanation of his dissatisfaction (*New Zealand Herald* 7 November 1979; *Auckland Star* 10 November 1979). Rata declined the 'open door'. He declared that his decision to leave the Labour Party had been an independent one and that he felt that 'the deteriorating state of affairs of the Maori people' required 'dramatic action' if any improvement was to be hoped for. The aim of his 'new movement', he said, would be to return to the Maori people their language, land, culture, and sense of self-reliance: 'above all we want our mana back' (*New Zealand Herald* 7 November 1979).

Support for Rata's dramatic move came in varying degrees from several quarters. Ranginui Walker declared publicly that Rata's bold resignation had been a major victory for the Maori rights movement (*Auckland Star* 7 November 1979). A Kingitanga spokesman, Bob Mahuta, called on Rata 'to go the whole hog'. Mahuta's 'whole hog' - a beast already rejected by Walker - was the abolition of the Maori seats, and the launching of the Maori into the country's political arena as full and equal competitors. As the Labour Party was usually the Opposition, Maori MPs were inevitably in a 'double minority', Mahuta contended: 'They were a minority of four within the Labour Caucus'. Maori youth were disillusioned with the present political system. He argued that if the special Maori seats were abolished, 'both major parties would scramble for the

Maori votes' and therefore take Maori concerns more seriously. Mahuta was reported as having extended an invitation to Matiu Rata: 'if Mr Rata was to move in this direction, the King movement would back him', he said (*Auckland Star* 8 November 1979). While many Maori feared that the loss of the Maori seats would lead to no Maori voice in Parliament, the NZMC observed that Rata's resignation had raised Maori hopes for increased representation. 'He has rekindled the imagination of the Maori people who are now reassessing their value within society' (*Te Maori* Feb./Mar. 1980: 43).

The exodus of Rata supporters from the Labour Party began on Rata's first tour of his electorate as an independent. Two key Northland Labour figures - Bob Tucker, chairman of the Whangarei branch of the party, and Hopa Brown, Labour Party leader in Te Kao (near the northernmost centre of Kaitaia) - both pledged their support before Rata's arrival in their districts. At Rata's public addresses other Labour branch members were joining the ranks of the fledgling Mana Motuhake movement (*Auckland Star* 9, 10 November 1979). A large number of Pakeha were also reported to have attended these meetings. There was no suggestion in the press that they attended with any feelings of hostility, but rather more out of political interest or curiosity. When asked whether he thought Rata would get the support of the Maori people as an independent, Bob Tucker, a Methodist minister himself, replied that in previous elections the Ratana Church had always been supportive of Mat Rata and was 'definitely behind him now'. Both men indicated that the Northern Maori people were grateful to Rata for 'standing out for our rights' (*Auckland Star* 9 and 10 November 1979). The early prediction that the movement could come to be regarded as a party, as was the Social Credit Party, was becoming an increasingly popular idea (*Auckland Star* 8 November 1979).

On November 9 the *New Zealand Herald* cast doubt over Rata's claim that the entire membership of the Northern Maori Electorate Committee intended to follow his lead in resigning from the Labour Party. The party president, J.P. Anderton, said that he had not yet received any other such notices. The Sunday meeting, where this pledge to follow Mat had ostensibly been made, Anderton claimed, had been called at short notice and a number of delegates had not been present. One senior member was quoted as saying that he 'had no intention of resigning'. The committee's chairman, I. Ihimaere, replied that because of petrol rationing not all members from the North could attend the meeting. He confirmed that the 'immediate executive of eight', who were present, had indeed resigned in support of Mat Rata. Notification of their resignations had been sent to the party the day after Rata resigned. Letters were also being sent to the various branches of the electorate - which consisted of about 300 financial members - urging them to take action 'as they saw fit' (*New Zealand Herald* 9 November 1979). Not only were the more ideologically committed members of the Northern Maori electorate willing to follow Mat in his quest for the promised land of political autonomy, certain idealists from among the traditional, conservative, and protest sectors of Maoridom were also giving him their support.

Te Matakite land activist Eva Rickard sought 'support for Mat Rata's Maori independence movement' at the Raglan's Te Kopua Incorporation annual meeting. She urged that a Maori political party be formally launched, as this, she said, would give Maori people a 'lawful power' in place of government 'charity'. Te Matakite's national president, Doug Sinclair, said that he saw Rata's move as possibly 'being the spark which sets off a long-overdue development of a united Maori movement ...'. However, he qualified this by revealing that he perceived Rata's role in this movement as being more one of contributor rather than leader (*Waikato Times* 10 November 1979).

Other protest organisations also wished to express an opinion about the form and purpose of the new movement. The *Star* declared that news of a radical new Maori civil rights movement had been 'leaked just days after Mat Rata's resignation from the Labour Party'. Its 'sources' appeared to be in the 'radical' Maori sector. The well-known activist, Syd Jackson, had indeed confirmed that plans to form an organisation which would 'take direct action over issues' had been 'going on for the past six to nine months ...'. A 'Maori Mana Motuhake Party', Jackson was reported to have said, would be launched in Auckland 'early next year'. It would be based upon 'the trade union movement and the unemployed'. Land, bilingual schooling, employment and other issues, which promote the 'right of Maoris to be masters of their own destiny', would be paramount. The new organisation, Jackson said, would attempt to 'band together the brown proletariat' (*Auckland Star* 9 November 1979). The kind of 'direct action' which Jackson saw such an organisation taking would be similar to trade union action. He confirmed that members of 'the new group' had had past affiliation or membership with the protest organisations of Nga Tamatoa and Te Matakite. It is inevitable, he said, that certain issues, particularly the taking over of Maori land, would 'bring the members of the new organisation into conflict with authorities' (ibid.).

Prime Minister Robert Muldoon expressed his concern to a press conference over the growing rumours of a new Maori movement. He said he feared it could mean an 'upsurge of Maori radicalism ... if Maori activists, who had caused a great deal of trouble, aligned themselves behind Mat Rata'. Muldoon added with a tincture of condescension that he thought Rata had 'too much sense' to let it lead to a 'disturbing situation' (*Waikato Times* 10 November 1979; *New Zealand Herald* 9 November 1979). In a speech delivered to the Auckland District Maori Council Rata, himself, called on the Auckland council to 'strongly endorse' the 'bold philosophy of Maori assertiveness', as this council had been willing to do in the past over various controversial issues. Rata clearly defined this 'assertiveness' as 'including the boycott of industries and organisations which fail to recognise Maori interests'. To make the New Zealand political system 'respond to our will' he proposed a mode of action which would not break the law but which would 'shake the system to its foundations'.[1] For example, Rata explained, before Maori clients support a bank, they 'should consider what support that bank gave them through staffing or grants' (*New Zealand Herald* 26 November 1979).[2]

While being prepared to espouse legal, political, economic, or union pressure tactics Rata was careful to deny any suggestion that the new movement would use illegal methods. 'Violence, radicalism and separatism are not part of the Mana Motuhake movement. Violence is something the Maoris, by and large, are strongly opposed to', he told the press. When asked about the risk of his movement 'becoming the tool of radicals' Rata responded with a careful explanation:

> The first essential move I must make is to encourage redistribution of leadership among the Maoris ... Each to his role and skill and function so no one will possess power over the other. My greatest contribution may well lie in the political field ... The action taken already has moderated the radical thought and behaviour ... Because Maori aspirations are over 140 years old, they cannot be radical. What is radical is the method of communicating the ideas.

> If you examine views and approaches of so-called radical thought you will probably find they are based on very long-established aspirations. Maori opinion is extremely conservative ... the Maori has never had the support and encouragement of the nation. New Zealand is going through a period where it is unaccustomed to people standing up eye-ball to eye-ball saying: "We are here for ever and a day with an absolute right to be here"... There is a demand by Maoris, and I think by the public generally, to have political institutions respond to the will of the people ... In effect what the Maoris are saying to the [political] machine is: "We have loyally supported you, now you support us" ... The principle of the movement is to see the Maori people have the will to stand on their own two feet again. (*Auckland Star* 17 November 1979)

The *Star* pointed out that the last report of the Labour Maori Policy Advisory Committee (17 May 1979), on which Rata served as chairman, gave an unheeded warning of events to come: 'the "we are one people" concept has, for the Maori, been an abject failure', Rata said. 'We have, as a people, never felt more let down, more insecure and more economically and socially deprived than we are today' (*Auckland Star* 10 November 1979).

The concept of 'mana motuhake', meaning 'self-reliance', 'self-determination', or 'permanent power', was not new. As early as 1861 it was pointed out in a letter to New Zealand's Governor, Sir George Grey, that the idea of 'self-sovereignty' was 'in the minds of the Natives'.[3] 'Mana motuhake' had been the motto of the Maori King movement. Since the Kingitanga established its Kauhanganui or Great Council in 1891, and the Kotahitanga movement attempted to set up an independent Maori authority at about the same time, the idea of political co-existence with the European had been a significant tradition in Maori thought.

On many occasions Rata publicly explained that the philosophy of mana motuhake was 'not anti-Pakeha but pro-Maori'. He claimed that he had no ambition to become the national leader of a Maori independence movement. His role, he said, was 'to expose Maori problems and aspirations using his skill on the public platform'. It was his objective to build the movement 'from the grass-roots', to 'co-ordinate' and to 'expose' the 'will of the people'. 'Only foolish Governments, whoever they may be, would ignore what is emerging', he said (*New Zealand Herald* 8 May 1980; *Auckland Star* 17 November 1979).

Professor Bruce Biggs, a distinguished Maori linguist at the University of Auckland who had spent many years trying to introduce an acceptance of Maori language education in schools and universities, explained that 'Maoris think of themselves as a separateness. It is the majority who have pushed this idea of integration'. Deep-rooted notions of Maori autonomy existed throughout a wide range of New Zealand social life. 'There have been Maori synods in the Churches, separate Maori courts, Maori land, Maori schools, and separate Maori units during the War' (Biggs, interview 16 December 1980).

Following several waves of social change - urban migration, widespread unemployment, and social disaffection in Maori youth - said Biggs, 'everything changed drastically'. In Biggs' opinion 'all these pressures' gave birth to the idea of an independent Maori political party. One of the aims of the mana motuhake movement was to emphasise to the European that the Maori did not want to be integrated into the ethnic majority of the country. 'This is not to say that they don't want to share in New Zealand's culture - materially. They want to benefit from these things. But they do want separate authority'. In describing this social and political separateness Biggs observed: 'We must think in terms of people. The social network among the Maoris is enormous. A Maori can go anywhere in New Zealand and find a place to stay, especially in the upper echelons where everyone knows everybody' (ibid.).

Rata's break with the Labour Party, and his foundation of an independent Maori political party, was a 'natural corollary to the rise of Maori assertiveness in the seventies', argued Walker (1981b: 8):

It is part of the unified creative attempt by Maori leadership on a broad front to bring about institutional transformation in New Zealand society. Mana Motuhake, in common with the broadly based thrust of assertive Maori leadership in the seventies, crystallises in the political arena their common concerns of self determination, recognition of Maori identity, control over Maori resources and cultural destiny and the devolution of power in harmony with our future as a bicultural nation.

This, of course, would be a fine summary, if it were describing the last stage of Maori political emancipation. But the fortunes of the movement were far from certain. With the social and political climate apparently ripe for change, a new organisation might at last break the barriers of resistance to power-sharing. Or it might prove to be merely the most recent transitory manifestation of the movement of Maori resistance which had secured only limited self-government for its followers in over a century of intermittent struggle.

Rowling moved swiftly in an attempt to heal the rift in the Labour ranks caused by Rata's resignation. In the company of Tirikatene-Sullivan of Southern Maori, and Wetere of Western Maori, 'Rowling flew to visit the ailing Eastern Maori MP Brown Reweti'. The objective, observed *Te Maori* (Dec./Jan. 1979/80), was to 'get Reweti's pledge of allegiance'. The leader of the Opposition called on Labour's Maori supporters to 'stand firm' in the face of Rata's breach of loyalty to the Labour Party. The party 'turned its guns on Rata'. He was accused of being 'anti-Labour', 'separatist', 'incompetent', 'a renegade', and 'derelict in his duties'. Labour had a 'proud record' on Maori affairs, the party claimed. It was demanded that Rata provide examples of Labour's 'insensitivity' to substantiate his allegations. Rata, however, declared that he did not wish to enter into a 'personalised mud-slinging match' with the party (*New Zealand Herald* and *Auckland Star* 9-20 November 1979). While Rata was coming under fire from the Labour Party for all kinds of alleged misdemeanours, he and his supporters were averring that Labour's network in the Northern Maori region was 'left in tatters' following mass resignations from the party.

Press reports demonstrated that Rata's first tour of his electorate attracted a generous and committed audience to his public meetings. 'With tears in their eyes' one elderly couple presented him with an envelope. Inside was 500 dollars in 20 dollar bank notes and a small message commending him on his independent stand. Although Rata did not win the hearts of all those who attended his meetings, he was left with the overwhelming impression from the excitement they generated that 'the North was rallying to the cause' (*New Zealand Herald* 12 November 1979).

On his return Rata triumphantly announced that over 200 people had resigned from the Labour Party to join him, resulting in at least four Labour Maori branches being dissolved. The Northern Maori Electorate Committee had resigned in his support and he had received unanimous motions of support from a meeting of 300 in Auckland, 300 at a Ratana Church function at Freeman's Bay, and 100 in Kaitaia. At Whangarei he had spoken to 50 people, 40 of whom resigned from the Whangarei branch. At Kaikohe he had spoken to 100 people on the Kotahitanga Marae. The Kaikohe Maori Labour branch of about 50 and at Te Kao 40 of the 90 Labour Party branch members he addressed also pledged to resign (*Auckland Star* 14 November 1979).

When he was asked about the possible emergence of a formal Maori political party he stressed that the movement was 'not a political party, in the accepted sense. It will have no hierarchy'. Non-Maori people, he said, were not excluded from this movement. The people who had joined him had a 'common interest'. 'They were pro-Maori'. The movement should not be a surprise to anyone, he said. 'The original alliance of the Ratana members with the Labour Party stressed they should be Maori members first and Labour members second'. The mana motuhake philosophy appealed, he said, to a wide range of people, and the movement claimed membership from ex-National, Social Credit, Values, and Labour Party followers (ibid.).

Although community hospitality was always generous, the new movement needed a fund to meet its growing administrative expenses. On this first tour, 1500 dollars was raised in collections. Other larger sums, in the form of personal donations from committed members, followed. There had been, however, little formality in the first few months of the movement's activities. The early following and structure of the Mana Motuhake Party grew initially from the base of pre-existing, converted Labour Party branches in Rata's Northern electorate - the independent MP's 'own people'. Rata had in fact forewarned trusted party associates in his electorate three days before his resignation (Rata to the author 12 October 1991). Within a week of his withdrawal from the Labour Party, Rata's loyal supporters had formed five Mana Motuhake branches in the Northland at Te Kao, Mangonui, Kaipara, Whangarei, and Hokianga. But although the movement had grafted itself upon, and took its shape from, the old Labour Party branch system in the Northland, its structure was still inchoate.

EMERGENCE OF A PARTY

After two major meetings Rata still had not officially formed the new party. Some of the movement's intellectuals - Ranginui Walker, Albert Tahana, and Toby Curtis - were becoming concerned. The second meeting, held in December, he had called an 'Us Day' - a get-together at the Orakei marae, Bastion Point, overlooking Auckland's sparkling Waitemata harbour. Bastion Point, the scene of one of the great land disputes of the 1970s, was redolent with Maori pride and political determination. It was a beautiful mid-summer's day and over 200 people attended. There was a growing fervour as people awaited the historic announcement. But, to the dismay of his closest allies, Rata let the opportunity pass. The party remained in the slipway, unlaunched.

Walker had left the Orakei gathering in disappointment, and decided to withdraw. Some of Rata's academic colleagues criticised him for appearing to assume he had sufficient personal following to campaign without an organisation. It was suspected that Matiu preferred to maintain his independence. Such a formal structure might restrict, control, or manipulate him. After entanglement in the web of Labour compromise and intramural warfare, perhaps he could not bring himself to accord defined authority to his friends and colleagues. But, without a role to play, the interest of his intellectual supporters would surely wane.

It was no doubt remembered that the forty year survival of the Ratana movement had been ensured once Ratana formed his church and delegated administrative responsibilities to a hierarchy of apostles, ministers, committees, secretaries, an Executive of Seven, and a president. This organisational structure had been extended to the 'political arm' of the movement when it emerged several years later. The contrast with Rata's apparent reluctance to organise the party caused some concern among his leading supporters, all the more so in the light of his rhetorical proclamation of a 'first essential move ... to encourage redistribution of leadership among the Maoris'.

It was the Labour Party which eventually forced Rata's hand. The party mounted a major attack on him through the media. While he had resigned from the Labour Party, Rata was still a member of Parliament. Labour began to challenge him on his right to the continued possession of the Northern Maori seat. Convinced that he could win his seat again at a by-election, Rata announced his intention to resign from Parliament. By January 1980 Rata had attracted a band of sympathisers. In the Northern hinterland supporters from his electorate, who were beginning to identify with 'Rata's new party', began to show their colours by resigning from the Labour party.

The formative meetings of the organisation appear to have occurred in March and April 1980. The minutes of one of the earliest 'Mana Motuhake Executive Committee' meetings (held at the University of Auckland for want of their own accommodation) on 26 March 1980, reveal an administrative hierarchy already taking shape. Twelve persons attended this meeting: Matiu Rata, Pat Hohepa, I. Ihimaera, Tui O'Sullivan, Toby Curtis, Albert Tahana, Hemi-Rua Rapata, Letty Brown, Eddie McLeod, Violet Norman, Titewhai Harawira, and Peter Muir. Five apologies were also received: H. Kaa, D. Hansen, J. Waerea, Waireti Rolleston and Hoori Tait. (Ranginui Walker's name, however, did not appear in these minutes).

At this meeting on March 26 Rata confirmed that he would resign from his seat in Parliament on April 30. It was becoming clear that, without the protection of a formal party affiliation or organisational structure, Rata would be vulnerable to attack from the established parties. As an independent his strength would depend too much upon his own popularity, rather than upon the acceptance of party philosophy. A new party would provide the machinery to mount an election campaign, and also a complementary focus for Maori loyalties. Plans for a Mana Motuhake policy hui on the following weekend were finalised. The areas in which Mana Motuhake policy was to be discussed and formulated were outlined. By-election preparations were also listed and it was agreed that a Mana Motuhake headquarters should be set up. The central body and the Northern Maori constituency needed the support of more Mana Motuhake branches and sub-committees in the Northland and Auckland regions. It was decided that the organisation of meetings with Maori groups - trade unions, churches, families, and marae - should take priority for April and May. Rata accepted an invitation to address Maori students at the University of Auckland the following week (Mana Motuhake Executive Committee meeting minutes, Auckland University 26 March 1980).

From May 6 Mana Motuhake's headquarters in downtown Auckland appeared in the minutes and in the first edition of the organisation's newsletter. Several more action sub-committees had been formed - The Mana Motuhake 'Social Services Committee', 'Publicity Committee', 'Women's Committee', and the 'Union-Employment-Industrial Committee' were visible, and there were possibly others. It was agreed that a Mana Motuhake logo and official stamp should be 'urgently settled'. The ordering of letterheads, envelopes, pamphlets, and other publicity material was to follow. Fund-raising events to pay for advertising, office supplies, and campaign expenses were planned. The organisation, it was stressed, must see that its members were correctly enrolled for the by-election. A small membership fee of two dollars per person, or five dollars per family, was also considered at this meeting (Mana Motuhake Executive Committee meeting minutes 16 April 1980; *Mana Motuhake Ki Tamaki* newsletter No. 1, 18 April 1980).

The plans being made at these early executive meetings were evidence of a purposeful approach to political organisation. Of several leaders in the inner circle Hohepa was most closely identified with Rata, being most intimately involved with the early conceptual and institutional foundation of Mana Motuhake. Walker, after his disappointment at the failure of the movement to take on a formal structure at the December 1979 gathering, had removed himself from the centre of events. Between March and June 1980 the rapidly developing movement began to recapture the attention of the Maori academics. Rata wished to draw them in to help the fledgling organisation. In April, Hohepa invited Walker to become involved again.

Plans were being made for the coming by-election and party policy needed to be finalised. Official meetings of the new party began after Easter (April 4-7). 'When your friend, colleague and comrade in arms asks you to a meeting', said Walker, 'although you don't want to go, you go'. 'About fifteen people were there discussing policy', Walker related, and it was at this meeting that he was invited by Rata to prepare a policy paper for the organisation to consider:

I said, "Mat, I need another sub-committee like I need a hole in the head. I can barely cope now without taking on any new interest". So he bided his time and then later on in the meeting leaned on me some more. But, of course, writing policy is near as easy as falling off a bridge because I like writing. So, finally, I said "Okay, Mat, I'll write a second section to the policy", which I did. (Walker, interview 10 December 1980)

This request was in keeping with Walker's perceptions of his role in Mana Motuhake: 'My role in Mana Motuhake was to help Mat set goals, to steer him, to set general aims, to provide a detached insight' (ibid.). The party's first official policy document came from this commitment. Key positions taken in Walker's paper on 'institutional transformation' were presented at the policy hui on the Waitangi Marae on 27-28 March 1980, and adopted by the new organisation.

The starting point of Walker's analysis was the proposition that New Zealand was a bicultural society in which 'cultural and language differences co-exist and enrich human experience'. Mana Motuhake, he contended, 'stands for total institutional transformation of New Zealand society from monocultural dominance to bicultural sharing'. Institutional transformation, he said, would entail giving the Maori language 'coequal' status with English as an official language; incorporation of Maori law and customary usages where appropriate in New Zealand statute law; bicultural consultation, planning, and execution of future legislation; increased recruitment of Maori staff into the public service, mandatory inclusion of Maori people on all statutory and government advisory bodies, and provision for co-option of Maori representatives to sit on local authority committees and education boards, hospital boards, etc.; an independent Maori radio network and prime-time scheduling of Maori programs on the state monopoly television channels; and contractual preference, wage incentives, and tax concessions to equal opportunity employers.

Walker's program of institutional transformation was as important for its silent repudiations as for its explicit desiderata. This was a vision of an equitably integrated society - of partnership, not of separatism. No mention here of a Maori Parliament and a sphere of political decision-making exclusively Maori. Rather, there was a demand that national institutions and public authorities be reshaped to reflect bicultural realities. Scarcely a revolutionary imperative, this was a statement of goals which Rata and others had long hoped could be achieved within the Labour Party. What was new was not so much the aims, as the instrument through which it now seemed they must be pursued.

In defining the political role of Mana Motuhake, Walker sought to position the organisation as an independent presence affirming Maori rights and needs, irrespective of whether National or Labour governments were in power. Taking the high ground of principle, he distanced Mana Motuhake from 'the ideologies of the left or right', asserting that it would 'promote Maori rights as human rights'. The 'ideology' of Mana Motuhake that held the promise of transforming New Zealand society was distilled in the claim that it 'stands outside the two-party adversary system as an independent variable and constant reminder that the essence of humanity is "aroha ki te tangata" compassion for fellow man' (*He Kaupapa Whakamaori I Nga Tari A Te Kawanatanga Na Te Mana Motuahake* ['Institutional Transformation of Governing Bodies to include Maoritanga from Mana Motuhake'], presented at the Mana Motuhake Policy Hui, 27-28 March 1980).

Walker's vision was carried forward and articulated in detail in subsequent documents. Successive policy statements drew together, refined, and expanded on a wide range of educational, cultural, welfare, economic, resource, land, administrative, and legal demands and aspirations. Central to the emerging philosophy and program was an insistence on co-operative enterprise as an alternative to 'competitive society which produces more losers than winners'. To assure the welfare of the Maori people, in times of adversity as well as prosperity, responsibility was to be firmly located in the whanau (extended family), hapu (sub-tribe), and iwi (tribe). 'The strength of the people will be encouraged in the development of tribal incorporations, and trust boards as the nucleus for tribal runanga (assemblies)'. Although the precise delineation of functions remained to be worked out, a comprehensive policy statement edited by Walker towards the end of the year pledged Mana Motuhake to 'restore to the community the right to determine, administer and conduct their own affairs within the runanga according to their will within the rule of law' (*Nga Kaupapa O Mana Motuhake: Manifesto*, October 1981).

This was a policy of local and regional self-determination within the larger framework of parliamentary authority. It looked backwards to a time when most of what mattered to Maori people was properly settled in the concentric domains of whanau, hapu, and iwi. However, it acknowledged the utility of modern legal forms (incorporation, trust boards) as devices to facilitate tribal land management and enterprise development. It was envisaged that there would be a stronger Maori presence in bureaucracies and government agencies, making all organs of government more representative and responsive. But the significant emphasis was on devolving authority to revitalised traditional structures (tribal runanga) rather than on seeking to overturn the balance of power in national institutions where the Maori voice would inevitably, and probably permanently, be in the minority. As Hohepa had declared three years earlier, democratic processes in which the Pakeha majority could 'outvote, nullify or submerge' the Maori minority were 'the most dangerous aspects of the Pakeha problem facing the Maori people' (Hohepa 1978: 100-1).

The rejection of the atomistic ethics and bureaucratised welfare delivery system of contemporary society was not inconsistent with the adoption of modern techniques of political organisation. Hohepa, as a seasoned Labour Party adviser, had a special role. In his own words, as one of the 'chief architects and theoreticians' of the nascent organisation, he had involved himself deeply with the practical establishment and running of the new structure. As treasurer and secretary-general of the organisation he acted as Rata's closest daily adviser and administrator. By contrast, Walker maintained an aloofness from the daily running of Mana Motuhake but responded to specific requests for assistance. The latter helped organise and chair significant gatherings and to draft policy. Walker and Hohepa complemented each other. By consciously adopting different roles they were able for some time to minimise the possibility of conflict and competition for authority.

Notwithstanding the paramount influence of Hohepa and Walker in the early organisation and maintenance of the party, the philosophy of Mana Motuhake was not solely drafted behind the 'sterile walls' of Auckland University. In a special article on the party, *Te Maori* reported (June/July 1980: 16) that Mana Motuhake policy meetings were always attended by a wide range of followers. 'Medical doctors, public servants, lawyers, clergy, university teachers and students, housewives, the elderly, the young, the unemployed, workers and trade unionists became part of Mana Motuhake'. From this rich pool of talent and experience many ideas arose and were shaped into party policy over the ensuing months. 'The main problem we faced then, and still face', stressed Hohepa in mid-1980:

is using the enthusiasm and talent of our Mana Motuhake people wisely and well ... For example, if we want legal advice from a Maori lawyer, it is not a question of how can we find one but which of our Mana Motuhake Maori lawyers to consult. The same problem occurs with choosing which trade union official, which educationist, which farmer etc. (ibid.).

Policy hui held between late March and early May (at the Waitangi Marae on March 27-28, Tira Hou Marae over Easter[4], and at Whangarei in the Ratana Church Hall on 3-4 May 1980) were acclaimed in the minutes of this period as 'a great success'. At the Waitangi hui, papers were presented by P. Hohepa on the 'Maori Affairs Legislative Paper'; by H. Baker of the Women's Committee on 'Mana Wahine'; by D. Clarke on 'Industrial Relations and Unemployment', and by M. Rata on the troublesome 'Electoral Roll'. There were also reports on health, finance, and organisation. It was at this meeting, reported the *Auckland Star* (7 May 1980), that the main points made by Walker in his document on institutional transformation were adopted by the organisation.

Remits were also received and presented from the Mana Motuhake township and urban branches of Poneke, Te Hapua, Mangere, Ngati Whatua/Naumai-Ruawai, Tokoroa, Kaikohe, Taupo, and Glen Innes. A wide range of topics was discussed including: Maori affairs legislation, land, electoral rolls, broadcasting and media, unemployment, judicial and legal practices, foreign affairs, health, the Treaty of Waitangi, culture and art, education, and recreation. A total of 36 remits was passed by the conference.

At the Tira Hou meeting the inner administrative council of the organisation was established. From this point onwards more regular meetings were arranged, policy was drafted, and the strategy for the by-election campaign became the focus of discussion. The Mana Motuhake Executive Committee consisted of the president, Rata, a general secretary, Hohepa, and a chairman, Ihimaera (a Northern elder). Walker was later appointed as a general policy adviser to the various sub-committees of the organisation. His attendance at the meetings over the next few weeks was irregular, but his name now appeared in the apologies of the minutes.

At the April 16 Executive Committee meeting it was moved that the secretary notify all branches, elders, and committees of the date of Matiu Rata's resignation from Parliament. Rather than allow the event to pass quietly, publicity would be sought by a gathering of supporters whose presence would confer additional significance on the occasion. With a new forum of their own, and a clean slate on which policy could be inscribed, Mana Motuhake's active inner group developed proposals on the issues that had long concerned them. A draft report was presented to the meeting from the organisation's newly established Judicial Committee. It was agreed that a revised version of the report should be presented at the next policy hui planned a fortnight later in Whangarei. Among its recommendations the Judicial Committee proposed that Mana Motuhake:

1. strongly endorse the total redrafting of the Maori Affairs Consolidation Bill through the NZMC;

2. favour the overhaul of the Town and Country Planning Act in order to enable Maori people to build homes, medical centres, and educational facilities adjacent to marae on their own land in rural areas;

3. seek to promote the repeal of the listed sections and clauses of various Acts which they considered were blatantly against the interests of the Maori people;

4. favour either the abolition or the restructuring of the statutory bodies of the Maori Land Court and the Waitangi Tribunal. [Suggestions to make these bodies more effective, and empowered to act retrospectively were offered]; and

5. support and assist in the establishment of neighbourhood law offices and other community-oriented legal services, in each of the tribal areas, the widespread distribution of booklets simplifying law and legal matters in Maori and English, and in the appointment of court workers to assist Maori people at all levels of the court system. (*Mana Motuhake, Judicial Committee Report* presented at the Whangarei Policy Hui, 3-4 May 1980)

Perhaps the most important element in these proposals was not an issue of substance but what superficially appeared to be a matter of conventional procedure. Notwithstanding the preponderance of conservative forces in the New Zealand Maori Council, it was not questioned that the Council was the appropriate forum in which a Maori approach to major legislation should be developed. To have challenged the legitimacy of the NZMC would have been premature and counter-productive.

A very early draft of Mana Motuhake's policy on Maori land, presented at the Whangarei hui on May 4, was also significant. It registered an objection to the system which split blocks of land and scattered ownership, sometimes among hundreds of different Maori shareholders across the country. This 'device', claimed the report, destroyed the 'unity of the iwi and hapu', often 'setting relative against relative'. Younger, urbanised, Maori rarely held land shares. They were separated both from their elders and their tribal origins. The elders were left alone to struggle with the running of small unviable farms and with the pressures from outside interests to take over or purchase their shares:

Mana Motuhake principles of Self-Determination for the Maori People require that control of the 300,000 acres of Maori Land in Tai Tokerau (Northland district) should revert totally to the people as a whole, young and old, whether they live in the home areas or the towns. Before we talk about "development" of Maori lands, we must first resolve this question ... Mana Motuhake demands that:

1. Maori lands must revert to control by the Iwi and Hapu structures of Maori Society.

2. Any development of Maori land must be decided by the recognised representatives of the Iwi, and shall involve the strengths and skills of all the people, young and old.

3. Special measures must be taken to increase the involvement of younger Maori people in Maori land matters. It is through their efforts that Maori lands will be retained and utilised for the benefit of the people as a whole.

4. All outside pressures to take control of Maori lands from the hands of the people must cease. The future development of Maori lands must be left to the people, not forced onto them by outsiders.

5. All legislation affecting Maori lands must be rewritten on the Maori people's own terms so that Maori ideals and aspirations are recognised by the laws and authorities of this country. (*Mana Motuhake, He Kaupapa mo o Tatou Whenua, Land Policies* 4 May 1980)

Mana Motuhake had quickly developed a standard practice of drafting a policy paper, having the paper scrutinised by members at a national policy hui, linking it to existing policies, and giving the acceptable policy the organisation's endorsement. By mid-May, reported *Te Maori*, 25 policy statements had already been released. These covered education, parliamentary representation, land, housing, youth, Waitangi, Maori enterprises, unemployment, women, justice, tribal authorities, 'Maorifying' New Zealand institutions, arts and culture, language, electoral reform, broadcasting and media, social welfare, sports and recreation, industrial relations, local bodies, forestry, sea-resources, foreign policy, and even theology. While Mana Motuhake was industriously breaking new ground in policy, Hohepa scathingly observed (*Te Maori* June/July 1980):

Labour was still content, if their publicity materials are a fair indication, with relying on bland statements e.g. "Education means a good deal - for everybody" ... Labour has only two policies released for Maori health - and their candidate is a medical doctor.

Feeling themselves liberated from the constraints of factional conflict and compromise endemic in Labour politics, the thinkers and organisers who charted Mana Motuhake's course were infused with passion and optimism. As long as policy could be declared, administrative machinery constructed, and opponents rhetorically vanquished, the buoyant mood could be sustained. The test of the ballot box would be a more sobering experience.

NOTES

1. On one occasion I witnessed Rata using this method when he was outraged with a particular newspaper for what he felt was distorted and misleading reporting. He threatened to refuse to give further interviews or news releases and to call for a Maori

boycott (i.e. refusal to purchase) of the offending newspaper. Rata later reported that the editor telephoned him and offered an apology.

2. During 1980-81 Maori leaders were seriously considering the idea of founding an independent Maori banking and finance company.

3. Alfred Domett to Sir George Grey, 6 June 1861 (*Governor Grey Collection*), Auckland Public Library GL:NZ, D12 (2).

4. Papers presented at this meetings are dated 29-30 March 1980. Records, however, indicate that a meeting was held on Easter weekend, April 4-7. It is likely that meetings were held over the entire Easter weekend between the Friday and Monday. The precise sequence of events is difficult to ascertain because of confused records of the Tira Hou hui.

V

THE BATTLE OF THE BY-ELECTION

The time had come for Matiu Rata to put his faith in the people. He drove the eight hour journey from Auckland to Wellington by minibus, accompanied by fourteen from the Auckland and Northland regions. Hohepa flew down to Wellington to help Sid Mead and other Mana Motuhake supporters arrange the welcoming party to greet the Rata retinue. Earlier that morning Rata had telephoned Parliament to order a hakari - a celebratory feast - for 40 of his supporters.

On April 29 Rata arrived at Parliament House 'amid traditional ceremony' to resign formally after seventeen years of service. At 2.30 pm Rata's wife Nellie, and twenty or so supporters, waited in the corridors of the Parliament buildings as the senior Maori parliamentarian presented his letter of resignation to the Speaker of the House. Although the media was present in force to record the event, the Speaker, J.R. Harrison, would not allow any cameras or tape-recorders into his office. As Rata's resignation would trigger a by-election for the Northern Maori seat Harrison felt that it would be improper for his office to be used as a springboard for an election campaign (*Auckland Star* 29 April 1980).

When Rata emerged from the Speaker's office 'his supporters broke into a haka while a cloak of rare kiwi feathers, traditionally worn only by those of high chiefly status, was placed over Rata's shoulders' by his elders. Whatever annoyance there may have been at his failure to warn or consult them before his move the previous November, here was a plain signal that he now enjoyed the confidence and support of his own people. At the end of this emotional display Rata stated that he hoped his resignation from Parliament would 'mark the end of political dependence and the beginning of political independence for the Maori people'. 'I shall return', he declared prophetically to the House (*New Zealand Herald* 30 April 1980; *Auckland Star* 29, 30 April 1980).

The Northern Maori by-election was set for 7 June 1980. Rata announced that he would fight for the seat on Maori issues. The question remained: would he do this as an independent, or would he campaign as the representative of the rapidly crystallising Mana Motuhake movement? At the policy hui at the Tira Hou Marae on March 29 and 30, the meeting had reached a compromise solution by unanimously endorsing Rata as the movement's independent candidate for the expected by-election.

The extent of the political handicaps confronting an independent candidate in an election had not at first been fully grasped. Approximately 60 percent of the voters of the Northern Maori electorate were in the small towns and rural areas of the Northland (north of Auckland) and 40 percent lived in the Auckland region. Unlike the typical candidate in a general constituency, which was likely to be socially homogeneous and to have common interests deriving from similar lifestyles and environments, Rata had to appeal to an electorate embracing isolated hamlets as well as most of the nation's largest city. Confident of support from former Labour allies, Rata initially appeared unconcerned by the poor track record of other independents in New Zealand elections. But by early May the very real problem of launching a full-scale, competitive campaign became abundantly clear. It was in these months, between March and June, that the first conscious attempt to found the Mana Motuhake 'Party' occurred. The significance of the by-election to the moulding of Mana Motuhake as a political organisation was highlighted by the words of one supporter:

The Mana Motuhake structure was precipitated by the by-election of the Northern Candidate. The actual Mana Motuhake structure had not begun to take shape until Mat's campaign for the by-election. It was like a trial run and began formation of the Mana Motuhake structure of branches. Before that, for some time, people were sitting around waiting for something to happen. (Wellington supporter, interview 17 July 1981)

By resigning from Parliament in May 1980, Rata wished to remove all doubt that he had a firm hold on the Northern seat, well before the general election due in 1981. Rata was betting on the theory that electors 'often vote for the individual instead of the party' in a by-election, knowing that their vote could not change the government. For a brief time he could stand alone and command the full attention of the press and television upon his 'single issue' campaign of Maori rights (*Te Maori* April/May 1980: 37). Because of the frequency of 'bloc voting'[1] in the Maori world Rata expected to do better than any independent before him. Now, with the growing capacity of his new party to mobilise Maori support, Rata felt confident of a clear win ahead for Mana Motuhake. Among his many well-wishers and friends there was general optimism. At the Whangarei hui Rata called for 'total commitment' from his supporters. 'We can't have people on a ten-bob-each-way basis', he said (*New Zealand Herald* 5 May 1980).

The approaching Northern Maori by-election held a particular fascination for other sections of New Zealand society. In an enquiring and not unsympathetic article, business journalist Colin James wrote:

Rata, it is clear from my conversations of the past week, is giving expression to a frustration - even an anger - which will not be assuaged with more houses or scholarships or Maori Affairs Department handouts. There are widespread misgivings about some of the methods Rata proposes - particularly his apparent espousal of radical tactics like boycott (of Waitangi Day for instance). But these misgivings may be submerged in a feeling that what Rata offers is an opportunity Maoris cannot afford to pass up to present a new Maori face to the establishment. All this concerns the Maoriness of the Maori voter. The [Labour] party is banking on the urban proletarian Maori voting Labour for class reasons rather than those of race. If the party is right, whatever response Rata gets from the depleted countryside and the intellectuals, liberals and radicals, will be overwhelmed by the Auckland city working class Maori. (*National Business Review* 11 February 1980)

The Northern Maori seat had always been held by a Labour Party member. Since the *en bloc* movement of a substantial number of Maori from Labour to Mana Motuhake, the Northern Maori Labour forces were falling into a state of disarray. The National Party began to consider whether it would run one of its own candidates for the traditionally Labour seat:

If Rata wins it will be a single humiliation for Labour. If the rank outsider National wins then of course it would be an even greater humiliation. But if Labour reclaims the seat, then it will be no great victory because they should never have lost it in the first place. "It's a marvellous opportunity for us to take the temperature" notes one National Party strategist. (*Te Maori* April/May 1980: 37)

His party having run a 'poor third' to Labour and Social Credit in the 1978 elections for the Northern Maori seat, the National Party president, G.A. Chapman, told the press that he could see little advantage in the Nationals contesting the seat. 'My personal position', he said, 'is that Northern Maori has a family squabble between the Labour Party and a former member' (*New Zealand Herald* [14] April 1980). Shortly thereafter the Nationals announced that they would not put forward a candidate for the Northern Maori by-election.[2]

With the new Maori party competing for the Northern Maori seat, the June by-election was brewing to be possibly the most important election for Maoridom in 40 years. 'His Mana Motuhake Party amounts to nothing less than a declaration of independence', declared the New Zealand Maori Council magazine *Te Maori*. 'For 100 years Maori aspirations have been filtered through European values and institutions. Governments and political parties have grafted Maori ambitions onto the mainstream of European objectives'. Rata wished to lead his people into a new age - a 'golden age' for Maoridom where compromise would cease. 'He demands that the Maori "control our own affairs as we did in the past. We must no longer depend on someone else to decide for us". "Control", he says, "must return to real tribal roots - to the Iwi, the Hapu and Whanau" ' (*Te Maori* June/July 1980: 14).

Between March and June the air was filled with well-aimed boasts and recriminations, as the media publicised a parade of superior intentions, scathing criticisms, and ideological platitudes. Seldom had a single seat stimulated so much political speculation or carried, for so many, such weighty implications. 'Renegade MP Mat Rata's announced scheme for a by-election in Northern Maori', commented *Te Maori* (April/May 1980: 37), 'has had the same effect as a brick thrown into a hot mud pool: things are bubbling everywhere'.

On April 14 the Labour Party announced the 'adoption of new and wide-ranging policies on Maori land'. Labour has given 'top priority', declared Bill Rowling, 'to updating Maori policy in all areas'. He promised to examine the contractual rights of Maori people in relation to the Treaty of Waitangi and to set up an authority to hear disputes arising from Treaty rights. Under Labour, there would be a revision of Town and Country Planning regulations with the aim of providing greater protection of Maori land rights. Labour would support an investigation into the possible return of all Maori land, taken by the Crown, which was no longer used for the original purpose for which it was taken. All outstanding Maori land grievances would be settled by a Labour government, he said. The Maori Land Court records would be updated, and all Maori land would be surveyed, titles clearly defined, and the information computerised (*New Zealand Herald* 14 April 1980).

Mana Motuhake responded the next day, criticising Labour for its outdated land and housing policies. Hohepa said he was surprised at Labour's proposal to upgrade the Maori Land Court. But who, he asked, would be expected to pay for the land surveys? It was 'still a sore point' with Maori land owners who had found survey charges which they did not want 'foisted on them'. Mana Motuhake offered a new system which would 'replace the Maori Land Court with a Runanga Whenua - a Maori-style land council', Hohepa announced. 'As well it would strengthen family and tribal ownership and management of their land, without Government interference' (*Auckland Star* 15 April 1980). 'Labour has a short memory', said Hohepa, remarking on Labour's proposal to set up an authority to hear disputes arising from the Treaty of Waitangi. 'Only five years ago, when in Government, Labour set up the Treaty of Waitangi Tribunal. But then the Caucus and Cabinet refused to give the tribunal the power to repeal laws already contravening the treaty' (ibid.).

On the following day Labour released a second batch of new Maori policies, this time concentrating on unemployment, vocational counselling, low-interest development finance, Maori programming on public broadcasting systems, and electoral law reform. Rowling also claimed that a Labour government would 'set firm conditions for any Maori land to be acquired for energy projects' (*Auckland Star* 16 April 1980; *New Zealand Herald* 16 April 1980). Rowling and the Southern Maori MP, Mrs Tirikatene-Sullivan, emphatically blamed Rata for 'the dearth of new Maori policy' between 1975 and 1978. Much of this policy, they repeated, had been held up by Rata himself. As the new chairman of the Labour

Maori Policy Council, Tirikatene-Sullivan said she planned to introduce a 'Treaty of Waitangi reconciliation charter Bill' which would strengthen Maori identity and remove the 'disparities between Maori and Pakeha children in educational and occupational attainment and health' (*New Zealand Herald* 16 April and 5 May 1980; *Auckland Star* 15 April 1980). Others came to Rata's defence. The 'blame heaped on the former Labour spokesman on Maori issues' by Rowling and Tirikatene-Sullivan was 'unjustified', declared political correspondent Tony Garnier (*Evening Post* 16 April 1980). The *Evening Post* 'has unearthed strong evidence to suggest Mr Rata had, in fact, put forward a comprehensive policy which was blocked by Mr Rowling himself'. The policy paper, to which the *Post* was referring, was that delivered by Rata at the Labour Maori Policy Convention at Rotorua in September 1979. The Maori people were said to have felt this had been rudely dismissed by Rowling at that meeting. The *Post* had acquired a copy of the paper which it described as being 'well written, detailed and fully backed by statistics' (ibid.).

As Rata was delivering his resignation from Parliament on April 29, the Labour Party was bringing to an end its search for a suitable Maori candidate to compete against him in the by-election. In the opinion of many Maori, stated *Te Maori* (April/May 1980), the difficulty the parties faced in selecting a candidate was 'to find a well-known person, very energetic, and with a strong degree of charisma, who can outpoint Rata ...'. During a weekend selection meeting for the new Labour candidate held in Auckland, Rowling related to the gathering advice which he had been given by a Moerewa Maori freezing plant worker: 'If the jockey falls off the horse during a race, you don't shoot the horse. You get a new jockey'. 'The anecdote', reported the *Star* on May 5, 'became instant Labour Party folklore', being woven into many a humorous moment over the weekend. A 43 year old Ngapuhi medical practitioner, Dr Bruce Gregory, was selected as Labour's 'new jockey'. When it was his turn to deliver an account of his tribal and political pedigree, during the selection process, Gregory added a bicultural twist to his tribal connections by claiming a family link with the former Labour leader, Norman Kirk.

In the speeches delivered by the Labour candidates and delegates there was some expression of feelings of betrayal by Rata's resignation after seventeen years in the Northern seat. In addition to directly blaming Rata for holding up Labour Party policy on Maori affairs, Tirikatene-Sullivan accused him of not returning certain party documents which he had in his possession. Gregory added his own allegation that 'Mr Rata had "ignored and insulted" the Maori people in his electorate by resigning from Parliament without consulting them' (*Auckland Star* 5 May 1980). Rata, confident of his own standing with the Maori community, defended himself by issuing a warning to the Labour Party to stop its personal attacks on him 'or lose the support of the Maori people'. He reminded Tirikatene-Sullivan that, as a long-serving member of the Labour Party, he quite properly had his own copies of certain documents. However, the papers to which she was referring were already in the hands of the Maori Policy Committee.

Although the Labour Party had accepted anything he had put up to it in the past, this acceptance, he stressed, had only been at the policy level of the party. In the House, the party had not acted in the interests of Maori people for some time. He warned the Labour Party that 'any attempts to "besmirch" his character would threaten the relationship the Party had with the people', adding that Tirikatene-Sullivan would be advised to return her attentions to her own electorate in the South. 'These are not the kinds of comments the Maori people will tolerate', he said. Mischievously, he told the press that 'he would not be surprised if Mrs Tirikatene-Sullivan was recalled to her electorate and asked by her people why she made the comments' (ibid.).

On his tour of the Northland, a week earlier, in an attempt to consolidate shattered Labour loyalties in this constituency, Rowling delivered a 'strong call for the Maori people to support the Labour Party and not the independent candidate' (*New Zealand Herald* 30 April 1980). Rowling, however, gravely under-estimated his former MP when, at a gathering at the Waimanoni Marae near Kaitaia, he attempted to coin a metaphor to describe Rata's falling away from the Labour Party: 'When a branch breaks from a tree it will wither and die', Rowling said. 'The tree may be scarred - and it is - but it will continue to grow ... Like that tree we will continue to grow and our policies will be built round the culture and tribal identity of the people' (*New Zealand Herald* 30 April 1980; *Te Maori* June/July 1980: 14).

Steeped in the lyrical and aphoristic style of Maori debate, Rata was not long in voicing his response. On May 7, before 225 people at the Te Unga Waka Marae, he opened his official campaign for the Northern Maori seat with a reference to the comment of his former leader. Shrewdly he turned his own name, which he shared with a certain native plant, to advantage: 'I want it known', he declared to his delighted audience, 'that the rata vine has also been known to strangle healthy trees'. 'Rata Vine Set to Strangle Limbless Labour Tree' read the headlines the next day (*New Zealand Herald* 8 May 1980).

Even the minority Social Credit Party waxed poetic. Its leader, Bruce Beetham, compared his party to the young great kauri tree which had been growing quietly and was 'about to push through the political undergrowth with the vigour of youth'. Social Credit, Beetham said, 'stood for the green of the soil and the gold of the life sustaining sun'. Amused by the proliferating arboreal imagery, *Te Maori* (June/July 1980: 14) concluded that the political atmosphere over the two months preceding the June 7 by-election had begun to resemble that of a 'steamy jungle'.

'A STRONG BASE OF SUPPORT'

The May Mana Motuhake Policy Hui at Whangarei was also attended by the press. It was reported that only 25 people were present at the opening session (although over the weekend about 150 people came and went). The press interpreted the attendance figures as evidence of meagre support for Rata. Later,

Walker attacked the newspapers for misreading the situation through the application of inappropriate 'Pakeha cultural references' ('Sunday Supplement' Radio New Zealand, 1 June 1980). According to Walker the mihi (traditional greeting to open the meeting) indicated 'a strong base of support for Rata from many different communities.' Maori people, he explained, read the 'tone' of the meetings to measure success, not the numbers present. Who is present indicates how many are present. Important elders could represent 200 or 300 members of their extended family or sub-tribe. The press had 'simply confused quantity with quality'. The following Tuesday, June 3, the *Star* editorial conceded that: 'Not too much notice should be taken of head-counts at Mr Rata's meetings, say the observers. A handful of elders, it is pointed out, can be at least as influential as a packed hall'.

By mid-May the spirit of the campaign had drawn members of many different interests - labourers, youth, elders, the conservative middle-aged, students, clerics, the unemployed, and a fringe of feminists. While the press and common room gossip suggested that a handful of Maori academics had goaded Rata into the creation of the movement, Rata at times was criticised by these same 'intellectuals' for being a little too independent. 'He does his own thing without reference to us', one of them stated later. 'We are only the servants of the organisation, not its leaders'. They were, however, 'servants' with vital directive roles.[3]

Both Rata and others who were influential in the movement's organisational structure professed the view that the real energy of the movement came from the ordinary people who joined it. 'The beauty of Mana Motuhake', Rata explained, 'is that it's a very grass-roots organisation, as distinct from something that is imposed from the top ... If and when the branches are established - fine. The next step they take is to expand that' (Rata, interview March 1981).

'Manu', a Maori language and culture expert from a northern tribe historically associated with the National Party, observed prosaically, 'Mana Motuhake may seem like a breath of fresh air' (Levine and Vasil 1985: 75, 180). In more ardent language Walker (1980) had proclaimed: 'Mana Motuhake is the people. It is the zeitgeist, the spirit of the ancestors and soul of the people. It is a force that no Maori can deny'. The fervour of the rank and file was channelled productively and with an eye to the welfare of individuals who could be helped by the offer of employment. A teenage girl, who had been unemployed, helped at the central office. The organisation's logo and other artwork were entrusted to a youth with skills in graphic design. Members, it was said, found a 'new meaning to their life' after joining the movement. 'Mana Motuhake released the creative and unharnessed energy of the people that built an *ad hoc* group into an effective party machine' (Walker 1980: 4).

Mana Motuhake campaign meetings generated what Walker - a lapsed Catholic - described as a 'spiritual fervour almost like a religious revival' (ibid.). A Maori clergyman who had moved across the political spectrum, from National through Social Credit to Labour under Norman Kirk and then to a disillusioned search for a more effective way of fighting 'Pakeha politics', described a similar feeling:

> What excites me is that I am meeting the butcher, the baker, the street cleaner, the guys on the dole, people who never really had a chance to articulate their feelings, and they are telling me that we could not get any change working through the existing political parties, and let us challenge the Pakeha parties. A vote for anything other than the mainstream of politics. That would be a vote for the spirit of our ancestors. It is almost a religious revival, but at a much more gut level. (Levine and Vasil 1985: 77, 180-1)

Even for the consciously detached observer it was difficult not to be swept up in the surge of hope and commitment to action. The gatherings were adorned with all the newly acquired symbols and regalia of the party. Brightly decorated tables, tended by the party faithful, offered a collection of pamphlets, rosettes, tickets for fund-raising functions, and membership cards. Gold and black ribbon rosettes, pinned to the chest, proudly displayed membership in the organisation. Rata explained the symbolism of the colours. Black, he said, represented the darkness of times past and yellow the golden years to come (*Sunday News* 8 June 1980).

Fund-raising was an important part of campaign organisation. Towards the end of May, 1200 tickets were sold for a social evening at Trillos, a 'fancy' Auckland nightclub and restaurant. The movement also attracted a few large donations. A sum of 50,000 dollars was offered to Matiu in mid-April 'in support of his independent political stand'. The unnamed Auckland donor, a retired Pakeha businessman, was hinted by the press to be a National Party supporter. The April 16 Executive meeting minutes confirmed that the donor, who wished to remain anonymous 'in case the donation starts a family war', planned to leave Mana Motuhake this sum in his will. It was to be used for Maori 'social, cultural, educational and economic development ... with specific programs to be determined by an elected Mana Motuhake Trust Board in terms of the will'.

A month later it was revealed that the still anonymous benefactor was an Englishman, with New Zealand citizenship, in his late 60s. He was mainly concerned for unemployed Maori, particularly the young. Mana Motuhake, he said, had already helped his unemployed part-Maori son. 'I have thought deeply about the whole thing and I support Maoris who want to help themselves ... I think Mr Rata is a very sincere man and could be a leader for all the Maori people'. But, he added, he did not think Rata would win the coming by-election. Although he felt both the National and Labour parties had done a lot for the Maori people, 'more needed to be done'. The first thing which needed to be done was to ratify the Treaty of Waitangi. 'The Treaty was a gentleman's agreement which had not yet been honoured', the benefactor said (*New Zealand Herald* 14 April and 13 May 1980; Mana Motuhake Executive Committee Meeting Minutes 16 April 1980).

Financial assistance was also offered to the organisation from a Maori land incorporation. Expressions of encouragement for Rata, and the hope that he would be re-elected to the Northern seat, were received from Maori regions as distant as Gisborne and Opotiki on the East Coast, and even the South Island. People were particularly sympathetic because Rata had given up the security of a substantial salary and had placed his political career at risk. To many this action spoke louder than words.

The support Rata was gathering inspired his membership with the feeling that he had at least a fifty/fifty chance of winning the by-election. When he resigned from Parliament Rata had been accompanied by a handful of Ratana and Northland elders. His party was now counting on the support of these two influential sectors to mobilise votes in the Maori electorate. The arrangement of meetings in the Northland, and the presentation of his message to the elders, became a central focus of the campaign. Nevertheless Rata was criticised for having failed to make an appearance in several Northland communities which had been expecting him. The 'vote' of those communities was said to be lost because of this oversight. Just as serious as any presumed slight was the sceptical realism expressed by a Maori public servant in the far North. 'Hikurangi', a man of strong tribal orientation, saw great similarities between the Tu Tangata program and Mana Motuhake's objectives. ' The difference to me is that, at the moment, Mana Motuhake is a dream' (Levine and Vasil 1985: 47, 174).

If rational self-interest might not compel support, could religious convictions be relied upon to yield votes for Rata? The Labour Party, claimed Rata, had severed the Labour/Ratana relationship by selecting Bruce Gregory, an Anglican, to run against him for Northern Maori. Although the Ratana Church had not yet taken a stand on the issue Rata believed that they would support him at the ballot box. 'This makes my re-election an even greater possibility', he said. Gregory dismissed this belief as 'absolute nonsense ... He (Rata) is a Ratana minister who resigned from the Labour Party ... He severed the links, not the party ... this by-election will be fought on political grounds - not on a religious basis', he said (*New Zealand Herald* 6 May 1980). The Northern Maori seat was already 'sewn up' for the Labour Party, said Gregory. In his opinion people were having 'second thoughts' about Mana Motuhake because they were beginning to find the 'ideas' did not relate to the 'reality' (*Auckland Star* 7 May 1980).

'Kare', a Maori woman active in South Island tribal affairs, was 'disgusted' with the Labour leaders' attempts to blame Rata for the party's failures:

And when Mat resigned, my world sort of dropped out, and I thought, "my God, what is going to happen now?" I thought of Matiu as a Ratana, I'm a Ratana. Is there going to be a split-up, is he going to go away from the Church? I'm not a Bible-banger, but I see a closeness. When Ratana was alive, and put his members in and then supported Labour, if he supported Labour, then there must have been something in it ... And then Mat leaves ... and I think, "why on earth have you done that Matiu, could you not stick it out," but obviously he was unhappy about something. My idea ... was that he had to resign, because they were stripping him of his mana - they being Rowling and Whetu [Tirikatene-Sullivan] ... I want to believe that Matiu has an idea, a good idea. (Levine and Vasil 1985: 78-9, 172)

The Reverend Wiri Toka Eruera, a Ratana Church minister from the North Shore parish, Auckland, openly disagreed that Rata's resignation from the Labour Party had anything to do with the Ratana Church. However, Eruera admitted, it was the founder's intention quite early after the alliance had been formed, that his church would eventually sever links with the party, and his members would stand as independents. This never occurred in Ratana's life-time. In Eruera's opinion the Mana Motuhake movement was the Maori people's 'last chance'. 'It is a very delicate situation ... the Northern Maori by-election has turned into a religious by-election', he said (*New Zealand Herald* 13 May 1980).

Rata realised that, in his enthusiasm to win the full support of the Ratana Church, he may have caused offence by drawing attention to his Labour opponent's religious background. At a meeting on May 13 on the Kotahitanga Marae, Kaikohe - a gathering dominated by Ratana members - Rata apologised. He said that he 'deeply regretted' and withdrew his statement that the Labour Party had severed its relationship with the Ratana people by appointing a non-Ratana as their candidate. As the Maori had always done in the past, 'Mana Motuhake stood firmly for church union ... I hope Ratanas will vote on the issues facing all the Maori people, not just on the basis of being a Ratana' (*New Zealand Herald* 14 May 1980). At this same Kaikohe gathering a leading Northland elder, Kiro Witehira, placed a kiwi-feathered cloak about Rata's shoulders as a 'measure of belief in the movement on behalf of Ngapuhi supporters'. Such an event is always seen to be imbued with spiritual significance and is spoken about in reverent and hushed tones. This particular cloak was certainly tapu. It belonged to Witehira's grandfather and was said to be over 100 years old.

After his selection as the Labour candidate Gregory also received a 'cloak of the Ngapuhi tribe of the Northland, symbolising the passing of mana to him'. Gregory said he felt 'humbled' by the whole experience (*Auckland Star* 7 May 1980). The manipulation of mystic symbols by different elders disclosed competing political interests, and this selective distribution of mana also signalled the later alignment of votes.

Further warnings to the Labour Party, about 'the dangers of being seen and not heard', came from its own Maori members at the May 1980 Labour Party Conference in Wellington. A standing ovation and prolonged applause followed the introduction of the Labour Party's new Maori policy, and new Northern Maori candidate. Speakers took care to begin their presentations with a few words in Maori. But the party was 'jolted' by Maori anger when many of the 600 delegates strolled out of the room 'in search of nothing more important than a cup of tea' during one of the Maori policy sessions.

Mrs Tiria Asher from Tauranga, a Maori delegate with close Ratana ties, strode to the microphone to upbraid the delegates for their snub of Maori aspirations. She reprimanded the conference for a series of actions which could be interpreted as 'patronising' or 'gratuitous'. 'How rude', reproached Mrs Asher observing the empty benches, that delegates should now see fit to interrupt this important debate. Her references to the remaining three Maori seats cut deeply with the party hierarchy: 'If you don't take notice, we will all go independent', she warned. 'Take heed!' The errant delegates were given a hasty summons from the stage to return to their seats (*Te Maori* June/July 1980: 16; *New Zealand Herald* 14 May 1980).

At this conference Tirikatene-Sullivan proposed that a bill of rights be introduced to prevent further erosion of Maori rights by successive National governments. Two days later she told delegates at a Maori Women's Welfare League Conference that she was drafting a Maori Rights Bill which would stop all further alienation of Maori land by the government, local authorities, or private sale, without the full consent of Maori land owners. This proposed bill, based upon the Treaty of Waitangi, would supersede the Public Works Act, the Town and Country Planning Act, the National Development Act and any other act of Parliament. It would also 'bind the Crown' to return land to Maori owners which was not being used for the purpose for which it was taken. In addition, this bill would make Maori an official language, equal in status with English (*New Zealand Herald* 14, 16 May 1980).

On May 17 the *Herald* threw doubt over Rata's chances in the by-election when it published a straw poll said to have been taken by one of its reporters after four days of interviewing Maori throughout the Northern electorate. This poll indicated there would be a 69.8 percent Labour vote for Gregory against a 22.4 percent Mana Motuhake vote for Rata and 7.8 percent for Social Credit (*New Zealand Herald* 17-23 May 1980). A number of pungent quotations from Maori interviews were printed in the *Herald* on that day (17 May 1980). These were overwhelmingly critical of Rata. He and his organisation were accused of creating disharmony in his own electorate; of committing a 'gross breach of etiquette by not consulting his people before resigning'; of wanting to create a 'mini-South Africa'; of 'stirring'; of having 'done nothing' for the Maori people in seventeen years; of having 'mucked things up' in the Department as Minister of Maori Affairs and of being an '"I" man, not a "We" man'. If he could not achieve things for the Maori as a Cabinet minister, was the message, what then did he expect to do as an independent?

Although Walker contended in a radio broadcast that the straw poll was 'unscientific' and challenged the view that Rata had little support, he could not undo the damage which had already been done ('Sunday Supplement' Radio New Zealand, 1 June 1980). Seeds of doubt had already been sown about the Mana Motuhake Party as a practical alternative for the Maori people to the time-weathered alliance with Labour's power structure and philosophy. Confidence in Rata had been shaken through the public accusations made against him by his Labour ex-colleagues and competitors. Labour, for its part, had been prodded into offering the electors a basket of new policies designed to answer a wide spectrum of Maori grievances, nightmares, and dreams.

During May to September 1980 two Victoria University political scientists recorded interviews with a number of Maori whose responses revealed a considerable degree of confusion and incomprehension about what Mana Motuhake stood for. Rata could have taken heart from the praise of a well-known Maori 'man of the cloth':

The formation of Mana Motuhake was a fantastic thing ... Maori problems and grievances which had remained below the surface for a long time have been brought out into the open. Everybody is talking about them and they are being kept constantly in the public eye. (Levine and Vasil 1985: 79, 180)

But not in everyone's eye. 'Hone', a shopkeeper, thought correctly that there was no Mana Motuhake branch near him. But he was interested to 'find out what it's all about'. Kanohi, an old woman who despised young Maori radicals as much as Pakeha, professed not to know what Mana Motuhake's ideas were; but if they were based on her ancestral heritage she thought the 'whole Maori race' would support Rata. The younger 'Kare', who resented the assumption of superiority over her South Island tribe's customs by linguistically accomplished northerners, thought Rata had been ill-treated by Labour. 'I hope like mad Mat gets in ... I don't fully understand it. But then I don't fully understand why I vote for Labour either' (Levine and Vasil 1985: 79, 175-6; 79, 173-4; 78, 172).

Into this climate of uncertainty a final and well-timed blow to Mana Motuhake came just four days before polling day. The *Herald* ran a large article on the five candidates, accompanied by photographs and minor particulars.[4] However, political correspondent Roger Fea focused mainly upon Mana Motuhake. The headline read: 'Separatism Fears May Hurt Mr Rata's Poll Chances'. The opening paragraph read: 'The Northern Maori by-election probably turns on whether an independent - as opposed to an established party - could usefully serve Maoridom in Parliament' (*New Zealand Herald* 3 June 1980). How effective, it asked, could one man be if returned to Parliament as an independent? Many Maori still believed, as they had for many years, that the effective voice lay within the party, not the man. The Labour candidate, Dr Bruce Gregory, was described as an individual rated highly among many Maori. Nonetheless, whether Rata was to win the election or lose he had 'forced Maoridom to take fresh stock of its political allegiances and the Labour Party to look anew at the Maori vote'. Maori policy 'will have high priority at the party's annual conferences, instead of allegedly being considered last' (ibid.).

Despite the new commitment it was Fea's opinion that the fresh Labour policies had a 'familiar look' about them. The Maori Affairs Department under the National Government was already making land development loans available to Maori land owners and incorporations, and providing youth employment opportunities. On the other hand, Mana Motuhake's desire to foster Maori autonomy and dignity was already being promoted through the National Government's Department of Maori Affairs Tu Tangata (community self-development) program under its innovative secretary, I.P. (Kara) Puketapu. The thing about which Maori felt most 'uneasy', concluded Fea, was 'Mana Motuhake's alleged "separatism", even though Mr Rata keeps emphasising that it believes in the rule of law'. The fear was based on a belief that Mana Motuhake would mainly attract Maori radicals and that a 'rift between Maori and Pakeha' would be created. It was suggested that some saw Mana Motuhake as harbouring within its philosophy 'the ingredients of racism and apartheid' (ibid.). To some Maori, not necessarily declared radicals, the idea of separatism - at least so long as it remained vague - was not repellent. 'I'm as racist as hell', a woman deeply involved in marae-based social work asserted. 'I like that idea of a separate party' (Levine and Vasil 1985: 79, 172).

But with many Maori valuing their family ties and friendships with their Pakeha neighbours, hints about incipient racial tensions were alarming. Graham Latimer described the fatal effect of Mana Motuhake's rumoured 'separatism' in the Northland. The major political parties, Latimer said, always have a 'trump card' up their sleeve, which they usually reserve until the last moment of a campaign:

> Up until the last week Mat Rata had the by-election almost won. But suddenly a fever swept through the North, where Mana Motuhake was concerned, and everyone was saying that they were racist. It was in that last week, that the trump card was played, that destroyed Maori confidence. (Latimer, interview 3 July 1981)

Who played the trump card? 'One will never know', said Latimer, 'but politics being what they are it is definitely played - it happens in every election' (ibid.).

In retrospect, what was surprising was not that so predictable a strategy was used against Rata and the new party, but that it was used so skilfully. Supported by further straw polls, Fea declared in the *Herald* on 5 June 1980 that a win for Labour in the by-election was certain. During the three 'surveys' of the Northern Maori electorate by the anonymous *Herald* reporter 'a significant number - but certainly not the majority - referred to their fears about separatism' (*New Zealand Herald* 5 June 1980). The questioning style used by the reporter was not explained and no-one seemed to know the source of the 'fever' of fear which 'swept' the North. But there was little doubt that the rumour received a drip-feed promotion by this newspaper's emphasis on racial separatism in its polling and reporting activities over these months. 'Despite predictions to the contrary', reported the *Herald*, Rata still believed he would gain a 'landslide victory'. Rata fought back, accusing the *Herald* of:

> doing harm and of the emotional use of words "that are aimed at cultivating an overly dangerous situation". The fact that 90 per cent of Maori youngsters failed at school and that the greatest number in jails were Maoris was separatism. "It is the kind of separatism which is going to keep us poles apart and which I intend to fight". (*New Zealand Herald* 6 June 1980)

In an unguarded moment Rata showed his hand to his opponents. He made it known that he believed Mana Motuhake adherents were more committed than Labour followers. Many Labour voters would not come out and vote, he said. When this prediction was reported, it presented a warning and a challenge to Labour to prove him wrong.

As the National Party had no contender for the seat some of the Kaikohe National supporters told the *Herald* that they had arranged a bloc vote for Labour, as they were 'worried by the "racial-separatism" threat posed by Mana Motuhake'. The *Herald* also took up the challenge. A 'wet weather test', reported Roger Fea, had been arranged whereby electors were probed about the degree of their commitment. If bad weather prevailed, would this keep them from the polling both, they were asked. After subtracting the 'fair weather friends' the *Herald* still had Labour 'trouncing' Rata in what it admitted was 'not presented as a scientific poll' (*New Zealand Herald* 5 June 1980).

'WE WILL FIGHT ON'

By the end of the campaign fifteen Mana Motuhake branches had been formed and 2,300 members had joined the party. Many of the members had contributed money, and had provided the party with a body of enthusiastic workers. On polling day the Auckland Mana Motuhake branches had Maori scrutineers assigned to most of the booths in their area. This level of commitment was not apparent in the Labour Party, which relied on Pakeha supporters (Walker 1980:5; *New Zealand Herald* 9 June 1980).

The Northern Maori by-election on Saturday 7, June 1980 did not bring a landslide victory for Matiu Rata - or a resounding win for Bruce Gregory. The Labour Party won the seat with 52.40 percent of the votes (3580) against Mana Motuhake's 37.90 percent (2589). A faded 8.19 percent (560) of the vote went to Social Credit, with 102 votes cast for 'other' parties. Rata had done considerably better than the 22.4 percent support which the *Herald*, at its last straw poll, had predicted for him (*New Zealand Herald* 6, 9 June 1980). In the 1978 general election he had won an overwhelming victory with 71.47 percent support (6071 votes) for the Labour Party. He had carried disappointingly fewer than half of this number of votes with him in the by-election. Nevertheless, it was a significant dent in Labour's massive majority. The *Herald* conceded this as a 'respectable performance' which 'raises the question of whether the movement will become a force in New Zealand politics ... ' (*New Zealand Herald* 9 June 1980). It also raised the question of how Rata and his counsellors might best sustain the enthusiasm of their inevitably deflated supporters.

Although he had been unemployed since his resignation from Parliament in April Rata claimed that he was not in a hurry to seek re-employment. He and his family had 'existed on less than nothing before'. It was his hope, with the consent of the members, that he would be able to work full time for the organisation - travelling extensively throughout the country. Mana Motuhake should not be seen purely in political terms, but in social terms as well, Rata said. He believed that the organisation was 'satisfying a Maori need'. 'Young people', he said, 'constitute 68 percent of the Maori population ... I have grave doubts that the Labour Party can contain or inspire them'. On the contrary, Bruce Gregory told the press, support for Mana Motuhake would erode during the next year's general election (*New Zealand Herald* 9 June 1980).

On June 8 the *Sunday News* reported that Rata would open his campaign for the 1981 general election the following day. Although deeply disappointed in the voters' 'punishing rejection' of Mana Motuhake the day before, he spoke calmly about his future plans. He appeared undisturbed about his personal situation, saying, 'Maoris have been good to me for seventeen years. I don't think I will go hungry'.

The 'unwarranted and unfounded' attacks on him by his Labour ex-colleagues, however, appeared to have deeply wounded him. He told the *Sunday News* (8 June 1980) that he had made a promise to Labour not to reveal any party secrets after his resignation. He was disappointed that 'they had not kept their side of the bargain'. Despite his loss of the by-election 'the movement will continue', Rata said. 'It's a beginning'. His party would fight on with 'determination for a better deal for Maoris'. In his last campaign speech Rata announced that, including the prospective bequest of 50,000 dollars, his movement had acquired assets of 62,000 dollars. Some of this would be used for the forthcoming general election campaign. Mana Motuhake, he said, planned to contest all four Maori seats, and possibly some marginal seats as well (*New Zealand Herald* 2, 6, 9 June 1980).

The fledgling Mana Motuhake political organisation had in fact done well in mobilising almost 38 percent of the votes in the Northern seat in the two months of the by-election campaign. But in the harsh light of the electoral arena, a new pro-Maori ideology had not been enough to convince the majority of voters that Maori interests would be better served by abandoning the loyalties of several generations. A simple question presented itself to many voters. What could one representative achieve as a lone voice in Parliament that he could not achieve as a senior member of one of the two major parties? But there was no doubt that for some electors the question was irrelevant. One observer visiting the North discovered that Rata was drawing on a vote of gratitude:

> the old people up there were blindly backing him no matter what because they thought that as a person he had done them a lot of good ... They were not going to vote for Mana Motuhake, they were voting for Matiu and what he had done. (Levine and Vasil 1985: 81)

Some professional commentators, however, saw serious faults in Rata's personal performance in the by-election campaign. 'He did not campaign well ... He did not communicate effectively over the media' (Garnier and Levine 1981: 132). Tempting as it might have been to dismiss such judgments by Garnier and Levine, an academic theorist and a Wellington journalist, Mana Motuhake strategists needed no tutoring in the weaknesses as well as the strengths of their leader. They were well aware that Rata's style was not universally attractive. But they did not make the mistake of equating his media appearances with his face-to-face campaigning.

For the Pakeha, like most Europeans and North Americans, the public meeting, indeed almost any public event, had lost much of its electioneering significance in the television era.[5] But Maori traditions of marae debate, with arguments and entreaties heard at length, had not yet been displaced by the 90-second news 'grab' or the 'photo-opportunity'. For Mana Motuhake, unable to afford extensive electronic and print media campaigns, it was possible to make a virtue of necessity. 'He Kanohi Kitea' (the face that is seen) was a Maori aphorism that affirmed the expectation that candidates would present themselves at gatherings as well as hold meetings of their own (Walker, 'Korero', *New Zealand Listener* 17 December 1983).

Ranginui Walker (1980: 5) took stock of the impact of the movement in the aftermath of the by-election:

> Mana Motuhake has shaken the Pakeha's faith in his ability to dominate and manipulate the Maori through the party political process. Labour asks, "what can one man do on his own", while at the same time putting its house in order in response to what one man has done.
> If the people are satisfied with the refurbished Labour policies and consign Rata to the limbo of independent politicians, then his gesture of resignation would have been in vain. As one prominent woman in the movement put it: "We owe it to the ancestors and ourselves that Mana Motuhake should succeed".

In Latimer's opinion Rata lost the by-election because he did not have as much support in the Northland as he supposed. 'I think that the Labour stalwarts put him in, in that first election', Latimer said. The first to follow Rata away from Labour were the idealists and the liberals of the Maori world. But the habit of voting Labour was much more difficult to break in the Maori working-class - as the straw poll indicated:

> From Auckland to Kaitaia, Kaeo to Dargaville, Maoris stopped in the streets, paused in hotels and cowsheds, or leaned on shovels in road gangs, to give their views ... Support for Labour, among those interviewed, was overwhelming ... Mr Rata ... may have vastly over-rated the rise in Maori nationalism. (*New Zealand Herald* 17 May 1980)

In the face of urban unemployment, and other issues of protest, Mana Motuhake hoped that it could draw a solid youth vote. But, unless one deliberately sought out the 'radicals', said the article, they were difficult to find in the random survey. Indeed, although unemployment and major protests over land had disturbed Maori people, 'to a surprising extent Maoridom - even Maori youth - appeared to be basically conservative' (ibid.).

The real 'stirrers', a 33 year old Moerewa freezing worker had told the press, were the young Maori university students (ibid.) - the sector of the Maori vote which a roving journalist would not find leaning upon shovels or in the cowsheds of the Northland to complete a 'random' straw poll. This group could not on their own have made up the difference of 15.5 percent between the *Herald's* estimate of 22.4 percent and Rata's poll of 37.9 percent. One has to assume that Rata won some working-class rural and urban votes, as well as some support from the small, but growing, minority of protesters, intellectuals, traditionalists, and middle-class liberals.

Although many Ratanas also said they would vote for Rata, at the time of the by-election it was clear that Rata could still not count on a bloc vote from the Ratana Church. 'The thing is', concluded Professor Bruce Biggs in an interview in November 1980, 'the protesting people are always the vocal ones. It's uncertain who are the majority - them, or the silent ones'. The bonds of loyalty to Labour among working-class Maori, in both the rural Northland and the urban areas, were apparent in all age groups. At the ballot box, it was they who emerged as the 'silent majority'. Ironically, nothing could have demonstrated more conclusively the success Rata had achieved over the previous seventeen years in convincing the electorate of the identity of interest between Labour and the Maori people than the tenacity of that belief in the face of Rata's own change of heart. When forced to make the choice, most Labour voters renewed their commitment to the party, not to its renegade favourite son.

What was uncertain - in some ways the mystery of the by-election - was the intention of the 2429 people who cast special votes but had them disallowed. Most of these votes - 84 percent of the special votes cast - were disallowed because the constituent was not enrolled (Stokes 1981: 88, 23). If, as therefore seems probable, the majority of them were irregular or inexperienced voters, the likelihood is strong that they were also trying to express their support for Rata. Thwarted by the complexities of the electoral requirements, they were perhaps the 'silenced' majority.

The evidence of public meetings and other first-hand observations was that youthful protesters, the urban disaffected, and middle-class liberals, were more immediately receptive to the Mana Motuhake Party's stand on current issues. Rata hoped to win the Ratana vote on the grounds of his long-term affiliation and service to the church. But the short period of the by-election campaign did not allow him time to cultivate the church vote. This would come later. Rata also had a potential following among the traditionalists who, steeped in the century old struggle, had kept alive the flame of 'mana motuhake' in the Kotahitanga enclaves of the North.

The rural conservative sector, Rata knew, would be harder to win. His long term in Parliament had resulted in a loss of contact with the community base over the years. As long as they voted for the party and not for the man, under Labour he was assured of re-election. His opponents, however, had been right to perceive that Rata's sudden decision to leave the Labour Party without consulting the elders of his electorate had not endeared him to some. Now he relied upon his Ratana and tribal elders to speak in favour of the new movement and to help mobilise support. Although the presentation of a persuasive message to the hinterland of the electorate became central to his campaign, not all communities could be visited. Some were offended when they were not included in Rata's packed itinerary before polling day.

Intense though his campaign tour of the Northland was over those two months, it was not enough to produce the spectacular reversal of Maori voting habits which Rata needed to regain the seat. Mana Motuhake gatherings in 1980 and the ensuing eighteen months clearly showed that Rata had not won the full support of any *one* of these sectors, but that he had attracted a discernible cross-section of followers from all of them. Although a wholesale transfer of loyalty from the Northern Labour cells to Mana Motuhake did not occur, Rata managed to split the Labour vote and to seriously disrupt Labour's Northland party support system. With the five branches that had resigned from the Labour Party in support of Rata, Mana Motuhake was provided with the first building blocks for its northern electorate structure. It was enough to encourage Rata to challenge in all four seats in the general election due in the following year. Once having embarked on the electoral path it would in any case have been a damaging signal of timidity or pessimism if Mana Motuhake were not to contest every seat reserved for Maori voters. To stand still would be tantamount to an admission of defeat. A movement, by definition, needed momentum.

NOTES

1. 'Bloc voting' refers to the practice of the group coming to a consensus upon whom or what they will vote for, and the group as a whole casting its vote in favour of the agreed delegate or proposal.

2. The Values Party leader, Mrs Margaret Crozier, announced that her party also would not contest Northern Maori as they 'wanted to endorse the Hon. M. Rata's Mana Motuhake movement. The movement's aim of Maori self-determination was already Values policy' (*New Zealand Herald* 8 May 1980). As the young Values Party still had only a very small following for its liberal platform on environmental, human rights, and welfare issues, this declaration was as much an exercise in self-promotion as it was a genuine offer of support for the new Maori party.

3. In addition to Hohepa, Walker, and Mead, other prominent post-secondary school educated Maori associating with the movement included Arapeta Tahana, Toby Curtis, and Amsterdam Reedy.

4. The five candidates for the 1980 Northern Maori by-election were: Dr Bruce Gregory for Labour; the Hon. M. Rata for Mana Motuhake; Mr H.Te K. Toia for Social Credit; Mrs P. Te R. Warner for the Reform Party; Mr T.K. Weal for the Christian Democratic Union Party.

5. About a quarter of the voters sampled in the Christchurch electorate of Papanui in 1978 claimed to have attended a political meeting during the preceding election campaign. But this self-reported figure was not checked against other sources of information about attendances (Deely and Trainor 1981: 25).

VI

A CAMPAIGN OF HOPE AND VISION

In the year following the Northern Maori by-election New Zealand witnessed a period of unprecedented political turbulence. Protracted national strikes and a tour by the South African Springbok rugby union team convulsed the nation. The 1970s had already brought a mounting tide of unemployment, inflation, national debt, strikes, land protests, and a frightening leap in urban crime. Widespread political unrest was reflected in volatile opinion polls.

With a rise in support for the Social Credit Party New Zealand's two party system had been replaced by a three party split which affected both Parliament and the local regions. MPs, fearing the loss of their seats, were kept busy fighting rear-guard actions in their electorates. They were reluctant to leave their own areas in response to other needs of their parties. The National Party government had plunged into a desperate 'Think Big' economic strategy, gambling on massive investment in energy projects to revive an ailing New Zealand economy and to insulate the nation from unpredictable fluctuations in overseas fuel supplies.

In this febrile climate the possible collapse of traditional Maori support for the Labour Party created a new dimension of uncertainty. Matiu Rata's resignation became a catalyst for a new wave of Maori political mobilisation, and for the revival of earlier ideals of Maori self-government and self-determination. While the major parties were preoccupied with a three-way electoral battle, Rata felt this was an ideal time for the Maori to contest marginal seats throughout the country. All that was needed was the party machinery to do so. The future success of Mana Motuhake as a political force, wrote Walker (1980: 5) following its loss of the Northern Maori by-election, would be determined by the movement's ability to raise the consciousness of the Maori voter; to develop a 'substantive infrastructure'; to establish its own constitution; and to withstand co-option by any of the major political parties.

CONSOLIDATION AND CONFLICT

Between August and September 1980, a draft constitution was circulated to all Mana Motuhake branches for review. There were proposals for an alliance with Maori activist organisations for the 1981 election. The chairman of Te Matakite O Aotearoa, Eva Rickard, had been considering contesting the Western Maori seat as an independent. At a September meeting Rata invited Te Matakite to join the ranks of Mana Motuhake - providing, he said, its members were prepared to 'act within the law' (*New Zealand Herald* 13 September 1980). Rata's terms for alliance with other radical groups carried a clear message that, whatever their agreed political goals, they would be pursued with tactical moderation.

Meanwhile, quiet overtures towards Mana Motuhake were being made by the Social Credit Party, which had polled nearly 17 percent of the votes in 1978 but had won only one seat. The smaller Values Party had declared publicly that it would not contest those seats which the Mana Motuhake Party was contesting. According to Mana Motuhake informants a similar assurance was given by Social Credit leaders in private discussions. But, as it was felt that for them not to put forward candidates would give the appearance of collusion, it was agreed that there would be only token Social Credit campaigns wherever there was a Mana Motuhake candidate. Indeed, it was believed that Social Credit candidates would actually encourage Maori electors to vote Mana Motuhake. In early June the *Herald* (10 June 1980) reported that the Labour Party was 'ready to talk' with Mana Motuhake about their policy differences, despite 'hurt feelings on both sides'.

While Rata affirmed the endeavour 'to get the major political parties ... to adopt Mana Motuhake's stated policies', he was also emphatically against any loss of his party's hard-earned independence through coalition or co-option (Mana Motuhake O Te Tai-Tokerau, monthly general minutes 11 June 1980). Encouraged by his capture of nearly 38 percent of the vote in so short a campaign for a new party, Rata launched his campaign for the general election the day after the Northern by-election. About one hundred people attended his first campaign meeting held at the Te Mahurehure Marae, Point Chevalier, on 8 June 1980.

The foundations of the election machinery were already in place. From early May 1980 Rata conducted his business from his head office, at its central Auckland city location, surrounded by a busy volunteer and part-time support staff. Office correspondence and a monthly newsletter were sent out on freshly printed stationery bearing the organisation's logo and colours. To support the growing administrative and campaign costs, members were invited to make a commitment of a dollar a week towards the movement over the next eighteen months.

Expanding activity made effective communication with Mana Motuhake's growing membership a quickly recognised problem. The only two office telephones had to be constantly attended in order to disseminate campaign information, answer enquiries, and conduct the president's regular business. In a letter circulated to all branches and area organisers on 9 July 1980, the president proposed that urban, tribal, and hapu bodies could assist their members by evolving a 'more effective communication network' by establishing a 'dial-a-tribe' and office circulation system. These units could act as 'central points of communication' to help facilitate the flow of information throughout the electorates.

With a membership of almost 5,000 Mana Motuhake's inaugural Hui-a-Tau (national annual conference), held at the Waitahanui Marae, Taupo, on 21-23 November 1980, attracted a large gathering. More than 200 delegates to the conference were to discuss and adopt the official party constitution; to elect officers to the Secretariat and the Policy Council; and to further plans for the election. The greater part of the first day was given over to mihimihi (greetings/ acknowledgements) and whaikorero (formal speeches). Elders - formally recognised as an Elders' Council - authenticated Mana Motuhake, linking its philosophy and aims with their historic roots (Walker, 'Korero' *New Zealand Listener* 3 January 1981). The purpose and objectives of the party, as adopted after vigorous debate the next day by the Hui-a-Tau, and outlined in (article 2) of *Mana Motuhake O Aotearoa Constitution and Rules*, were:

a) To foster, promote, assist and sustain the social, economic, cultural, spiritual and political interests, self-reliance and advancement of the Maori.
b) To foster and promote the election of able and competent men and women to Parliament, Local Government, public and Maori authorities and organisations.
c) To foster and promote the lawful recognition and honouring of agreements and guarantees entered into in the Treaty of Waitangi, and to obtain reparations for past injustices.
d) To enlighten the public towards the better understanding of the Maori and Mana Motuhake.

There was scarcely a breath of separatism in this charter. With the possible exception of the unspecified ultimate meaning of Mana Motuhake itself, there was nothing in the stated aims to which even the most conservative of Maori could object. Nor could there be any question among Pakeha about the legitimacy of attempts to obtain better Maori representation in public bodies. While there might be some basis for apprehension about the potential scope and magnitude of 'reparations for past injustices', this had become familiar liberal rather than revolutionary language.

The membership arrangements blended conventional individual (annual and life) and branch categories, with provision for whole families (kin-group or hapu), junior members (under 16 years old), and associate members, including non-Maori (article 3). The structure of the Mana Motuhake Party was to comprise: a) branches; b) area councils, the governing body within the area or district of their jurisdiction; c) four electorate councils, the governing body within their respective electorates; d) a secretariat, the supreme governing body for Mana Motuhake (article 4).

An Elders' Council, Women's Council, Youth Council, Industrial Relations Council, and other advisory groups were established by, and under the control of, the Secretariat. The Secretariat was to consist of nineteen members, nine elected and the rest to be appointed by the Electorate Councils. Each year at the Hui-a-Tau, elections for the Secretariat, Policy Council, and the party presidency were to take place. Nominations for these positions would be called for by the general secretary several weeks prior to the annual conference. As a primary body of the organisation, the function of the Policy Council was to design policies based upon the general philosophy and rules of the party constitution. Major constitutional revisions could only be made at the Hui-a-Tau.

Each branch, area council, electorate council, and the Secretariat - according to the size of their membership - would be represented by their chosen delegates at the Hui-a-Tau. All bodies of the Mana Motuhake would be invited to raise issues for discussion by remit to the general secretary. Conference decisions would be taken by consensus, or vote when consensus was not reached, following the normal Maori debate and discussion period. When the supreme decision-making institution of the Hui-a-Tau was not in session the Secretariat would act as the governing administrative body. The president was to preside over the Policy Council and the Secretariat (*Mana Motuhake O Aotearoa: Constitution and Rules*, adopted by the Mana Motuhake O Aotearoa Conference, 21/23 November 1980, Waitahanui Marae, Taupo). In effect, the methods of administration used by the Mana Motuhake were a combination of the well-ordered customs of modern marae life and those imbibed over a 40-year period of Labour Party affiliation.

At Mana Motuhake's first Hui-a-Tau Matiu Rata was confirmed as the party's president. Following intensive lobbying, the occupants of other key positions of leadership on the Secretariat and Policy Council were elected from among the outstanding community leaders, or highly educated elite, of the organisation's membership: Dr Patrick Hohepa, senior lecturer in Maori Studies, Auckland University; Sid Mead, Professor of Maori Studies, Victoria University, Wellington; Dr Ranginui Walker, senior lecturer, Continuing Education Department, Auckland University; Amsterdam Reedy, senior lecturer in Maori Studies, Wellington Teachers' Training College; Arapeta (Albert) Tahana, senior vocational guidance officer, Labour Department, Auckland; Maree Woodcock, school teacher, Avondale Primary School, Auckland; Hanna Baker, housewife, Northland; Toby Curtis, lecturer in Maori Studies, Auckland Teachers' Training College; Te Pare Josephs, government farm manager, Mangakino, Waikato; Joe Toki, elder, Mangamuka, Northland; Ihimaera Ihimaera, freezing worker, trade unionist, Onehunga, Auckland. The following year further representatives were to be appointed from the Elders', Women's, and Youth Councils and from the remaining three electorate councils, once they were established.

In depicting the flow of power, the constitution represented Mana Motuhake's administration in the shape of an inverted pyramid. Under article 4, section 1, local branches were listed at the top of the power hierarchy and the Secretariat at the bottom. This was consciously a 'Maori structure'. There was a stated desire to avoid replication of a Pakeha model - where the greatest power is reserved for the smallest number, positioned at the apex of the administrative pyramid. 'We want people power - not power politics', said one member. Decision-making within Mana Motuhake, it was contended, should rise from the membership branches, by remit and delegation. It was the function of the area councils, electorate councils and, finally, the Secretariat to formalise and carry out the objectives and aims of the members. These bodies, and their officials, were the 'servants' of the majority. The national conference, or Hui-a-Tau, was the supreme decision-making body of the people.

Unsurprisingly, as the New Zealand Maori Council had found, the ideal was sometimes difficult to sustain. Maori democracy, on one hand, and Maori leadership, on the other, were conceptual contradictions which the underlying influences of kinship could successfully balance within the tribal arena. Decisions to place authority into the hands of a favourite son were either predetermined by customary inheritance of title, or were taken by community consensus in recognition of the special merit of a particular individual.

The attempt to balance Maori democratic ideals and organisational necessities in a pan-Maori context, however, created a number of problems for Mana Motuhake. First, the modifying influence of traditional kinship priorities was frequently overborne and disrupted by inter-tribal jealousies. Second, there was an innate tension between the facilitative and guardian role of Mana Motuhake's administrative bodies and the functional inevitability of decision-making on behalf of their members. Inevitably, the powerful encapsulating currents of the national political system induced the Secretariat to act as the governing body, empowered to interpret and to implement the constitution.

While often hailing him as an inspired and tireless leader, disgruntled members and frustrated officials were sometimes heard to criticise Rata for his 'authoritarianism', his habits of 'parliamentary remoteness', and his tendency to act as a political 'one-man-band'. Some of those closest to Rata wanted to share a little more of the leadership limelight. Members with administrative expertise to offer criticised the party for its lack of internal democracy. What was occurring would have been no surprise to those familiar with the Weberian antithesis between charisma and rationality, or with Michels' diagnosis of the oligopolistic dynamic of political parties. But there were other elements, peculiar to the time and place. Bickering and incipient factionalism within Mana Motuhake on the question of the delegation of power and responsibility were accentuated by the diverse tribal, party-political, and ideological backgrounds of the membership. Some members brought old hostilities with them.

In the months leading up to the general election there was restlessness among Mana Motuhake's adherents. One of Rata's admirers admitted that he was 'beginning to hear a groundswell of opinion' in favour of younger leadership. 'I suppose that those of my age group, the late 30s and the early 40s, are all feeling that but none of us is willing to come out and say that at this point because we admire the person too much' (Levine and Vasil 1985: 80). 'An acknowledged leader of Maori radicalism' was convinced that Rata 'should step down and become a patron of the movement'. He wanted 'fast and dramatic change' and was sure that Rata could not lead the 'direct assault on the political scene' that was needed (ibid.: 80, 178). Despite his longevity as a parliamentarian (he was first elected at the age of 28) Rata himself was still only 47 years old during the 1981 election campaign. He had no thought of retiring. It was not going to be easy to retain the full-hearted involvement of those who thought Rata was now a barrier to change rather than its vanguard.

Another unhappy faction was also appearing. By the end of 1980 a feminist group had emerged, increasingly assertive and vocal. At the November conference they were seeking a constitutional guarantee of 50 percent representation for women in Mana Motuhake's administration. As positions were based upon election as well as nomination, this demand conflicted with party philosophy and intended practice. With the rejection of the feminist lobby's claim the women resorted to recriminations and accusations of sexism against the male members. They threatened to withdraw their vote in the next election, and their practical support at meetings and functions. These attacks incensed a large majority of the male and some of the more conservative female members (Walker, 'Korero', *New Zealand Listener* 3 January 1981).

Internal division was accompanied by unwelcome external interest. Following a rather bizarre burglary of the parliamentary office of Maori MP Whetu Tirikatene-Sullivan in December 1980, the Wellington branch reported to the Secretariat that some of its executive members had been picked up for questioning by the police about the break-in. There were suspicions that the whole episode had been set up by New Zealand's intelligence service (SIS) as a means of cross-examining Mana Motuhake officials about the organisation's membership and purpose. One Wellington official reported that the police enquiries 'were more of an interrogation' and had caused considerable distress. Another member referred to 'harassment and enquiries' from the police.

Professor Sid Mead, a Secretariat official from the Wellington branch, expressed his concern about efforts to 'implicate Mana Motuhake' in the crime and the suggestion of 'subversion and radicalism' in the police investigation. Deep concern was expressed by the president and a motion was passed at the December meeting to officially 'condemn the burglaries of Maori Members of Parliament' (Minutes of the Secretariat 19 December 1980). At the following meeting it was resolved:

That the president write to the Minister of Police regarding the matter with a copy to the Minister in Charge of the Legislative Department and Leader of the Opposition, and an appropriate public statement being made in due course. (Minutes of the Mana Motuhake Secretariat 18 January 1981)

Against the forces which would fragment the new Maori party, other activities promoted growth and consolidation. By January 1981 Mana Motuhake had formed 59 branches (36 being in the Northland), comprising a financial membership of almost 7,000 (*New Zealand Herald* 24 January 1981).[1] The party was said to be supported almost solely by 'Maori money', acquired by fund-raising, membership fees, levies, and contributions. A campaign fund target of 50,000 dollars had been set at the Hui-a-Tau in November 1980, and each member was invited to make a personal commitment of ten dollars to this special fund. In addition to meeting their own needs, branches were encouraged to undertake local fund-raising for the national campaign fund. Although limited publicity, travel, and office expenses were met by the organisation, the president and his staff received only small honoraria for their labours. General hui expenses of food and accommodation were borne by the host communities.

By March 31 membership fees, affiliation fees, and donations amounted to 13,460 dollars; the finance committee and campaign fund accounts stood at 1,695 dollars; and income which had been expended by Mana Motuhake since its inception amounted to 25,967 dollars. But, as branches established their own fund-raising committees to finance local campaigns, the total income generated by the movement was considerably larger than this. Mana Motuhake's three roomed head office had become the focus for campaign planning, publicity activities, the registration of new members, the distribution of membership cards, correspondence and telephone enquiries, and the design of press statements and pamphlets on a broad range of Maori and general issues. Head office kept its printers busy with pamphlets and circulars distributed by the national campaign committee. Minutes and policy papers also needed to be duplicated for distribution, and on August 14-16 the party sponsored a National Mana Motuhake Youth Conference for its younger members.[2]

By February the president's itinerary was full with daily campaign and administrative meetings. Not only did he have to win new recruits in the northern seat, he also wished to establish strong branch networks in the other three electorates - each with its own candidate for the coming election. The excitement of rapid growth raised hopes of winning the four Maori seats in Parliament. Mana Motuhake officials speculated that at least two Maori seats could be won in the 1981 election and that the results in another thirteen marginal seats on the general roll might also be affected. Voters, who were sceptical about the potency of a lone member in Parliament, might well think more optimistically about the prospective influence of a party with several parliamentarians and a number of other candidates who could determine the outcome of particular constituency contests.

In his opening speech at the inaugural meeting of the Secretariat, Rata warned that growing industrial unrest in the country might encourage the National government to seek an early election. Mana Motuhake, he said, must prepare itself for this likelihood. The instability of the New Zealand political climate, could be seen in the erosion of support for the two major parties to Social Credit. Pointing out that Mana Motuhake would be composed of differing

MANA MOTUHAKE IS THE FUTURE OF THE MAORI PEOPLE.

RATA AND MANA MOTUHAKE

our dignity and mana demand that we control our own affairs as we did in the past. We must no longer depend on someone else to decide for us. Control must return to real Maori tribal roots – to the *iwi*, the *hapu*, the *whanau*. People – the elderly, the very young, the adolescents and men and women – must be our first priority. People, land, forests and fisheries, language and culture are crucial areas for Mana Motuhake not only in the 1980's, but also in the 1990's the year 2000 and the century which follows . . ."

Marae
● that Marae subsidies and grants be increased to complete the backlog of needs within 5 years. Automatic yearly increases of grants to Trust Boards.

The Young
● our first concern.

Tribal Authorities
● our Tribal Authorities should replace the Dept. of Maori Affairs using former Departmental staff and resources to assist ● that to the Treaty of Waitangi has been long regarded by the Maori people as the Charter which protect our rights ● the Treaty be legally honoured ● all laws which contravene the Treaty be repealed ● compensation for all injustices.

MANA MOTUHAKE

Arts, Culture, Artifacts
● that a Maori Arts Council, fully funded, be set up independent of the QEII Arts Council ● that no pre-1900 artifacts be sent overseas for any reason ● that it will be an offence to abuse or misuse Maori culture in New Zealand or overseas.

Land
● that Maori Land Courts be replaced by our own Runanga Whenua.

Language
● our Maori language be a right to all Maori children ● that the Maori language be made available to all children from pre-school to University ● that the mass media have 10% of all productions in Maori ● our Maori place-names be reinstated, starting with "AOTEAROA" instead of New Zealand ● that Maori and English be accepted as the official languages of this country.

MANA MOTUHAKE

THIS IS FOR YOU VOTE RATA

opinions he appealed to members to 'bear in mind the necessity for agreeing to the right to disagree'. The only way to avoid conflicts of interest within the party, Rata concluded, was to strengthen and safeguard the autonomy of every branch, area council, and electorate of the party. He reminded members that Mana Motuhake was not a substitute for the Maori world but its 'political arm' whose task was to 'reinforce' that world (Minutes of the Secretariat, 19 December 1980). This was, of course, a strategic objective rather than a reality vindicated by popular acclamation. The extent to which the new party could credibly present itself as 'the' political arm of the Maori world was soon to be put to a profound and public test.

From the beginning of the 1970s the celebration of Waitangi Day, February 6, had become the focus of protest for Maori rights by a group of young Maori activists, latterly calling themselves the 'Waitangi Action Committee'. The nature of the debate over the Treaty of Waitangi had changed very little over the last century and a half. The original Waitangi orators were still referred to on marae. Their words were used to support modern grievances. Maori thought telescoped time and blended generations when issues, and the positions people occupy, were thought to be the same. It was the immemorial duty of Maori leaders to ensure that Maori land and well-being were secure.

The grievances of land loss and loss of autonomy remained undiminished by the passage of time. But the methods of protest had changed, with new strategies of civil disobedience and use of the media. One of the central issues of the latest phase of protest was the validity of the Treaty of Waitangi. In the committee's view the Treaty had never been honoured and was therefore not a legal document. As the New Zealand nation-state was said to have been founded upon the Treaty of Waitangi - which was not a legal document in national or international law - by deduction then, all agencies of the state (police, courts, and government) were therefore illegal and not to be recognised. This view was not shared unequivocally by other sectors of Maori society, but there was from the outset some sympathy for it.

The capacity of Maori leaders to manage complex political cross-currents, and the role which would be assigned to the newest aspirant for power, were to be revealed in the events surrounding Waitangi Day 1981. The official celebrations of that day were to include an investiture, when imperial honours would be conferred upon two renowned Maori leaders, Sir Graham Latimer and Dame Whina Cooper. Royal honours had been incorporated into the Maori status system since the early twentieth century. 'Pakeha medals', however, had always been more popular with loyalist and conservative Maori than with the strongly traditional, or the more recent liberal and radical sectors.

Latimer was not only the president of the NZMC, he was also the chairman of the powerful Northland subdivision of the NZMC, the rural based and largely conservative Tai Tokerau District Maori Council. The Tai Tokerau and other Northland supporters and relatives of Sir Graham and Dame Whina were immensely proud of their leaders, and passionately wished these honours for them. In the reasoning of Latimer and Cooper, 'an honour conferred upon one of

MANA MOTUHAKE

IS CONCERNED ABOUT THE FUTURE
OF THE MAORI PEOPLE . . .

MANA MOTUHAKE
SAYS . . .

"that our dignity and mana demand that we control our own affairs as we did in the past. We must no longer depend on someone else to decide for us. Control must return to real Maori tribal roots — to the iwi, the hapu, the whanau. People — the elderly, the very young, the adolescents and men and women — must be our first priority. People, land, forests and fisheries, language and culture are crucial areas for Mana Motuhake not only in the 1980's, but also in the 1990's the year 2000 and the century which follows . . ."

Eva Rickard

MANA MOTUHAKE CANDIDATE FOR WESTERN MAORI

Eva Rickard
56 years Maori woman, mother and grandmother, descended from Waikato tribes and Ngati Toa, educated in the Ponga houses of my Tupunas, conditioned in the Colonial Schools.
"Maori Land Consultant, Activist for Human Rights, Land is Life."

MANA MOTUHAKE
IS CONCERNED ABOUT . . .

- High unemployment rate (5 out of 7 unemployed in the North are Maori)
- High imprisonment rate • High infant deaths • High educational failure rate
- High incidence of child abuse • High health risk • Maori land • Maori forestry
- Maori fishing rights • Maori language and culture • Maori heirlooms and artifacts.

VOTE EVA   VOTE EVA   VOTE EVA

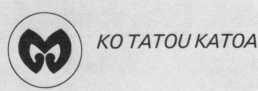

MANA MOTUHAKE   KO TATOU KATOA

their members was an honour conferred upon the whole'. They felt compelled to gracefully accept these honours on their people's behalf. Latimer was well aware of the history of controversy surrounding Maori acceptance of royal honours. He proposed that the ceremony be conducted on Te Tiriti O Waitangi Marae - the Waitangi national marae - to ensure that the investiture had the blessings of the Maori people. 'It was my people who put me up for the honour', he explained, 'this was my way of returning it to them' (Latimer, interview May 1981).

In the climate of the day the disruption of the investitures was a wholly predictable symbolic gesture on the part of the Waitangi protesters. The Northland supporters of Latimer and Cooper were as determined to have their investiture ceremonies conducted on the national marae as the protesters were determined to disrupt them. The ensuing conflict erupted in a violent clash of wills during marae debates and meetings over several weeks before the ceremony. Words exchanged were highly emotive and explosive, rapidly concluding discussions between the parties. By the morning of the appointed day no consensus had been reached. Both were to proceed with their intentions.

Dr Patrick Hohepa agreed to put forward the protesters' complaints to Sir Graham and Dame Whina. This was done in a dignified manner before the visitors arrived. Peacemakers among the elders decided to allow the protests to 'have their say' to the Governor-General, Prime Minister, and other invited dignitaries before proceeding with the official ceremony. The abundant presence of the police - alerted to likely trouble from the protesters - and their apparent disregard for the role of the volunteer Maori wardens within the marae grounds, fuelled the resentment. A series of incidents - the intensifying hostilities of the marae debates the evening before, the undisciplined behaviour and offensive rhetoric of the protesters, and the ill-judged impulse of the Minister of Maori Affairs, Ben Couch, to make a little political mileage out of the situation - all escalated tensions on the day.

The determination of the young protesters to voice their grievances about the 'broken promises' and to obstruct the proceedings climaxed in a display of defiance staged by one young man who leaped to the dais at the moment the Governor-General was performing the investiture for the elderly Dame Whina Cooper. The police swept on to the marae grounds and carried off nine of the protesters. The arrests and subsequent court hearings provoked an ideological battle that touched the loyalties of most Maori and many Pakeha over several months. Some of the most powerful figures in the Maori and Pakeha worlds became caught up in a series of verbal exchanges, acerbic correspondence, and public sparring - reported in detail by the media (for a fuller account of the Waitangi Day incident see Hazlehurst [1993]).

PETITIONING THE QUEEN

The 1981 Waitangi Day incident, and its contentious aftermath, presented Rata with the ideal opportunity to demonstrate Mana Motuhake's capacity to act as the 'political arm of the Maori world'. Following the disturbances it was decided that Mana Motuhake would launch a petition, seeking the ratification of the Treaty of Waitangi, on the same marae where Sir Graham and Dame Whina received their controversial honours. It was the intention of the party to present the petition to Queen Elizabeth II during her visit to New Zealand planned for October 1981.

The date for the Waitangi Policy Hui was set for the weekend of March 27-29. The majority of the participants arrived at Te Tiriti O Waitangi Marae before 5.00 pm on the Friday evening. The evening debates began about 9.00 pm, and continued through the night. Over 200 guests were accommodated in the marae meeting house. Mattresses lined the walls and central floor-space. Listeners reclined on their beds. Individuals rose in turn to speak. Sleepers - 'eyes closed and ears open' - awoke when they heard a name or issue of interest to them. Rata, weary from the day's travel and preparing himself for the morrow, withdrew early to acquire a night's rest in a nearby hotel. He knew that 'someone would wake him if anything important was happening' (field notes, 27 March 1981).

In response to a request from Tai Tokerau elders, other business had been suspended to allow debate on 'the issues underlying the invasion of Waitangi marae by police to arrest protesters' (Walker, 'Korero', *New Zealand Listener* 25 April 1981). The youth, alternately chastised and indulged by the senior members and elders, aired their angry justifications. By morning some common ground had emerged from the evening debates and from private exchanges between the participants. The Waitangi protesters would make their formal presentation to the party on the Sunday morning. Business matters, submitted beforehand by branches and area councils to the Policy Council, were scheduled to be dealt with on the Saturday. Between 6.00 am and 7.00 am each morning sleepers were stirred by a chanted prayer offered by an elder or church official. People rose to wash in the cold water of the ablution block. Breakfast was already waiting in the large dining hall, prepared by a team of helpers. Rata joined his members for breakfast, and an update on the night's discussions.

Saturday's agenda included the presentation of several formal papers on a range of policy issues concerning the new Maori Affairs Bill, health, employment and industry, women, the electoral roll, institutional transformation, and political organisation. During the day views and conclusions arrived at the night before found their way into the presentations and questions. After dinner the brooding members of the Waitangi Action Committee and the Women's Committee met privately to discuss the developments of the day. The feminists and the protesters, who used similar pressure tactics, were disgruntled by the disapproval expressed by some of the other Mana Motuhake members. Feeling that their causes might not receive the support and recognition they deserved, they reviewed their strategy for their official presentation the following morning. A 'disco' dance boomed loudly from the dining hall for the teenagers and pre-teens. Some adults stayed to dance and sing with the Maori band, others drifted off to bed.

Following breakfast on Sunday morning, members gathered outside the marae grounds for the day's business and the combined church service. A long table, decked with crisp white tablecloths, had been arranged for the seating of Mana Motuhake dignitaries, elders and churchmen. Today was a special day - the day of the Queen's petition. The arrival of the president stirred a sense of history and occasion among his supporters. His round, radiant face and stocky build emitted an aura of power and confidence as he crossed the grass and entered the marae courtyard. His approach was announced by the sedate and mellow tones of a favourite Ratana hymn. Flanked by the Ratana brass band and other Ratana supporters (conveyed by bus, especially for the event, the night before) the procession marked a new development in Rata's mobilisation campaign. The bright purples, whites, and greens of the apostles' robes and band uniforms of the Ratana Church mingled with the black and gold T-shirts, aprons, rosettes, and medallions of the party colours. The petition had generated interest and support from other quarters of the Maori world. At its launching a visible swing of Ratana support behind Rata had occurred.

The Policy Council convened to hear the presentations from the Women's Committee and the representatives of the Waitangi Action Committee. The women launched angry accusations against the Secretariat. They claimed that demands they had made for equal representation within the party administration, first presented at the November Hui-a-Tau, had been ignored. This was clear from the small number of women in higher office throughout the whole organisation, they said. Gasps and mutters rippled through the crowd when one feminist shouted that the Secretariat had better 'pull up its socks' and circulate the women's paper to all member branches, as it had promised.

The president addressed the feminists. 'I will not tolerate implications of interference on the part of the Secretariat. We have said that these papers will be circulated, and they will be circulated'.

'You'd better!' interjected the indecorous feminist to the shock of the other members.

'It is your right to be critical of the Secretariat', continued Rata. 'We welcome constructive criticism, or even destructive criticism, but', he added, 'I hope you will support the resolution, now before us, for the members to help provide the financial resources which will enable the party to print and circulate material'. The protesters were advised not to carry out their plan to defy the court by failing to appear when their cases arising from the Waitangi Day protests were heard. 'The elders, who are willing to come to court as witnesses, cannot help you if you don't attend', the protesters were told.

From these encounters it was clear that there was a rift in understanding and expectation between the protesters and feminists - the so-called 'radical' sector of the party - and the more conservative, traditionally oriented and liberal sectors. The grievances of the feminists appeared to overshadow their interest in the other victories of the party. The Secretariat's explanation that they could not be guaranteed 50 percent representation on the administration, because positions were allocated by democratic vote, was not acceptable to the militant women.

The protesters, seeing the party as a vehicle for their own version of social change, were not interested in modifying their strategies or in bowing to the wishes of more senior members.

Those with a deeper sense of Maoritanga saw the Mana Motuhake movement as part of a political and spiritual continuity. Indeed, to them its mana and authority sprang from the tap-roots of the Kingitanga and Kotahitanga movements - sixty years before the Ratana/Labour alliance established more conservative habits in the Maori. To these followers the concept of 'mana motuhake', now embodied for the first time in an independent Maori political party, was the fruit of the seeds of self-determination first sown in the late nineteenth century. Although the two sectors of the party could appreciate and to some extent respect each other's perspectives, their motives and goals seemed increasingly irreconcilable. The main body of the party felt deeply offended by the way the activists 'trampled upon the mana of the people'. The protesters and feminists felt betrayed.

During the Sunday morning debate Walker had left the gathering to seek solitude under a cluster of trees in a gully near the upper marae. Drawn to this spot he found a large pohutakawa tree - its red flowers, he recalled, 'still damp with the morning's dew'. There in the shade, looking over the 'sparkling waters of the harbour', he felt inspired to complete his task of drawing up the petition to 'Her Majesty Queen Elizabeth II'. As he returned to the lower marae, another 'intuitive insight' came to him:

> Instead of rejoining the meeting on the marae, I walked past the paepae [threshold] almost in a state of automation, and entered the Tiriti O Waitangi meeting house. I at first thought to place the document in the middle of the floor under the ridgepole, but instead I was drawn to the pakitara [back wall] where I placed the document to be sanctified and made tapu (sacred).

Walker only learned afterwards that the centre of the back wall was where the Ngapuhi lay their dead for a tangihanga.[3]

With the official business over, Walker laid the petition before the gathering, relating to them the circumstances surrounding its preparation. The initial discussion with Matiu Rata on the contents of the petition had occurred in the dining hall, a noa (common) place. Walker later wrote:

> The Treaty ground where the original Treaty was signed was the appropriate place for the preparation and writing of the petition about the Treaty and the redress of Maori grievances. Placing it in the meeting house to make it tapu completed the process. So the petition began its realisation in the realm of the profane and was transformed into the realm of the sacred (Ranginui Walker, Notes on the Treaty of Waitangi Petition 2 April 1981).[4]

The elders approved of the manner in which Walker had conducted his assignment - convinced that the ancestral spirits were fully participating in the auspicious event. Thus endowed with both spiritual and human confirmation, the document became imbued with tapu and historical significance. It could properly command support as an instrument of appeal to the Queen. Rata then related that he had written a letter to the Prime Minister, asking that Mana Motuhake be granted permission for a delegation of Maori elders to have an audience with Her Majesty. This petition, Rata declared, 'will be sent throughout the length and breadth of New Zealand'. It will be 'circulated to every branch everywhere'. He then read the document to the gathering. Its three requests were for ratification of the Treaty of Waitangi, pardon for the chiefly ancestors who had resisted the Crown,[5] and the appointment of a person of Maori descent as New Zealand's next Governor-General.

As Rata placed the petition upon the table Tawai Kawiti, paramount chief of the Ngapuhi, came forward as the first to sign it. A long time advocate of the ratification of the Treaty, Kawiti was a direct descendant of the original Kawiti who refused to sign the Treaty in 1840. Only after all the other chiefs had signed, so the story goes, did his 'grandfather' add his mark at the top of the Treaty document. The spectacle of the 'grandson', now elder and leader of his own generation, coming forward to be the first to exhort the Crown to keep its promises under the Treaty, had a breathtaking effect upon aware onlookers. 'I know it is an honour for me to be the first to sign', Kawiti said in Maori, 'yet at the same time it is a weight pressing upon me'. With the spirit of the moment heavy upon them, the document was passed from one to another down the official table and then laid in front of the chairman, at the centre of the table, for the members to sign. The signing ceremony was accompanied by a gentle and moving hymn from the Ratana band which formed a semi-circle behind the dignitaries.

Suddenly a large white seagull swooped down upon the gathering, hovering and almost settling on the petition. Another elder crossed the marae grounds, chanting an incantation as he strode. Reaching Kawiti he grasped his hand and greeted him with a hongi (pressing of noses), sending a frisson through the crowd. Addressing the crowd in Maori the second elder, Walsh, declared, 'I believe because the Treaty of Waitangi which was signed by this man's grandfather, and then signed by this grandson, the Treaty has returned'.

Walsh was a descendant of Aperahama Taonui - the famous Ngapuhi prophet who warned his people at the unveiling of a stone engraving of the Treaty of Waitangi in 1881: 'Do not cover the Treaty with the flag of England, cover it with the Maori cloak'.[6] Twice the cloak had been removed and replaced by the British flag. The third time Taonui did not replace it with the Maori cloak. Instead he said to his people: 'Ngapuhi, I will leave you and soon your house will be occupied by spiders and cobwebs'. Taonui then left his people and was adopted by the more southern tribes. 'When his grandson crossed the marae grounds and grasped the hand of Kawiti, in so doing he healed the breach of 100 years ago, and put honour back into place', an informed Maori observer later explained. In Maori exegesis, the prediction of spiders and cobwebs had been interpreted as referring to the secularisation of the Waitangi marae. What had happened that day signified the 'return' of his ancestor to Waitangi and was thus a portent of spiritual regeneration.

A combined church service was conducted by the Ratana, Roman Catholic, and Anglican ministers (all of Maori descent) seated at the official table. Each rose to conduct his portion of the service, invoking a blessing on the petition. The ceremony, rich with prayer, music, symbolism, and historic resonance demonstrated the inseparability of religion from politics in the Maori world. To all but the resolutely unbelieving, it imparted unique authority to the new undertaking. After the service the second elder related the prophecies of his forefathers and explained the significance of the events of the ceremony. In the characteristic oratorical manner of an elder - strutting and thrashing his 'talking' stick vigorously at the air - Walsh told of a time 'when a seagull will unite us'; 'when a man will come with the Bible in one hand and the Treaty in the other'; 'when the holes of the Ngapuhi would be filled up'. (The saying, 'Ngapuhi of a hundred holes', referred to the loose association between the dispersed hapu of the Northland tribe.) [7]

Like Ratana before him, Rata was also seen by some elders as fulfilling this prophecy. He also was a man with 'the Bible in one hand and the Treaty in the other'. [8] Thus the missions of Taonui, Ratana, and Rata were mystically linked in a fashion typical of Maori political cosmology. [9]

The feminists and protesters seemed oblivious to the meanings of these spiritual references. They drifted off behind the dining hall to talk among themselves of their challenges and victories of the morning. The elders had spoken only in Maori - an inaccessible tongue to most of the young people from the cities who were not sufficiently interested to seek an interpreter. An atheist member of the activist group later confessed that during the entire Sunday morning she and her comrades had been 'pushed further and further back' by the crowd from the sacred heart of the ceremony. Finally their backs were against the wall of the dining hall, the most noa (common/devoid of tapu) part of the marae.

Believers attributed this, and other strange happenings during the weekend, to the powerful spiritual forces which had been aroused by the launching of the historic petition. These same forces, it was said, disapproved of the actions and attitudes of the young people. The most outspoken feminist experienced more severe retribution. When she returned home to Auckland on the Sunday night she was tormented by terrifying ghostly visitations, which were only exorcised by the performance of cleansing rituals over her person, clothes, and home by a tohunga. Distraught and fearful, she fled the next day to Wellington, remaining there for some months.

The gulf between Maori and non-Maori speaking sectors of the party, between conservative and radical, old and young, was deepening. Much of the poignancy of the ceremony was lost upon the young people. Most were unaware that the old world had been 'reunited'; nor would they have cared. To them the past provided the source from which they drew proof of injustice and oppression to sustain their anger and to fuel their cause. They sought little moral or spiritual sustenance from the wellspring of Maori heritage which, for those who had not lost their culture or language, brought confirmation, renewal, and a sense of continuity with revered ancestors who had never surrendered (field notes and interpreter translations during ceremonies and political debates, 27-29 March 1981).

BUILDING THE ELECTORAL MACHINERY

During the year Rata conducted extensive speaking tours throughout the Northland, the Auckland and South Auckland districts, the West and East Coasts, Wellington, and other districts of the North Island. Visits were also planned for the South Island. Monthly Secretariat meetings were held at different marae locations to provide the president with opportunities to promote the party through public meetings and the local media. Minutes of the Secretariat indicated that head office was now handling hundreds of calls and visits a month, and a heavy flow of inward and outward correspondence.

To attract wide support the fundamental philosophy of the party had to have an appeal transcending and reconciling existing Maori loyalties and attitudes. The concept of 'mana motuhake', Rata pointed out, had been in existence since the mid-nineteenth century: 'It represents tribal authority. It represents "freedom fighters". It represents the whole state of Maori well-being'. These, he reasoned, were concepts to which all Maori could relate (Rata, interview 4 March 1981).

The Northern Maori electorate and the Ratana Church were two sectors from which Rata could hope to draw some political support. More remote were the prosperous and land rich East and West Coast tribes, and the fiercely independent Kingites of the Waikato. In February 1981 the president addressed a gathering of the Waikato Maniapoto tribes. He compared the Kingitanga movement with the Mana Motuhake movement. The idea of self-government, he acknowledged, was not new but had emerged in Maoridom at the time of the formation of the King movement. Ranginui Walker had reminded readers in his 'Korero' column the previous August that the term mana motuhake 'appears as the motto on the coat of arms called Te Paki o Matariki (the widespread calm of the Pleiades)'. Literally translated, mana motuhake means 'power cut away' but its broader meaning was 'distinct or discrete power, namely self-determination for the Maori people' (Walker 1987:107). Rata suggested to the Kingitanga people that they might think of the new Maori party as their 'political arm for the bringing into being of the concept of mana motuhake'.

A few weeks later Rata held another meeting in the neighbouring district, 76 kilometres north of Otorahanga - the territory of the Maori Queen. The meeting was near enough for Kingites to attend. In a private interview on March 4 he related the events of that meeting. He had been pleased to observe Henare Tuwhangai, chief adviser to the Maori Crown and spokesman for the Waikato people, sitting among the elders. Addressing Tuwhangai, Rata said:

I am here not for anything new, except to recommit ourselves to a concept which you were the first to arouse to the Maori consciousness. I bring only one new element to this old dream of mana motuhake - the element which may make it succeed - political action.

Rata explained the obstacles confronting a possible alliance between the Kingitanga people and his party: 'If ever a people have been badly dealt with, it is the Waikato people. They were the most persecuted. Their people have suffered the most'. When the King movement first formed, he said, it was others who controlled them politically. During that period of massive European settlement, the Maori could see the rapid erosion of their way of life and land resources. 'The Governor had absolute power. The only way out for the people at that time was to place their mana under the banner of the Maori King'. The formation of the Kingitanga movement, and its Kauhanganui Council (internal government) was to meet the pressures of the colonial government in the Waikato Maniapoto region. 'They were the first to institutionalise the concept of mana motuhake. It is a matter of pride for them to maintain their independence'. Addressing Tuwhangai again, Rata said:

I am saying, you support me and I'll support you. I'll get you the political success needed and will help you achieve the role of traditional leadership by my supporting a request to Queen Elizabeth II of having the mantle of Governor-General placed on Dame Te Atairangikaahu. We will include your ancestors among those we seek pardon for on our petition.

'After all', Rata reflected later, 'why just put the Maori people under the Maori Queen? Why not put the whole of New Zealand under her next time the position of Governor-General comes up?'

I say, you support me and I will support you and I will ask the four quarters to support you in this request. It will achieve the debt which is owed to the Waikato Maniapoto. It would be symbolic of old hurts healed, old debts repaid and new ones built.

'Mr Tuwhangai said nothing', Rata related, 'he just gave me a quiet smile'. Well versed in traditional meanings and wise to Rata's political ingenuity Tuwhangai's smile, at that point, was non-committal. But Rata believed that it was also a smile of 'reflection' and 'acknowledgement'.

When Henare Tuwhangai finally spoke he referred to the prophecies of the Kingitanga people and those of Ratana. He also referred to a discussion between the Maori Queen and Queen Elizabeth II, when the latter had said that she saw the division of the people as one of the main problems facing the Maori. Tuwhangai concluded that 'mana motuhake is not possible unless unification occurs'. This unification - whether spiritual or political - would have to rise above and not threaten existing divisions of Maori identity.

'The Mana Motuhake and the Waikato people are both caught in cleft sticks', Rata explained privately:

We can't approach them for fear of being accused of interference and they can't approach us without appearing to lose mana. Yet they will ask - "Why hasn't the Mana Motuhake come here? Are they not interested in us?" So the approaching between us is being done in a round-about way. We have received a round-about invitation from them. Independence must mean exactly that, right through the Maori world. We do not want to be oppressed, but we must be careful to avoid oppressing ourselves.

Matiu Rata was aware that those under the Maori Queen's protection represented all party political followings - the National, Labour, Values, and Social Credit parties. Already there were several Mana Motuhake branches established in the Waikato, and there was 'no opposition', he felt, to the formation of more branches. What Rata really hoped for was an invitation 'from the throne itself' to visit the Waikato people. 'The Queen and her Council would not tell their people directly how to vote'. This would offend the various political interests in that region and would interfere with people's options. However, 'if the Maori Queen would convey her pleasure on Mana Motuhake, this would have great influence', he suggested. For the party to secure her blessings 'the implication of support would be there - the command would have gone out. I would expect I will get an invitation in the near future to visit the Waikato people from the Maori Queen', he confided (Rata, interview 4 March 1981).

The president's depiction of Mana Motuhake as a means by which the Maori people could become masters of their own destiny was attractive. He presented political mobilisation as a preferable alternative to inactivity or despair. 'The Maori people suffer from a simple lack of faith', he said. 'Mana Motuhake is looking for a political solution to a political problem. I walked out of the Labour Party to illustrate that "you don't own us". "You have misused our loyalty". "You have turned our loyalty into an ownership deal"' (Rata, interview February 1981).

The special appeal which Mana Motuhake held for Maori people was explained by an up-and-coming young Maori leader and spokesman for the Social Credit Party, Maanu Paul. Social Credit, he said, had drawn younger Maori members equally from the National and Labour parties - Maori who were 'tired of the "Think Big" policies of the National Government and the cloak and dagger attitudes of the Labour Party'. At a lecture delivered at Auckland University (30 June 1981), Paul pointed out that:

Mana Motuhake has the emotive appeal which Social Credit doesn't. It is a Maori Party ... For the Maori the appeal is a strong charismatic leader in Matiu Rata; a strong organisation, getting branches all over the countryside. Leadership, and followers, are respectable 30-plus, conservative, successful

Maoris. There is an *avant gardeness* about these men and their thinking - but it is certainly a spiritual, thrilling experience for the believers.

The Social Credit Party would have difficulty competing against this, Paul concluded, particularly if Mana Motuhake 'epitomises all the policies seen to be needed by Social Credit for Maori people as well'.

The formalities of Mana Motuhake's campaign began quietly in April, 'reflecting the genial, easy-going nature of its president', wrote the *Auckland Star* (14 August 1981). The election was not due before November 28, but growing industrial and social unrest throughout the country led Rata to press for the hasty establishment of Mana Motuhake's electoral structure in anticipation of an early election:

> We have been saying for months that the National Government's complete failure on just about everything affecting the interests of our people and country will mean that a major diversion, such as the Springbok Tour and its implications will be used ... to submerge the other important issues ... hopefully the public is not so gullible. (Mana Motuhake press statement, 3 August 1981)

With nearly 8000 financial members and 66 branches there was considerable optimism by February that the movement would have some impact upon the Labour monopoly of the Maori seats. At a meeting of the Tai Tokerau Electorate Council, held at Kaikohe on February 14, Matiu Rata was unanimously re-elected as the Mana Motuhake candidate for Northern Maori.

The monthly meetings of the Secretariat provided the opportunity for the executive to plan the next development of the party machinery and to gear itself for the campaign. By early June all four electorate councils were functioning and the party claimed 70 branches totalling approximately 10,000 financial members. However, as Mana Motuhake was seen as a 'family organisation', where members were encouraged to join their children as well, a large proportion of these figures included children and youth under the voting age of eighteen.

Nominations for the Southern Maori seat were called for, shortly after the establishment of Mana Motuhake's Southern Electorate Council. On May 10 the party announced the selection of Amsterdam Reedy, a 37-year old member of the Ngati Porou tribe employed as a senior lecturer in Maori Language and head of the Maori and Multi-Cultural Studies program at the Wellington Teachers' Training College. In mid-May Mana Motuhake announced that it would also contest the constituency of Eastern Maori. From the seven nominees, two of whom were women, Albert Arapeta Tahana was selected on June 28. Aged 36, university educated, and an active representative on Public Authorities and Maori organisations, Tahana was a descendant of the Te Arawa tribe and worked as a senior vocational guidance counsellor with the Department of Labour in Auckland.

Tahana and Reedy were both founding members of Mana Motuhake and served the party in executive capacities. It was confirmed late in June that the Western seat would be contested. Of the two female and thirteen male contestants Mana Motuhake's only woman candidate, Eva Rickard, was selected on August 9. At the Western hui, lasting until 3.30 a.m., aspiring nominees 'entertained the house with their skills in repartee, oratory and singing'. Following a formal selection meeting the five short-listed candidates spoke again (Walker, 'Korero', *New Zealand Listener* 7 November 1981). Most noted for her long-time advocacy of the Maori land rights movement, Rickard, a 56 year old descendant from Waikato tribes and Ngati Toa, mother of nine and grandmother of eighteen, resigned from the presidency of Te Matakite following her selection.[10]

Finding a candidate selection process free from kin group promotions of 'favourite sons' or 'favourite daughters' was a matter of experimentation during the 1981 campaign. Some felt that the selections should be done the 'proper Maori way', by all-night discourse. Eventually the Secretariat chose a blend of Maori consensus and more formal examination procedures. In the first instance each electorate council, stressed Rata, must have complete autonomy in deciding whether to contest Maori (and eventually marginal general) seats in their area. Nominations could be submitted to head office by any Mana Motuhake body under the jurisdiction of an electorate council. Under the constitution, a selection committee, consisting of seven persons appointed by the electorate council and one appointed by the Secretariat, was to be established. This selection committee would act as a panel of judges whose function was to evaluate the suitability of nominees for candidacy in their electorate.

Nominees were invited to address the selection committee and gathered members at a special selection hui. The presentation given by candidates for the Eastern seat, for instance, consisted of a ten minute speech, ten minutes of answering questions put forward from a panel, and a period of answering questions from the floor. Questions from the floor were written on slips of paper and handed to the selection panel. From these the best questions addressing the issues were put to the nominee by the panel. The address provided each nominee the opportunity to display verbal skills in English and Maori. Some even used waiata (singing) or chanting of whakapapa (genealogy) to demonstrate their worthiness. Competitors spoke sometimes with humour, sometimes with passion, about the Mana Motuhake movement, what it meant to them, and what role they felt they could play in its promotion.

Selection hui drew lively gatherings of up to 400 members and officials. A one page 'biography' on each nominee had been supplied to all branches and committee members before the hui, and more copies were available for the audience during the event. Competitors were graded by the panel against a series of criteria: general appearance, voice, content of speech, knowledge of Maori language and etiquette, knowledge of English, formal qualifications, tribal ties and standing, ability to answer questions and to speak upon the philosophy of the party. The candidate's availability to undertake campaign activities over the next three months was also taken into consideration.

In addition to these evaluations the selection committee could call for an open vote from the floor, as a 'guide' towards consensus. As nominees might be supported by groups of unequal size the audience vote was not to determine the outcome. The final decision was in the hands of the selection panel. Under Article 12, section 3(d) of the Mana Motuhake *Constitution and Rules*, the selection committee was required to have regard to 1) Maori customary practice of collective decision-making; 2) the collective opinions of all financial members of Mana Motuhake in the electorate as expressed at any selection meeting or in any vote undertaken for such purposes; and 3) any other means which ensured the just and fair selection of a candidate.

This system for candidate selection proved widely successful and acceptable throughout the electorates. The announcement of Albert Tahana as the Eastern Maori candidate brought a lusty ovation from the audience. 'I can go to bed with a clear conscience tonight', the chairman of the selection committee told the people, 'because the decision was made unanimously by the panel and was endorsed by you, the hui. These votes will go into archives'. He also encouraged branch and council members not to allow the other nominees to return home with a sense of defeat. 'The merit and calibre of the remaining six ... should be recognised by providing for them a place of authority in the electorate council'.

At the close of the Eastern Maori Selection Hui Matiu Rata, who had taken no active part in the selection process, turned to the unselected nominees saying, 'Don't go back now and cower in your committees - they look to you for leadership'. And to the membership he said:

> You take the knocks, don't let your candidate take them. We can ill afford to let our candidate take them. If your nominee did not win this selection don't let him go to waste. Use his or her talents in your own area - put them to work on building up Mana Motuhake. (Mana Motuhake Eastern Maori Selection Hui, 28 June 1981)

The public meetings held by the president were seen by him to be essential for the promotion of the movement and the foundation of the party's branch network. Once the regional campaign machinery was in place and the electoral councils and their candidates were elected, much of this responsibility could be assumed by the newly elected officials of each area. Rata took a keen interest in every hui and development within the party. At campaign meetings he undoubtedly drew crowds. Likewise, his presence at formal party gatherings was a powerful one. The attendance of Rata and head-office officials gave mana and authority to the meetings organised in virgin territory.

Despite his staggeringly full itinerary Rata helped the candidates launch their own campaign tours by accompanying them, at least at their opening public meeting, and sometimes on part of their tour. These campaigns attracted considerable interest and curiosity from among the Maori, the general public, and the media. Candidates were invited to give interviews and to participate in radio talk-back programs. Rata, constantly reminded 'the New Zealand people' of their obligations towards the Maori. Yet his style of oratory included a flair for softening the sting of admonition. His public criticisms, cleverly entwining logic and appeals to higher ideals, were tolerated and even enjoyed:

> I would venture to suggest to you that what we are in search of is equality and not conformity. That is to say, a New Zealand that embodies us, in mind, spirit and soul. A New Zealand that understands that a Maori isn't a bound person who has now moved from country to town. A New Zealand which regards its Maori people as an integral part of its life. And a New Zealand which adopted some of our practices, customs, laws and standards of behaviour and values as part of the everyday system of this country. That's what we are in search of; and we have always been in search of this despite the labours we have imposed upon ourselves over the years. I attribute it to the young for reminding us of our obligation to ourselves. (Rata, Mana Motuhake election campaign speech, Wellsford, 6 October 1981)

The president's close oversight of the party that year had angered some of his senior officials. There was an increasing sense of urgency and impatience among these men, themselves the cream of the Maori intellectual community and leaders in their own right, for a greater delegation of responsibility within the party. Their desires were not always communicated to, or perhaps recognised by, Rata. Towards the end of the year their frustration declined into indifference and diminishing commitment. Rata, however, remained the indispensable man. By accompanying new candidates in their respective electorates some of his charisma rubbed off on them. In the public arena there was no figure in the party with quite the same aura as Rata - the man who had abandoned the safety of Parliament and had dared to establish a Maori party.

NOTES

1. 'Financial membership' represented voting members, and children and youth under voting age.

2. As in the Labour Party, 'youth' was defined by Mana Motuhake as full or junior members 30 years old and under. Representatives on the Mana Motuhake Youth Council were to be elected at the annual National Youth Conference, in a fashion similar to the elections which took place at the annual Hui-a-Tau of the party executive.

3. The practice of other tribes varies. Walker's people, the Whakatohea, lay their dead at the front of the marae during a tangi.

4. The events of that morning had such a profound effect upon Walker that four days later he committed them to writing. A much abbreviated version was published in his 'Korero' column (*New Zealand Listener* 25 April 1981).

5. A royal pardon for 'rebel' leaders, who had resisted the British, would be central to later claims for the return of large tracts of land confiscated by the Crown from 'rebel' tribes during the Land Wars.

6. There are many different translated versions of this saying. Another is: 'Do not cover the Treaty with the cloak of England [the Union Jack], but cover it with the cloak of the land' (Walker 1987: 79).

7. I received these translations and explanations of the prophecies during the ceremony on Sunday 29 March 1981. They were oft repeated sayings on Ngapuhi marae and usually varied a little according to the speaker. See also footnote 8.

8. The vision of the Maori prophet Aperahama Taonui, believed to relate to the coming of Ratana and his church, was recorded this way by Henderson (1973: 12):

O chiefs of the Ngapuhi, listen to me; let not the Treaty of Waitangi be covered by the flag but let it be enshrined in a cloak of this land ... Seeing that you Ngapuhi will not listen to me, a spider will inhabit this house. There is a man coming, however, who will carry two books: the Bible and the Treaty. You will listen to him.

9. The telescoping of past and present is common in marae rhetoric and cosmology.

10. By 1984 Eva Rickard had taken up and revived the Kotahitanga movement, becoming its spiritual leader and president, and encouraging the movement's members to vote Mana Motuhake.

Matiu Rata leaves Parliament House after his resignation, 29 April 1980 (courtesy *New Zealand Herald*).

Te Tokanganui-A-Noho, the elaborately carved wharenui, or marae modern meeting house, at Te Kuiti, 1972 (photographer: Cyril A. Schollum, courtesy Anthropology Department, University of Auckland).

Left to right: Sir Peter Buck, Sir Apirana Ngata, and Sir Maui Pomare, thought to be at Huramua Station, Wairoa ca 1925 (courtesy Sir Henare Ngata).

Tahupotiki Wiremu Ratana, the Ratana Pa and Church, ca 1935 (courtesy National Art Gallery Museum, Wellington, NZ).

Norman Kirk, Prime Minister 1972 to 1975 (courtesy Public Relations Department, Parliament House, Wellington).

Sir Robert Muldoon, Prime Minister 1975 to 1984 (courtesy Public Relations Department, Parliament House, Wellington).

Sir Wallace Rowling, Prime Minister 1974 to 1975 (courtesy Public Relations Department, Parliament House, Wellington).

The Hon. Matiu Rata with his wife Nellie, after announcing his resignation from the New Zealand Labour Party, 7 November 1979 (courtesy *New Zealand Herald*).

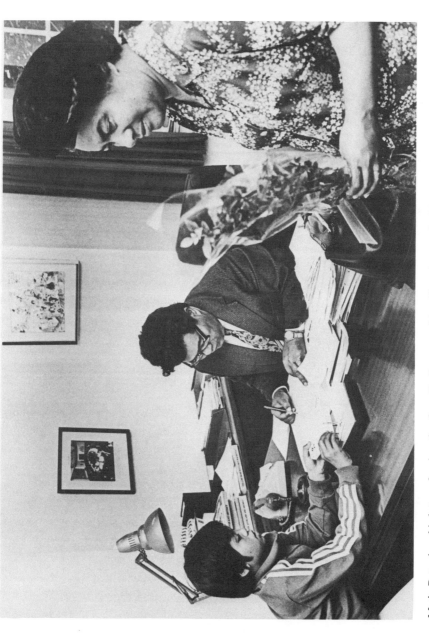

Matiu Rata signs his letter of resignation from Parliament as his wife and son wait, 29 April 1980 (courtesy *Auckland Star*).

Matiu and Nellie Rata count votes on polling day, 1980 Northern By-election, 9 June 1980 (courtesy *New Zealand Herald*).

Campaigning in the rain, Matiu Rata during the 1980 Northern By-election campaign (courtesy *Auckland Star*).

Dr Ranginui Walker, Chairman, Auckland District Maori Council, political adviser to the Mana Motuhake Party, 1981 (photographer: Kayleen Hazlehurst).

'Hey Maori people get up and fight for your rights'. The Waitangi Action Committee asserting their grievances in a protest song, Waitangi Day, 6 February 1981 (courtesy *New Zealand Herald*).

Hone Heihei, a Northland elder wearing a Mana Motuhake badge, urges restraint in the protester Arthur Harawira, in his address to the Governor General, Waitangi Day, 6 February 1981 (courtesy *New Zealand Herald*).

Sir Graham Latimer in a feathered cloak, escorted by Maori wardens and Arch-
bishop Paul Reeves following the disrupted investiture, behind them (left back)
Prime Minister Robert Muldoon, 6 February 1981 (courtesy *New Zealand
Herald*).

Dr Patrick Hohepa, Secretary, Auckland District Maori Council and Secretary-General to the Mana Motuhake Party, 1981 (photographer: Kayleen Hazlehurst).

Professor Sidney Mead (Hirini Moko Mead), executive member of the Mana Motuhake Party, 1981 (courtesy S. Mead, 1988).

Amsterdam Reedy, Mana Motuhake candidate for Southern Maori, 1981
General Election (courtesy A. Reedy).

Arapeta Tahana, Mana Motuhake candidate for Eastern Maori, 1981
General Election (courtesy A. Tahana).

Eva Rickard, Mana Motuhake candidate for Western Maori (courtesy Mana Motuhake Party).

VII

A DISTINCTIVE ALTERNATIVE

At a meeting of the Mana Motuhake Secretariat in August 1981 the president 'urged all members to get behind their candidates now that the campaign was in full swing', and 'not be distracted from this task'. In his 'Leader's Report' Rata advised that he had appointed his fellow candidates as 'spokesmen' for Mana Motuhake on various issues: Tahana was to cover finance, economic development, labour and employment, industrial relations, trade and industry, energy, works, skills and trade training, mining, and Pakeha affairs. Reedy would be spokesman on education, health, sport and recreation, art, culture and language, planning, local government, environment, and tourism. Rickard would be responsible for lands, agriculture, fisheries, forests, women's affairs, youth affairs, and Post Office; and Rata himself would be spokesman on Maori affairs, foreign affairs, defence, state services, broadcasting, housing, electoral, communal affairs, social services, transport, and justice (Minutes of the Secretariat monthly meeting, 28 August 1981).

After the long subjugation of Maori people to Pakeha 'Maori affairs experts' the ironical inclusion in Rata's list of a Maori specialist on 'Pakeha affairs' titillated the press. But the headline in the *Herald*, 'Spokesman on Pakeha Affairs', aroused not a murmur of political reaction (*New Zealand Herald* 19 September 1981). The appointment, and the bemused response to it, quietly turned a century of European paternalism on its ear.

Mana Motuhake wished to promote increased functions and powers for the Waitangi Tribunal. Under the present arrangement, explained Rata, Maori people were denied an effective 'judicial process' through which outstanding claims could be lodged against the Crown. If the Treaty of Waitangi were made a legal document by Parliament, he reasoned, this would provide court jurisdiction to handle these claims. 'It may also mean that the very things which we believe in, and stand for, might be embodied into law' (Matiu Rata, Mana Motuhake campaign speech, Wellsford, field notes 6 October 1981; Mana Motuhake Report to all members, 18-20 September 1981).

The first edition of the pamphlet, *'Ratify the Treaty of Waitangi'*, was circulated internally on June 30. On July 24 head office informed Secretariat and Policy Council members that 20,000 copies of the Waitangi pamphlet, along with copies of the 'Queen's petition', were being printed for general distribution. Electoral councils were asked to seek support for the petition in their electorates as soon as copies became available. The objective of the ratification, the pamphlet declared, was to have the Treaty of Waitangi 'recognised by and enforceable by law':

> It is more than a solemn pact. It is a binding contract between the Maori people and the Crown. A Charter which guarantees the rights of the Maori and the interests of a nation ... .
>
> There is a duty to honour the treaty agreement. Regarded only as a symbol, to the Maori it is a reality; for he has long endured the injustice of minority status, lost prestige, massive land losses and a partnership of hardship and increased disparity.

The three requests to be made to Queen Elizabeth II in the Mana Motuhake petition were outlined in the pamphlet. First, the Maori elders were to petition Her Majesty to have the Treaty ratified. A full pardon was to be sought for 'our chiefly ancestors for the miscarriage of justice'. And finally they would request the appointment of a person of Maori descent as New Zealand's next Governor-General. In addition the pamphlet proposed that the Treaty be 'honoured' before the Maori accepted any further honours from the Queen or took part in any annual celebrations at the Waitangi Treaty Grounds. The establishment of a fully functional Treaty of Waitangi Tribunal, empowered to enquire into, adjudicate upon, and amend, all matters resulting from miscarriages of justice under the terms of the Treaty of Waitangi, was proposed (*'Ratify the Treaty of Waitangi'*, *Election Policy '81, Mana Motuhake,* 30 June 1981).

Not all Maori were in favour of ratification. Once the Treaty achieved legal status, some argued, any unfavourable government could terminate it simply by amending or repealing legislation. It was safer to leave it as it was - as part of the New Zealand heritage - where at least governments could be exhorted to act within the 'spirit of the Treaty'. This argument ignored the fact that successive governments had frequently enacted legislation that was inconsistent with the Treaty. Dr Bruce Gregory said he strongly opposed any attempts of Mana Motuhake to have the Treaty ratified. The circulation of a petition calling for ratification, the implications of which were not fully understood by many of the signatories, was 'irresponsible', said Gregory. Furthermore, the Waitangi Tribunal had proved to lack any real power to bring about change. Under a Labour Government the Northern MP indicated that this would be replaced by a more effective authority (*Western Leader* 17 November 1981).

None denied the advantage of a royal pardon for chiefly ancestors who, in defending their territory in the Land Wars, had been deemed guilty of treason. The implications of such a pardon were far reaching. Thousands of acres of

Maori land had been confiscated by the colonisers as retribution for Maori resistance.

> We inherited the stigma of our forefathers who were branded as "rebels" in their own land ... I am suggesting that the Crown acted unlawfully. We cannot successfully secure redress from our claims to the Government until we secure also a pardon. (Matiu Rata, Mana Motuhake Secretariat Meeting, Tuwharetoa ite Aupouri Marae, Turangi, fieldnotes 28 February 1981)

A royal pardon, even granted a century later, would strengthen the position of Maori claimants seeking the return of seized lands. The proposal for a Maori Governor-General was also widely acceptable in the Maori world, although the idea of appointing the Maori Queen to the post was canvassed circumspectly outside her traditional strongholds.

With the growing consolidation of the party structure, and the increasing demands for campaign publicity material, Mana Motuhake began to clarify and define its position on a wide range of Maori grievances and aspirations. The heart of the campaign, between April and October, was marked by a proliferation of policy papers, press statements, and pamphlets distributed to campaign committees throughout the regions. The party drafted policy on human rights, social welfare, educational, and land related issues. Comment was also made on current public concerns: the Springbok Tour, the Race Relations Act (1978), and New Zealand's interpretation of the Gleneagles Agreement (1977) on sporting contacts between South Africa and the Commonwealth; social attitudes and values promoted through the media and advertising; New Zealand foreign aid; abortion; the Marginal Lands Board Enquiry; strikes and other union issues; violence and the courts; policing; employment and unemployment; natural resources and mining; Air New Zealand; the national budget; taxation reform; the fishing industry; and other aspects of the New Zealand economy.

In a comprehensive rejection of state dependency and control, and of the National Party's 'Think Big' development policies, Rata announced that Mana Motuhake's basic policy was to seek:

> communal autonomy by restoring to the people the power of decision-making on all matters affecting their affairs. What we further seek is communal prosperity and the beginning of a co-operative society ... It was Society that needed to be restructured and not industry. ('Mana Motuhake's Basic Policy', press statement 11 May 1981)

At a public address to release the party's new policy paper on 'Employment', the president asserted that Maori communities and regions must take greater responsibility for creating work for their people. 'The State has failed us, so-called private enterprise has failed us, and we must not fail ourselves', he said (*New Zealand Herald* 18 June 1981):

The ownership, control and means of all production, goods and services must therefore ultimately be undertaken by communal direction. The concept of communal direction, enterprise, control and ownership is essential if prosperity is to be ours. To enable us to achieve this goal, the Treaty of Waitangi must be ratified. The New Zealand Government must be made to pay their accounts to us. Whether by land or funds, or both, or by any other means, it must be paid. Further, all Maori leasehold must be re-negotiated. All agreements between Maori owners of land with timber forests and mineral rights must be re-negotiated for increased returns or increasing our interest in the industry concerned.

Advocacy of 'communal direction' was an attempt to blend a socialist objective with familiarly Maori forms of decision-making. Radicals were likely to welcome the uncompromising aim to own and control 'all production'. Conservatives could construe 'communal' as a synonym for 'traditional' while sensing that Rata and his principal advisers had in mind a more democratic communal form of government than had been common in the past. There was good news for rural communities with a proposed expansion of agriculture and horticulture. The introduction of a 35-hour week implied benefits for the employed as well as the possibility of job creation. The suggestion of an increased interest of the trade unions in their respective industries 'to aid and stabilise the interests of their members' was a bid to detach powerful and wealthy union support from Labour. And the general introduction of 'affirmative action based on New Zealand conditions' was a cautiously qualified step towards equality for minorities and women (Mana Motuhake Employment Policy 1981, delivered at Tira Hou Marae, Panmure, 17 June 1981).

Tantalised by the notion of 'communal direction', the New Zealand Socialist Unity Party (the major communist party of New Zealand) invited Mana Motuhake to join its seminar on the 'Rights of Maori People'. Rata responded coolly to a solicitation which carried overtones of co-option and entailed 'guilt by association'. 'We may be more socialist than they are,' he said confidentially. 'Certainly Maori socialism has been around a lot longer but we are against state socialism. They must learn to listen. We must find our own solutions' (Rata, interview 3 June 1981).

Severe criticism was levelled at the government for the state of the Maori rolls and enrolment procedures; the political manipulation of the Maori population figure; the inequitable determination of the number of Maori seats; and the inexplicably large number of Maori votes disallowed at the last election. Mana Motuhake joined its voice with other Maori organisations in objection to the lack of remedies offered in the forthcoming revised legislation. As the proposed changes in the 1980 Electoral Amendment Bill did not meet Maori concerns, the party general secretary stated, Mana Motuhake would consider approaching the 'United Nations and the International Court of Justice to lay charges against the government for political oppression'. So too would the

NZMC, Te Matakite, and Maori women's organisations, Hohepa warned, if these problems were not addressed.

'The fact that over 33,000 Maori names were removed from Maori rolls at July 1979', and that there were no avenues of appeal or correction when enrolment errors occur, should make the problem a legislative priority, Hohepa wrote. A message to be delivered to the Minister of Justice by the New Zealand Maori Council was in accord with Mana Motuhake policies and confirmed by the party. Hohepa wrote an uncompromising summary of these demands:

1. a return to the past view that Maori population, for political purposes, be the Maori census population. The situation is oppressive when the number of Maori people is calculated from the number of registered voters on the Maori rolls, and their children (and to add insult, half the children of mixed marriages), and the other seats are determined from the balance of population;
2. a return to the view that the Maori seats shall be determined on the basis of the total Maori (census) population;
3. a return to the past view that Maori people decide which roll they want to go on, even during an election year. The argument used that we must not be allowed to decide during election year because we are not capable of making balanced and wise personal decisions really smacks of racism. Are we, the Maori people, naive, simple, immature and stupid? That seems to be the impression. (*Mana Motuhake O Aotearoa*, Newsletter No. 1 September 1980)

The Electoral Amendment Bill was introduced in Parliament in August 1981. The next period when Maori voters could exercise their enrolment options would be during March and April 1982 - a reduction from a three month period to two months. Although there was some realignment of the Maori electorate boundaries, Tirikatene-Sullivan pointed out that the four electorates were still 'inexcusably large'. The Southern Maori seat contained 45 general seats in the same geographical area (*New Zealand Herald* 29 August 1981). In response to the bill Rata forwarded a fifteen point submission to the Chairman of the Parliamentary Electoral Law Committee, P.I. Wilkinson, on behalf of Mana Motuhake (Mana Motuhake submission on the 1981 Electoral Amendment Bill, 11 September 1981).

In the absence of legislative solutions Mana Motuhake, meanwhile, looked at ways in which it could take practical action on behalf of Maori voters. Votes were frequently disallowed because voters, though having officially exercised their option, were not registered prior to the election. At the inaugural meeting of the Secretariat it had been agreed that Amsterdam Reedy and Sidney Mead would approach the Justice Department and the Postmaster-General to request that Maori students be invited to canvass Maori electoral areas in order to promote Maori enrolment (Minutes of the Inaugural Secretariat meeting, 19 December 1980). Mana Motuhake canvassers were instructed to carry the electoral roll and enrolment cards with them, wherever they went. They were encouraged to start with their own families and branch members. 'Register people on the roll', wrote the central campaign committee, 'and your candidate will get them to the polls'. A guide to the conduct of 'door-knocking' canvassing was circulated to all branches. Head office also provided information on how regional campaign committees could obtain copies of Roll and Habitation Indexes from their respective Registrars. Candidates and committees were reminded to adhere to the provisions of the Electoral Act in campaign expenditure (the statutory limit in 1981 being 4,000 dollars), and to ensure that all fund-raising activities were licensed where local law required it. Before polling day, Mana Motuhake Electoral Councils appointed their own scrutineers. Area organisers and scrutineers were provided with head office directions on polling day organisation and their respective responsibilities.

For some time Walker had been toying with the idea of shaping Mana Motuhake policy into a single manifesto. Party philosophy and practice was loosely formed and scattered on 'scraps of paper', he said. Even during the candidate selection process, party philosophy and purpose was as much a product of the imagination and views of the successful nominees as it was the published commitments of the Policy Council. Mana Motuhake supporters still had a dim understanding of what it all really meant, and frequently complained that they had difficulty answering queries from other Maori about the party. The party had to spread its message as best it could by word of mouth, publication of its own campaign materials, and public meetings. In 1981 there was no specific Maori news programming on television and only spasmodic reporting in the popular press. There were few authoritative speakers available to travel - and most audiences wanted Rata to bring them the new doctrine.

Walker reasoned that candidates and supporters were in need of a single document with which they could promote the party and be uniformly guided on its policies. While head office kept files, the staff had little time to maintain archival efficiency as well as run a campaign. As the party had established a number of committees to work on different policy areas it was unlikely that the policy files of even top party officials were complete. Walker himself did not have a full set of such papers. He approached the president on the subject towards the end of May. In an effort to 'unify' this material he asked head office to send him copies of all papers on policy, offering to edit them into a single manifesto. By July he was still waiting for the papers to arrive. There appeared to be no head office opposition to the proposal. But the task of gathering together the material was too daunting for an already overworked staff (field notes 9, July 1981). Finally Walker went ahead and edited those papers he could acquire, incorporating them into the nineteen page draft, *Nga Kaupapa O Mana Motuhake: Manifesto*. When this document was circulated among the executive and the candidates in October 1981 it was far from complete and, more significantly, it was not published before the 1981 election.[1]

Mana Motuhake councils and branch members were urged to make 'every effort' to 'acquire support and signatures' for the Treaty of Waitangi petition. It was suggested that Mana Motuhake public meetings could be organised around the launching of the petition in their respective areas (Rata, letter to Secretariat, Policy Council, councils and branches, 30 March 1981). By September 30 over 7,000 signatures had been collected on the petition, but securing the co-operation of the government to approve its presentation to Queen Elizabeth II proved more difficult. In April Prime Minister Muldoon turned down Mana Motuhake's request for an audience with the monarch, on the grounds that it was 'not proper' to do so: 'It is not customary for a small political group, without elected representation, to claim the right to speak on behalf of the Maori people'. Only a body such as the New Zealand Maori Council, where elected members represented all tribes and districts, had such authority, the Prime Minister asserted. This was a shrewd argument, taking advantage of divisions in the Maori world, of which Muldoon was well aware through close personal and political relations with senior NZMC figures. Obviously, Rata could not yet present Mana Motuhake as the primary mouthpiece of the Maori people.

Rata wrote again to the Prime Minister explaining that the audience sought with the Queen was not only for Mana Motuhake supporters but to enable a cross-section of 'tribal elders and leaders to represent us [the Maori people] before their sovereign'. Maori support for this audience was clearly manifest in the signatures on the petition. The NZMC and other Maori groups, Rata said, would be consulted on the matter (*New Zealand Herald* 22 April 1981).

Towards the middle of the year invitations to address the New Zealand Maori Council were extended to the leaders of the Social Credit, Labour, Mana Motuhake, and National parties. The state of the Maori economy and the protection and development of Maori resources were central to these dialogues with the leaders. When delivering his pre-election speech to the Council on September 11 Prime Minister Muldoon stated that he did not feel the Maori people were making best use of their land and human resources:

All of New Zealand needs more jobs, more intensive use of resources, but I fear that the Maori resources are the most under-used and it is not something that the Government alone can do. In fact, without the will and desire of the people to progress little can be achieved.

The answer to economic development, concluded Muldoon, 'lies in more effective use of our land resources' (Robert Muldoon, speech notes delivered to the New Zealand Maori Council, 11 September 1981).

The Council members responded with comments. 'The problem is', said Maanu Paul, 'we don't have the power to make decisions. We can't utilise our lands because we don't have the financial wherewithal to utilise them'. Muldoon replied that the Maori people must plan their projects together and approach the government for development funds in the right order of priority. Eva Rickard commended the Prime Minister for his references to Maori spiritual beliefs in the land during his speech. However, she reminded him, there are '100,000 out there who don't even have a spiritual concept of their land'. The Maori people, she said, were more than willing to dedicate their energies to the utilisation of their land and resources but 'we need financial assistance for our programs to succeed'. 'I will end with a Pakeha saying', she said. ' "If you've got the money, honey, I've got the time" '. The Prime Minister and the entire council collapsed into delighted laughter at this daring wit.

As frequently occurs in Maori debate, the good humour of the speakers broke the ice and prompted more relaxed discussion. Muldoon showed interest and respect for the Maori leaders as they presented their various community and land development concerns, promising to look into some of the issues which they had raised (NZMC Meeting Minutes; field notes, 11 September 1981). The following day Matiu Rata addressed the Council. In an attempt to defuse political rivalry Rata opened his speech by saying:

> I want to share some of our hopes over the next few months. If we are to be masters of our destinies, we must master our political destinies also ... Mana Motuhake will not be seeking votes from the National Party, the Labour Party, Social Credit, or the Values Party, but rather we seek them from people who share our values and our hopes.

This forecast meant both more and less than it seemed. It did not mean that Mana Motuhake expected support only from previous non-voters (though some response was sought among those not hitherto politically active). The unstated assumption was that Maori who had in the past voted for one of the principal parties might share 'values' and 'hopes' to which none of the parties gave sufficient priority. Without directly attacking the established parties Rata was implying that some of those Maori who gave their allegiance in the past had done so for want of a Maori alternative. Rata went on to congratulate the Council for winning the responsibility for developing a new Maori Affairs Bill. He reminded the members that the Council's success would depend ultimately on the support it received from members of Parliament - particularly the Minister of Maori Affairs. In outlining the purpose of the Treaty of Waitangi petition being organised, Rata stressed that it was a request for ratification from all Maori people and that he had expected the delegation to contain 200 to 300 elders. 'I spent nine years of my parliamentary life on the Treaty', Rata claimed. Since the petition was first approved by 'our elders' in March, he said he had written to 'every district Maori council, to Church leaders, elders and others' seeking their support:

> Our objective is to remind Her Majesty of her obligation to the Maori people. We are seeking royal pardon for our ancestors who fought honourably for their land ... We have sought royal favour because Parliament cannot grant pardons. The principles of the Treaty are as important now as they were in 1840 ... We have never at any time asked that this petition be launched by, or for Mana Motuhake, or even by Mana Motuhake people.

Rata said he could not see the point of having a monarchy, if the monarch could not be approached, and spoke of the alternative of a republic for New Zealand.[2] The Maori people were still losing their resources. 'They've found a new way of alienating Maori land,' he said, 'through leasing our land'. It appears to be 'not the colour of the skin which interests us, but the colour of the money':

> Over the last twelve years 200,000 acres of Maori land was leased to forestry. That's a quarter of the total land under forestry now. These leases are under 45-99 year leases. Either we are being taken to the cleaners once again, or it has got away on us.

Rata suggested that the Maori people approach the government and ask to 'renegotiate all their leases which affect forestry, timber and mineral rights' and that an 'independent advisory group' be established to help Maori land owners in the negotiation of more favourable lease arrangements. Mana Motuhake would also soon be seeking the support of the United Nations in their efforts, he said.

There was an urgent need to 'increase the skills capacity' of the Maori people, Rata said. Maori women and girls were 'socially and economically the most oppressed' of all in New Zealand:

> You can't expect to have our people on the dole and to improve their lot, their attitude towards their fellow man, while their land is under lease! We want to be a part of the arrangement, a part of the industries which the leases are under. Not just receivers of payment [land rent]. We want to put a time limit on ake ake [long-term or indefinite] leases.

The Maori people are 'artists at debate', Rata concluded. 'We must use it more in order to benefit from our collective wisdom and our ability to change'.

Rata also expressed his concern to the Council about what he saw as a growing 'multitude of voluntary groups' in Maori society. He feared these were being constructed as mere 'leaning posts' - substitutes for the real social and political unity which he envisaged for his people: 'Our world needs reconstructing according to the reality we live in today'.

The Maori people are looking for material prosperity, he said, but they are also looking for 'a new social order, based on human worth ... Mana Motuhake wishes to reconstruct our country, influence government policies and laws. We wish to do things ourselves. These are things which each and every one of us can subscribe to' (NZMC Meeting Minutes, 12 September 1981; field notes 12 September 1981).

Rata was vague about the form of the desired 'new social order'. By warning that voluntary groups continued to fragment Maori social and political relations, he might have seemed at variance with Walker's earlier portrayal of voluntary associations as vital to community construction, identity, and self-determination. It was not that the proliferation of Maori organisations and associations presented a contradiction to Mana Motuhake's ideal of Maori self-determination

- quite the reverse. But Rata had rightly grasped a more subtle point: that voluntary organisations had fostered a degree of satisfaction with, and complacency about, the political structure within which the Maori worked. In their success, there was a danger that larger issues concerning the redistribution of power and resources in New Zealand, which affected the capacities and well-being of Maori people at all levels, might be neglected in favour of lesser goals. In the election campaign Rata did not develop this idea any further, no doubt sensing that its implications would be unacceptable to the hundreds of community-based leaders whose status derived from their roles with the very organisations he was criticising. The thought that voluntary groups, upon which so many relied, might stand in the way of major reform was a conclusion better left unsaid.

When by July it became clear that the itinerary of the royal visit provided no opportunity for a deputation of Maori elders and leaders to present the petition to the Queen, Rata called a 'special conference' of his Secretariat and Policy Council to 'consider and endorse' Mana Motuhake policy on the monarchy. 'Clearly we are to be denied the last vestige of constitutional redress on this important matter', wrote the president. Many Maori people will be 'deeply disappointed that our efforts to do things properly and in keeping with the due process of law have been rejected'. 'For over a century, Maori people have been loyal to the Crown and it has brought us to nothing but misery and a sense of futility', he said.

In addition to the Maori elders - many of whose genealogies, he had once pointed out, matched that of Queen Elizabeth II in both length and distinction - Rata had wished to invite each Maori MP and other Maori leaders to join the delegation. With the exception of the Auckland District Maori Council, Church leaders and the Maori Women's Welfare League, most of the Maori organisations and Members of Parliament he contacted did not reply. 'Despite the widespread support from Maori people', Rata claimed, the majority of those invited to support Mana Motuhake's royal petition chose to stand aloof from the initiative. Their refusal to be drawn into Rata's campaign earned them a robust rebuke:

> We can only assume that their lack of interest and encouragement for our petition simply means that they do not believe that there is ever likely to be any Maori who may be suitable to serve as Governor-General, or that our chiefly ancestors do not deserve to be fully pardoned, and that they have no answers on the Treaty of Waitangi.

Rata believed that the 'continued rejection of our endeavours as a people' left them no alternative but to:

a) consider withdrawing from the monarchy;
b) consider moving towards establishing the 'Republic of Aotearoa';
c) require the Republic to honour the Treaty agreement;

d) consider expressing our disapproval by disrupting the Royal Tour. (Mana Motuhake press statement, 15 July 1981; *New Zealand Herald* 16 July 1981; Mana Motuhake Royal Tour Report to all Secretariat and Policy Council members, 24 July 1981; Mana Motuhake Report on the Royal Tour and the Treaty of Waitangi Petition, ca. 18 September 1981)

In a private interview Rata again expressed his exasperation when 'our efforts to do things properly' and to 'remain within the law' were rejected. How much longer, he asked, can 'we be expected to be responsible for our actions?' Such a rejection of the request to have an audience with the monarch could only be viewed 'as an act of aggression against us from the other party' (Rata, interview 16 July 1981). Rata, however, was not acknowledging what was at the root of the government's refusal to countenance the presentation of a petition to the Queen. New Zealand had long enjoyed 'responsible' government. It was a sovereign nation to which, many constitutional theorists maintained, all the previous obligations of the Crown under the Treaty had passed many years earlier.

There was a long tradition of Maori attempts to appeal directly to the Crown and there was much to be gained from seeking to revive the memories and obligations of a more direct relationship between the British monarch and the Maori people. But no modern government was likely to give any encouragement to a tactic which so obviously sought to by-pass its own authority. Nevertheless, whether or not the campaign was successful, Rata stood to gain by pressing the issue to a conclusion. If the petition could be presented, it would be a triumph. If the opportunity was denied, it would be further proof of entrenched injustice. Because of his personal influence with the Prime Minister, Mana Motuhake sought the assistance of Sir Graham Latimer. In his capacity as chairman of the NZMC Latimer declined to act. But in mid-September he agreed to approach the Prime Minister personally to seek an opportunity for the presentation of the petition (Mana Motuhake letter to all branch chairmen and secretaries, 15 September 1981). In return Mana Motuhake members were advised not to mar the October tour of the Queen and the Duke of Edinburgh. It was agreed that, as they 'should not blame the Queen for the indifference of Mr Muldoon', no disruptive action would be taken. The party, said its president, 'wanted to avoid adding to the divisiveness of the country'.[3] Rata, however, declared that he had personally turned down two formal invitations to royal tour functions - including a reception on board the royal yacht, *Britannia* - as a statement of protest.

Latimer's private conversation with Muldoon about the presentation of the Treaty of Waitangi petition had brought no change in the Prime Minister's disposition towards the proposed delegation of Maori elders and leaders. When it was learned that one of the duties of the royal couple would be the presentation of a silver dog collar on behalf of an Auckland greyhound racing club, Rata was quoted as having remarked bitterly that 'even the dogs have had better reception from the Queen than the Maori people' (field notes, 16 October 1981). That Rata should enlist Graham Latimer's aid in these circumstances was an extraordinary

testament to the mutual trust and bond of unity that transcended their party
political differences and potentially conflicting ambitions. But it also was an
unambiguous acknowledgement of the unshaken pre-eminence of the NZMC
leader, at least so long as the National government was in power.

The Pakeha-dominated macro-political system still provided the framework
which defined and delimited the roles available in the bridging system of Maori
brokerage. While Latimer enjoyed the access and influence denied to Rata and
his new party, his obligation was to act for all Maori people. While Rata
remained excluded from the realm of personal influence in the governing party,
it was his obligation to ask for Latimer's intervention. For Rata not to seek help,
or Latimer to refuse it, would be to repudiate that which they shared as Maori.
In this ultimate joint venture they demonstrated the national Maori network in
action.

A SOCIAL AND POLITICAL ALTERNATIVE

The old debate over the advantage or disadvantage of keeping the Maori seats
once again became an issue during the 1981 election. Neither among politicians
nor among Maori generally was there agreement. The four seats had, at different
times, been condemned as 'electoral apartheid' and hallowed as 'a unique and
enlightened system' which guaranteed political equality. Koro Wetere, now
Labour's shadow Minister for Maori Affairs, stated a firm view in favour of the
seats. 'Maoris look upon these seats as a way of airing their views, and to try to
rectify the wrongs of yesteryear. It's going to be some time before that process is
finished' (*Tu Tangata* November/December 1981: 2)

Other Maori argued that only by the abolition of the Maori seats, and the
transfer of Maori voters to the general roll, would the Maori people be removed
from a state of 'political limbo'. 'To operate effectively', said Robert Mahuta
'we have got to move towards political and not symbolic representation'. Mahuta
believed that the potential political force of the Maori people was handicapped
rather than protected under the Maori roll system. Both the Labour and National
parties supported the maintenance of the Maori roll, he argued, because the
sudden influx of 150,000 Maori voters on to the general roll would upset the
already precarious balance of power - adding to it an 'ethno-class element' (*New
Zealand Herald* 28 March 1981). Some Labour voters blamed Labour's loss of
the last election upon the Maori seats. Intuitively, they felt that a more even
distribution of Labour-voting Maori throughout the general electorates would
undermine the National Party hold on a large number of marginal seats. On
balance, it was to the National Party's advantage to retain, but not increase, the
Maori seats.

The Social Credit Party characterised the guarantee of only four seats in a 92
seat Parliament, for over 10 percent of the New Zealand population, as an
institutionalised guarantee of inequality. Bruce Beetham strongly advocated the
elimination of the Maori seat system. If a system of 'proportional representation'

were introduced under a Social Credit government, Beetham said, this would put 'an end to the discrimination which is involved in separate representation ... As long as we have Maori seats, they will be controversial' (*Tu Tangata* November/December 1981: 3).

The chairman of the Eastern Maori Labour electoral committee, G.R. Ormsby, called for an increase of Maori seats because of the sheer size of the Maori electorates. 'Our electorate extends from Coromandel to Gisborne. It covers the area of eight of the general electorates'. These electorates were too large for one person to manage, he said. Maori electors were lucky to see their member once a year (*New Zealand Herald* 28 March 1981).

Opponents of the Maori roll proposed that, as some 60 to 70 percent of the Maori voters had withdrawn from the New Zealand political process, this clearly constituted a condemnation of the present system and made a mockery of the retention of the Maori seats (*New Zealand Herald* 20 April 1981).[4] The chairman of the Maori section of the National Council of Churches, the Rev. Hone Kaa, argued that the 'non-voting Maori' may be 'a reflection of the scepticism that prevails in our society about the effectiveness of Parliament'. The Maori seats under the present system were 'only symbolic', he said, 'and not a political reality'. If the Maori were to have 'ethnic representation' Hone Kaa proposed that 'there should be eight Maori seats' (*New Zealand Herald* 6 April 1981). The Labour Party promised that if it were elected to power it would tackle the objectionable issues arising out of the disorder in the Maori rolls and introduce a fairer allocation of guaranteed Maori seats.

The New Zealand Parliament consists of one chamber - a 92-member House of Representatives. National elections are held at intervals of not more than three years. The 92 seats (including that of the Speaker) are allotted on the basis of single member electorates. Elections are by a 'first past the post', or simple plurality system. This electoral system naturally tends to work in favour of the political party which has support spread evenly in the greatest number of electorates, namely, the National Party, rather than those whose supporters are highly concentrated in urban areas (especially the Labour Party). As Bean states, the 'inherent weakness in the simple plurality electoral formula', that the party which wins the largest number of votes may not necessarily win the majority of the seats in Parliament, became apparent in the 1978 and 1981 elections (1982: 1). In 1978 the Labour Party won 40.41 percent of the votes compared to National's 39.82 percent. Nevertheless Labour secured only 40 seats, compared to 51 seats secured by National (*New Zealand Official Yearbook 1984*: 924). Electoral boundaries, which produced larger numbers of electorates per capita in the rural districts, were firmly maintained by successive National governments.

In 1972 Labour's majority of 23 was the outcome of 'the third biggest two-party swing since the formation of the modern party system in New Zealand' (Bean 1982: 1). Against all predictions in 1975, Labour lost its majority by an enormous two-party swing of 8.4 percent. This time it was the National Party which won a 23 seat majority. In the 1978 and 1981 elections the feeling was that 'anything' could happen (ibid.). Adding to the political instability of the time was the rise of a third major party - the Social Credit Political League. Social Credit jumped from 7.43 percent of the vote in 1975 to 16.07 percent in 1978. The New Zealand electoral system, however, discriminated the most against small parties. In the 1978 election Social Credit secured only one seat. Social Credit, more than any party, pressed for a change in the electoral system.

In the late 1960s there was little unemployment in New Zealand, but the 1973 world oil crisis, the agricultural policies of the European Economic Community, and increasingly adverse terms of trade with overseas markets had a crippling effect on the New Zealand economy. Unemployment and inflation began to accelerate by leaps and bounds.[5] When the National Party's 'Think Big' industrial and natural resource development policies had not succeeded in curbing inflation or unemployment during its two terms in office, National focused its 1981 election campaign upon its pugnacious leader, 'Rob' Muldoon. The 1981 election campaign turned more on the personalities of the party leaders than on the controversial issues of rising unemployment, national strikes, and the socially disruptive tour of the South African Springbok rugby team which had driven thousands into the streets in protest (Henderson 1980; Chapple 1984; Bean 1982: 7-11).

Muldoon's blunt political style provided a striking contrast to the Labour leader's rather gentlemanly demeanour. Rowling was never able to project the image of a tough decision-maker. Muldoon, shrewd politician that he was, played this up. He showed a readiness to tangle in public with the noisiest heckler or the most annoying critic. He had a particular dislike for 'intellectuals' and 'journalists' who publicly denounced him - a few of whom were Maori. Mounting libel suits against the Prime Minister attested to his imprudent public assaults upon his enemies. In the meantime, the somewhat more intellectual persona of the Social Credit leader, Bruce Beetham, was beginning to capture the attention of a few more voters. Contesting elections since 1954, Social Credit made a strong bid for votes from both National and Labour quarters. Was New Zealand shifting from a two party to a three party system? The confusion in the electorate in the 1978 election foreshadowed the widespread ambivalence of the New Zealand voter in 1981.

Studies undertaken by New Zealand social and political scientists - David McCraw (1979); Stephen Levine 1978, 1979; Clive Bean (1980); G.A. Wood (1978); D.C. Webber (1978) - indicated that the popularity of both the National and Labour parties declined between 1975 and 1980. Conservative voters, disillusioned with the National government's inability to control the economy, or disenchanted with the stubborn and abrasive Muldoon, increasingly registered their protest by not voting for the National Party. Likewise, lack of confidence in the Opposition to provide strong leadership was reflected in a similar response from traditional Labour Party voters. The success of the Social Credit Party, stressed McCraw (1979: 55), must be partly attributed to voter dissatisfaction with the two major parties.

In addition to a deterioration of the popular image of Bill Rowling, a significant decline in Labour Party support from within trade union ranks had been occurring over several elections. From being a party of the masses in the 1940s, said Webber, by 1975:

> Labour had ceased to be either a mass party or a party of the working class, organised or otherwise. Having relinquished or been dispossessed of the power that they had once exercised in the party, trade unions ceased (as of 1975) to be active participants in Labour's internal politics. The party's working class branch membership appears to have been almost totally wiped out. (Webber 1978: 191)

In 1976 the allegiance of the 'organised working class' to the Labour Party was weaker than 'at any previous time in its 69 year history', Webber concluded. The upswing of Labour's popularity since Webber's study, in the 1978 general election, was still not sufficient to upset the National Party or to give the Social Credit Party the balance of power. The National Party still held its ground in the majority of the seats. However, disunity and an attempted party coup while Muldoon was overseas in October 1980 were followed by internal strife and Cabinet reshuffles on the leader's return.

Mana Motuhake claimed to offer Maori people a distinctive political alternative in the 1981 election. There had to be something better for Maori representation than the perpetual occupation of only four seats in Opposition, it was argued. For a Maori party, a party which truly understood and represented Maori interests, the Maori seats, and possibly some marginal seats besides, hung ripe for the picking. Furthermore, Rata hoped to convince other New Zealanders that there was nothing like a 'homegrown party with homegrown ideals'. Many who joined Mana Motuhake shared Rata's exhilarating optimism. It was envisaged that the Maori party, while not likely ever to be in power in its own right, would one day exercise real influence in Parliament and perhaps even hold the balance of power. Others joined Mana Motuhake motivated by feelings of impotence and frustration about the present parliamentary system. Beyond the politically active Maori voter, whether pessimistic or optimistic about the system, lay the untapped thousands of disillusioned or apathetic non-voters.

Rata declared that he did not want protest votes. He was only interested in votes which reflected an endorsement of the party's policies - the alternative social course which Mana Motuhake offered New Zealand (*New Zealand Herald* 2 November 1981). 'The primary objective of Mana Motuhake is to transform New Zealand practices and laws so as to reflect the true nature of a bi-cultural country', wrote Rata in a pre-election article:

> Mana Motuhake believes in achieving commercial prosperity by advancing, with co-operative means, enterprise and control and ownership. Mana Motuhake seeks equality not conformity and believes the rights of the family must be restored. The present insistence on the rights of the individual must give way to family and collective decisions and obligations. (*Tu Tangata* November/December 1981)

The human family has 'taken a beating', stressed Rata. The youth of today drift in uncertainty. The strength of the New Zealand family must be reasserted, he said. Party policy on the welfare of the family, and related issues, included papers on health and housing; land development; education and skills-training; gangs and crime; and the retention of Maori language, culture, and art. In furtherance of their new social vision Maori people, it was asserted, must share rights of decision-making in broadcasting, in the design of Maori programs, and in ensuring that a percentage of media time and revenue 'goes into promoting human and family worth ... The image of the nuclear family - Mum, Dad, the kids and a lot of plastic furniture was a norm which Mana Motuhake did not promote', said Rata. 'Our concept is of the extended family and this concept needs to be embraced in the laws of the country. Law aimed at helping families ... families are part of New Zealand's capacity to rebuild itself as a nation' (*New Zealand Herald* 2 November 1981).

Drastic measures were needed to counter the chronic homelessness, landlessness, joblessness, and aimlessness experienced by the Maori people. High unemployment and urbanisation were the result of a long process of land alienation. Maori land-use and family businesses should be supported in order to make the family economically, socially, and culturally viable. 'Land is economic and social power'. Not less than 10 percent of New Zealand's total land holdings should stay in Maori ownership, Rata contended. The government should return all Maori land wrongfully taken (*Tu Tangata* November/December 1981).

Rata's emphasis upon the distinctiveness of the Maori family had the potential to touch feelings both of pride and of guilt. To the extent that the misfortunes of Maori people could be linked to the breakdown of kinship ties and obligation, the revival and official support for the Maori family might be seen to offer a uniquely effective way forward. It epitomised a Mana Motuhake strategy of redefining the political domain so that it encompassed Maori 'values' and 'hopes'. Likewise, Mana Motuhake sought to 'restore the power of tribal assemblies [runanga]' to deal with the affairs of the Maori in their respective areas. This would directly foster and return decision-making responsibilities to the hands of the people. The establishment of an elders' tribunal in every community was a recorded policy of the party. 'Mana Motuhake seeks a social order based on our forefathers, an order that sees Maoris sharing responsibility and obligations' (ibid.).

There was an attractive logic in Mana Motuhake's goal of greater and more effective Maori representation. But the quest for the improvement of the quality of Maori social life, in the face of breakdown and fears of disintegration, held a more fundamental and emotional appeal. Mana Motuhake held out to both the frustrated and the idealistic the vision, and perhaps even the credible vehicle, for overcoming minority helplessness. But would the dream materialise through the ballot box?

BY FAIR PLAY OR FOUL

By October Mana Motuhake was claiming 15,000 financial members (voters and their families) distributed over 92 branches, four electorate councils, and a proliferation of area councils and special committees. Because of the brevity of the 1981 campaign, and the financial strain on its members, it was decided that only the four Labour-held Maori seats would be contested.

Of all Labour Party candidates, the Northern Maori MP, Dr Bruce Gregory, had reason to feel most threatened. Over a third of Mana Motuhake branches were located in his electorate and Rata was once again its candidate. In the Northern Maori Labour newsletter Gregory mounted a stinging attack upon his opponent:

The Mana Motuhake Party, I believe, is a contradiction of the very name it proposes to represent. It has the trappings, structure and the emblems of a minor Pakeha political party, totally non-Maori, with the added major flaw; to divide the unity of the Maori people, with little, if any likelihood of delivering its policies. Let's not be hoodwinked by the mechanics by which the Mana Motuhake Party will achieve its objectives, whether it be by so-called by-elections, blackmail of other political parties and ... by the use of violence - matchboxes [he had heard] would be distributed to Auckland members to set the city alight!! - as a last desperate resort!

Governments alone can deliver their policies - rule the country. The Maori people can best achieve these goals by building on to what they already have within this political system - namely by adding on to the four Maori seats they already have and having a greater voice in Parliament. To achieve this the Maori people must remain united in their resolve and not be side-tracked by violence, false hopes, bribery and disunity. (*Te Manu Korero* No. 5. 22 May 1981)

On June 25 Rata publicly condemned Gregory's allegation that Mana Motuhake promoted violence as 'blatantly false and irresponsible':

For a Member of Parliament to circulate such trash is unforgivable ... Mana Motuhake will not tolerate criminal behaviour or seek redress for the many problems faced by the Maori people other than by means within the rule of law ... The strong language used is clearly an indication of political desperation or that Mana Motuhake will face a smear and foul campaign from Labour. (Mana Motuhake O Aotearoa, press release, 25 June 1981)

In October it was rumoured that Gregory claimed he had been receiving threats to his life from an anonymous phone caller who claimed to be a Mana Motuhake member. Gregory's determination to inform the police and the newspapers about the threats brought ridicule in some quarters, and critical

comment from others. It was said that other prominent figures, such as Henare
Ngata and Graham Latimer, had on many occasions through their careers
experienced such threats. But they did not feel it was worth setting up a 'hue and
cry' over them. In going public, said Rata, Gregory risked discrediting himself
and the Labour Party by appearing to resort to slander to harm Mana Motuhake.
Furthermore, it strained credibility that such a caller would declare his party
membership. It was more likely that an outsider was bent on discrediting Mana
Motuhake by using Gregory as his mouthpiece. Maori figures from several
political camps expressed disapproval of the caller's cowardice. But they also
reproved Gregory for allowing himself to be provoked - and possibly
manipulated. No-one was very happy over the incident, least of all Gregory,
who was finally persuaded to drop the matter.

Gregory could be more pleased with the impact of some of his other
arguments. For a movement which needed above all to be seen as a unique
alternative, it was a palpable hit to be described as just another 'minor Pakeha
political party'. Few electors could be aware that Mana Motuhake's 'trappings,
structure and emblems' were not Pakeha but universal characteristics of political
parties. It was undeniable that, while a new party might one day be a force for
unity, it would inevitably, at the outset, be a cause of further fragmentation.
There was just enough truth in Gregory's attacks for them to be damaging, but
not enough for them to be fatal.

The election provided the Northern Maori opponents with several
opportunities to engage in public debate. An early hui held on the Ratana Pa (22
January 1981) attracted an estimated 20,000. They came in large numbers,
reported journalist Selwyn Muru, partly to celebrate the birthday of the prophet,
Ratana; partly because a new building was to be dedicated by the church; and
'partly because of the highly charged political and ecumenical climate'.

Rata arrived, 'flanked on all sides by defiant kaumatua from the north with
Mana Motuhake black and gold rosettes and ribbons ablaze in the Aotea sun'.
Their mission was obvious, Muru said. 'To give support to their man of the
hour, Matiu Rata':

> Impromptu sparring in the evening against northern counterpart Dr Bruce
> Gregory and other Labour stalwarts we're told, showed Rata in top form. He
> threw left jabs, right hooks, and counter-punched effortlessly. Before the end
> of the final round, he threw two finely executed upper cuts, leaving half a
> dozen opponents dazed and flabbergasted. An over-confident Rata however
> fails later to draw the church hierarchy into an open-slather punch-up on the
> marae. Their reply is terse and to the point: 'This is a church hui; boxing is
> not on the agenda'. (*Tu Tangata* August/September 1981: 82)

A special interview program, held by Radio Pacific on October 5, gave each
contestant for Northern Maori an opportunity to present his or her case to the
voters. Gregory stated that he recognised he was 'going into a political arena
where a great deal of force, foresight and strength' was needed to 'put the view

of our people forward'. 'I believe I have done this,' he said, pointing out that he had already presented one private member's bill and had assisted in a second. The policy of the Labour Party was to increase the total number of seats in Parliament from 92 to 120. 'Of those extra seats a percentage of those will go to the Maori people,' Gregory explained. Under a Labour government, all those who could claim Maori descent would 'automatically go on to a Maori electoral population figure,' he asserted. On the basis of this, the number of Maori seats would be determined in a manner similar to that used to determine the number of general seats. A 'critical issue' facing Maori people, Gregory argued, was unemployment. In the Northern Maori electorate it was the highest in the country.

Rata was the second speaker. His desire to return to Parliament after seventeen years of representing his people there was, he said, not 'to simply take up a seat.' Mana Motuhake's 'expressed purpose' in the forthcoming election, said Rata, 'is to re-establish the claim of the Maori to be politically represented in the institution of Parliament. It is our hope ... that this will be the first occasion in many a year that the Maori people will have a realistic alternative to consider when they go to the polls ... Mana Motuhake firmly believes that the time is long overdue when New Zealand should begin to reconsider establishing a new order, or an order which includes the Maori'.

Rather than being a 'brown version' of everyone else, there are things which the Maori values and regards as purposeful, Rata said. The Maori wished to 'elevate those human strengths and values that have been part of his life, to establish them clearly in the social fabric of this country'. It was the time now, he said, for his people to 'see if we cannot establish whatever practices, attitudes and laws' which will incorporate 'those things that are held dear by Maori people':

We must do our utmost to persuade our fellow countrymen that the social course that we have been following has become engrossed in simple materialism and obsession in collecting possessions, as distinct from caring for people and fulfilling obligations to others ... People have a duty to make their contribution as citizens of this country ... Above all Maori people have an opportunity to play an important role in the changes that must now be made.

The candidate for the Social Credit Party, Patrick Campbell, had failed to arrive. This was interpreted by Mana Motuhake members as a confirmation that the Social Credit Party would not seriously contest the Northern seat. The National Party candidate, Marie Tautari, invited her people to 'pause' and take a 'long look' at this election. Recently they had witnessed the tour of the Springbok team 'coming out of the country where the Black people do not have the vote':

But let's not throw away our chances in our own country ... Here our vote has to count for us ... We cannot afford to take a solution lightly. The way you vote can make your people, and the way we vote can break our people too. I believe when I hear these other candidates talking tonight, they are talking about a broken people, and I put it to you tonight that you've got what you voted for ...

I will tell you why I stand for the National Party. It's the party that's governed this country for most of my life. It was the party most chosen by Europeans. No matter what we want as Maoris, it is what the majority wants, that Maoris have to live with.

Tautari urged her people not to be satisfied with having members only in the Opposition, but to seek to place members into 'the governing party'. 'I do not deny my Maori side by going and standing in another party', Tautari said. Many issues of Maori concern were conservative issues, and the Nationals were not a 'trendy' party:

I've been involved in struggles for Maoris for a long time now. I have been part of this activist movement of this country. I have been in the forefront too. And I know that you cannot keep protesting. The secret is to put a man [sic], a Maori voice, into the party that governs this country.

With its 'conservative, traditional attitudes and philosophy', she said, the National Party 'stands for Maoris'.

Turning to the other two candidates, she asked Gregory, 'What's the use of increasing the Maori seats if the Maori doesn't have representation already, and his seats are all in the Opposition benches?' To Rata she said, 'Matiu, you're talking about a movement that is separatist':

While you are all going on with your dreams, what's happening to us? ... To say that you don't think that we have to carry on with the present system is to indicate to me that you want us to just live in a vacuum until you've got your own set-up. (Radio Pacific interview with the Northern Maori candidates, 5 October 1981)

The three Northern Maori candidates were offering three quite different political strategies. Gregory's position was that Maori allegiance to Labour was a political and ideological tradition that ought to be maintained. All that was needed, it was proposed, was to remove the flaws in the present system; to increase and improve Maori representation; and to make efforts to ensure that Maori grievances were systematically addressed. The Rata alternative was that a completely new voting pattern be established through a Maori party which would advance Maori issues, undistracted by major party concerns. By assertive action, and an independent stance, Mana Motuhake proposed that it could open the way for Maori access to the four Maori seats, and to certain general seats as well. The third option posited that the Labour and Mana Motuhake parties were unrealistic, peddling false hopes to a people doomed to impotence if they were taken in by dreams and rhetoric. Vote with the majority, the National candidate said, and you will then have the opportunity to influence the law makers of the dominant party. Irrespective of ideals, in the end this was the political reality which the Maori 'had to live with'. Though the most pragmatic, this last position was the least popular with voters. It bore the acrid fragrance of assimilation and submission. 'If-you-can't-beat-'em, join-'em', was an unequivocal admission of defeat. The Labour and Mana Motuhake parties were akin in their assertion of the Maori right to separate representation within the wider political system. They were the real competitors for the Maori seats.

For Rata to succeed he had to persuade the majority of voters that everything he had told them over the previous seventeen years about the harmony of Labour and Maori interests was no longer tenable. It had never been enough to be a Maori in Parliament without allegiance to one Pakeha-dominated party or another. Now, the Maori must believe that their representatives should be completely uncompromised by Pakeha philosophies and goals.

There was growing support for the new Maori party in the Northern electorate. Even some Labour supporters admitted during the closing stages of the campaign that Mana Motuhake was 'in good shape' and would come 'close to winning' the seat. Rata's confidence in regaining the Northern seat from Bruce Gregory was reported to be high. He also believed that Albert Tahana stood a good chance of winning the Eastern Maori Electorate. Mana Motuhake, he said, would concentrate its energy in the last lap of the campaign on winning these two seats (*New Zealand Herald* 26 May and 28 September 1981).

Earlier in the year the *Herald* had conducted another survey of Northern Maori, speaking 'to Maoris on farms, streets and roads and in homes and hotels'. The poll did not support Rata's optimism, or Labour's pessimism, the press claimed. 'Mana Motuhake seems to have kept its grip on the support it gathered in the lead-up to the by-election, but it is struggling to narrow the advantage held by Labour' (*New Zealand Herald* 26 May 1981). With increasing public respect for Mana Motuhake there was a discernible reduction in the mischievous press comment of the by-election days. In an article bearing the large headline: 'EASY RIDING DAYS OVER FOR LABOUR', the *Herald* declared that:

> The once predictable, almost traditional, general election voting trends in the four Maori seats could go awry on November 28, and the catalyst which could seriously alter the successful formula that has in the past led to the domination of all the Maori seats by one party is Mana Motuhake. (*New Zealand Herald* 5 October 1981)

In the last two months of the campaign the press was increasingly less confident about predicting the outcome of the election:

Mana Motuhake has the potential to create shock waves. It may do so in this election if it wins a seat or two off Labour; but it is more likely at this stage to cause ripples - though of a sort that mask deep currents underneath ... no-one is prepared to make a firm prediction as to how well he [Rata] will do in November. (*National Business Review*, 'Outlook', October 1981)

Uncertainty about the fate of the Maori seats was matched by the unpredictability of the election as a whole. The outcome of this 'razor edge' election, reported the *Herald* - an election displaying 'wild and fluctuating voting trends' and 'curious conflicts' - was difficult to forecast. Until the last hours of vote counting the first minority government in 50 years seemed imminent (*New Zealand Herald* 30 November 1981).

As the final recounts in disputed seats were made, the National Party again emerged as victor with 47 seats (38.78 percent of the total valid vote). The Labour Party increased its representation by three seats, winning a total of 43 seats (39.01 percent). For Social Credit, a surge to 20.65 percent of the total vote translated into a meagre two parliamentary seats. Rata and his fellow candidates, however, were all decisively defeated in the Maori seats, with Rata himself garnering 22.96 percent of the vote in Northern Maori (for further analysis see Tables 1-3 and Postscript).

Before the tinsel of the election had been taken down the newspapers were reminding the public of the grim realities to which they had to return. Unemployment had passed 70,000, New Zealand credit overseas was depreciating, and the country faced a record budget deficit of 2,100 million dollars (*New Zealand Herald* 30 November 1981). Voters' 'faltering faith in the government' and their lack of confidence in the Opposition had left the country in a 'betwixt-and-between political period'.

For Mana Motuhake, the disappointment was severe. With even Rata unable to win back his seat a dream had failed to materialise.

NOTES

1. By the 1984 election the manifesto was still incomplete and, as a project, seemed to have been abandoned.

2. Rata was here skating over the constitutional complexities inherent in the evolution of the monarchy as a symbol of unity since the mid-nineteenth century, and the dispersal of the executive authority of the Crown among the organs of the State (Cleave 1989: 51).

3. In the early part of 1981 the country was beset with months of national strikes followed by massive street marches and convulsive public disorder during the South African Rugby Tour (Chapple 1984).

4. According to Sorrenson (1986: B-82), of the 279,225 estimated Maori population (half or more Maori blood) in 1981, 147,130 were of voting age. Of these 75,704 (51.5 percent) were registered on the Maori roll that year. All other Maori (presumably the

remaining 48.5 percent) who did not specify preference for enrolment on the Maori roll in the previous census were, as is the rest of the New Zealand voting public, placed automatically on the general roll. But as ethnicity of voters on the general roll is not determined, the actual numbers of Maori voters in non-Maori seats cannot be known. The assertion that 60 to 70 percent of adult Maori have withdrawn from the New Zealand political process is, therefore, a speculative calculation which apparently assumes that four out of five Maori on the general roll are regular non-voters.

5. The total registered unemployed of 4166 in 1975 jumped to 24,904 by January 1979 and 26,889 by December of that same year (*New Zealand Official Yearbook 1980*: 777). The 1981 census, including many unemployed who had not 'registered', found 60,860 unemployed - 62.4 percent of whom were between the ages of 15 and 24 years.

Maori Seats	Election Year	Labour No.	%	National No.	%	Social Credit No.	%	Mana Motuhake No.	%	Others No.	%	Total Valid Votes
Northern Maori	1975	#5988	69.98	1837	21.47	500	5.85	-	-	231	2.70	8556
	1978	#6071	71.47	1049	12.35	1227	14.44	-	-	148	1.74	8495
	+(1980)	(3580)	(52.41)	-	-	(560)	(8.20)	#(2589)	(37.90)	(102)	(1.49)	(6831)
	1981	6368	54.09	1004	8.52	1573	13.36	#2703	22.96	124	1.05	11772
Eastern Maori	1975	8491	73.98	2230	19.43	548	4.78	-	-	208	1.81	11477
	1978	9085	74.79	1685	13.87	1195	9.84	-	-	182	1.50	12147
	1981	8222	63.79	1505	11.67	1172	9.09	1990	15.43	-	-	12889
Western Maori	1975	10145	81.58	1220	9.81	821	6.60	-	-	250	2.01	12436
	1978	11176	81.88	893	6.54	1457	10.68	-	-	124	0.90	13650
	1981	10523	67.17	1547	9.87	1697	10.83	1899	12.12	-	-	15666
Southern Maori	1975	7708	74.60	1256	12.16	598	5.79	-	-	770	7.45	10332
	1978	10250	82.33	1070	8.59	1013	8.14	-	-	117	0.94	12450
	1981	10685	71.64	1060	7.10	1149	7.70	1740	11.66	280	1.87	14914

TABLE 1: THE MAORI SEATS: VALID VOTES AND PERCENTAGES BY POLITICAL PARTY 1975-1981 ELECTIONS

Maitu Rata as candidate

+ 1980 Northern By-election following the withdrawal of Maitu Rata from the Labour Party.

(Sources: *The General Election 1975-1981, Northern Maori By-election 1980, Journals of the House of Representatives of New Zealand*).

Maori Seats	Labour		National		Social Credit		New Zealand		Mana Motuhake		Others		Total Valid Votes
	No.	%	No.	%	No.	%	No.	%	No.	%	No.	%	
1981													
Northern Maori	6368	54.09	1004	8.52	1573	13.36	-	-	2703	22.96	124	1.05	11772
Eastern Maori	8222	63.79	1505	11.67	1172	9.09	-	-	1990	15.43	-	-	12889
Southern Maori	10685	71.64	1060	7.10	1149	7.70	-	-	1740	11.66	280	1.87	14914
Western Maori	10523	67.17	1547	9.87	1697	10.83	-	-	1899	12.12	-	-	15666
Total	35798	64.80	5116	9.26	5591	10.12	-	-	8332	15.08	404	0.73	55241
1984													
Northern Maori	10471	69.49	949	6.29	373	2.47	492	3.26	2783	18.46	-	-	15068
Eastern Maori	12285	84.18	1055	7.22	277	1.89	400	2.74	575	3.94	-	-	14592
Southern Maori	11792	78.28	982	6.51	226	1.50	427	2.83	1297	8.61	338	2.24	15062
Western Maori	11325	78.59	1215	8.43	523	3.62	298	2.06	1049	7.27	-	-	14410
Total	45873	77.57	4201	7.10	1399	2.36	1617	2.73	#5704	9.64	338	0.57	59132

TABLE 2: THE MAORI SEATS: VALID VOTES AND PERCENTAGES BY POLITICAL PARTY 1981-1984 ELECTIONS

Mana Motuhake also won 285 votes in general seats in the 1984 election, (94 votes Otara, 21 West Auckland, 45 Whangarei, 125 Porirua) bringing the party's total valid votes to 5989.
(Sources: *The General Election 1981-1984, Journals of the House of Representatives of New Zealand; New Zealand Yearbooks 1984-1989*).

149

Maori Seats	Labour		National		Social Credit/ Democrats#		New Zealand		Mana Motuhake		Others		Total Valid Votes
	No.	%	No.	%	No.	%	No.	%	No.	%	No.	%	
1987													
Northern Maori	7760	57.91	1079	8.05	329	2.45	-	-	4231	31.57	-	-	13399
Eastern Maori	10653	74.11	1321	9.19	442	3.07	-	-	1957	13.61	-	-	14373
Southern Maori	10130	76.88	1030	7.81	344	2.61	-	-	1282	9.72	390	2.95	13176
Western Maori	9990	74.48	1024	7.63	539	4.02	-	-	1861	13.87	-	-	13414
Total	38533	70.88	4454	8.19	1654	3.04	-	-	+9331	17.17	390	0.72	54362
1990													
Northern Maori	5789	48.98	1195	10.11	.	.	-	-	4833	40.89	-	-	11817
Eastern Maori	9085	70.92	1484	11.58	.	.	-	.	2241	17.49	-	.	12810
Southern Maori	9024	74.50	1287	10.62	.	.	-	-	1410	11.64	391	3.2	12112
Western Maori	7851	66.56	1287	10.91	.	.	-	-	2385	20.22	272	2.30	11795
Total	31749	65.41	5253	10.82	.	.	-	-	10869	22.39	663	1.36	48534

TABLE 3: THE MAORI SEATS: VALID VOTES AND PERCENTAGES BY POLITICAL PARTY 1987-1990 ELECTIONS

In the 1987 general election the Social Credit Party changed its name to the 'Democrats'.

+ In 1987 Mana Motuhake won an additional 458 votes in general seats (77 votes Gisborne, 156 Mangere, 225 Porirua) totalling 9789 votes.

(Sources: *The General Election 1987-1990, Journals of the House of Representatives of New Zealand; New Zealand Yearbooks 1988-1990*).

VIII

THE MEANING OF MANA MOTUHAKE

HOPE, CHARISMA, AND IDEOLOGY

For several generations the Maori people have been integrated into the New Zealand party political system - not only through the creation of separate Maori seats, but increasingly, through the choice of Maori voters to join the general roll. The emergence of the Mana Motuhake Party was, in part, a challenge to both political integration and to voter satisfaction, apathy or indifference, by the provision of an avenue for votes in protest at the failure of the political system to meet significant Maori concerns.

It was also, in part, a claim for recognition of Maori political maturity, of Maori entitlement to their own political party within the national system. Considerable recognition seemed willingly granted to Mana Motuhake, particularly by the National, Social Credit, and smaller party interests which felt they had little to lose by portraying open-minded goodwill towards the infant party. Such displays could hardly hurt the standing of these parties among their staunch Maori voters. The Labour Party, which was subject to, and stood to lose the most by, Mana Motuhake criticisms of the 'existing system', was least accepting.

For all its shortcomings as a reform party, Labour had a strong and habitual hold on the four Maori seats. Of the parties which could in the conceivable future govern New Zealand, Labour had enjoyed the widest appeal among Maori intellectuals and workers. Nevertheless, the perennial frustrations of both office and opposition had bred disaffection. Matiu Rata's sensational resignation, and the excitement of participating in a new organisation, could dissolve some traditional allegiances. But, however much Rata and his ideological mentors might seek to stake out Maori concerns as Mana Motuhake prerogatives, the majority of Maori voters in 1981 concluded that the best hope for the advancement of Maori interests still lay in the established parties.

The efflorescence of Mana Motuhake was a triumph of hope over the harsh realities of a political system dominated by mature and well-endowed major parties. The 1975 and 1978 elections had demonstrated growing Maori disillusionment with the choices offered. The emergence of a new party, attuned to Maori discontent, provided a voice for the idealistic and the disenchanted - those who believed in a different political future for the Maori people, and those who calculated that the threat of defection in unprecedented proportions might at least precipitate policy concessions from the recalcitrant Labour machine. In the media and throughout the country at marae and party meetings the advent of the new Mana Motuhake Party, and its challenge to the Labour dominance of the Maori seats, gave increased publicity to Maori interests.

In many Maori communities power struggles were occurring between Mana Motuhake and Labour factions - to the delight of National and Social Credit supporters. Labour Party organisers worriedly scouted the country for areas thought most vulnerable to Mana Motuhake campaigns. Moribund Labour branches were propped up, or given reinvigorating injections of attention and funds. The rapid spread of the Mana Motuhake movement, and its establishment of branches throughout the Maori electorate, were cause for concern. Even some loyal Maori Labour supporters were blaming their party for Rata's resignation and were demanding that the Labour Party rethink party policy on Maori affairs.

Did Mana Motuhake succeed in effecting any significant shift in Maori political allegiance and voting patterns, or did the events of 1981 bring merely the illusion of change? Any analysis of the impact of Mana Motuhake based upon its first two or three election campaigns will naturally reveal the fragility, the ebbs and flows, of infancy. Historians will, no doubt, discern a variety of meanings in the 1981 general election (Sorrenson 1986; Chapman 1986). But all accounts must begin with a fact that requires explanation. Mana Motuhake secured 8332 Maori votes, coming second in each contest in competition with established parties in all four electorates. What was the appeal of this new political presence?

The administration, action, and mobilisation techniques of the Mana Motuhake Party are closely linked to the philosophical basis of the movement. The party portrayed itself as the fruition of modern Maori politics, and the positive symbol of 'Maori' spiritual unification. 'Mana Motuhake is the mauri (life force) and wairua (spirit) of the Maori people. It is a force that cannot be denied because it embodies the spirit of the ancestors and the soul of the people' (*Nga Kaupapa O Mana Motuhake: Manifesto*, October 1981).

Mana Motuhake was presented as the vehicle, 'created by the people', by which 'Maori identity, cultural aspirations and the social values of sharing, co-operation and fair dealing' would be expressed (ibid.). To the believer, the beauty of Mana Motuhake colours and regalia, the dignified enactment of Mana Motuhake ceremony, the inspiring delivery of Mana Motuhake speeches, the orderly execution of Mana Motuhake business, all acquired an added significance. They bore witness to the promise and possibility of Maori unity. 'The spiritual unification of the Maori world is stronger than its political division': this was the message of Motuhake. Rata was confident that this was a message of 'broad appeal'. His belief that the emergence of the Mana Motuhake Party would excite the interest of all Maori was seen in his willingness to involve Maori leaders of all walks of life, of all religions, and all socio-political philosophies. Maanu Paul, chairman of the Waiariki District Maori Council and an up-and-coming Social Credit intellectual, recalled with amusement a Mana Motuhake meeting which he had been asked to chair:

> At the outset I said: "Right, everybody knows who I am. Everybody knows I am a Social Credit man. Now I am going to operate a brilliant piece of Maori aroha here. I am going to ask a Ringatu, National man to open our meeting with prayer", and he did. "I, a Social Credit, Catholic man will chair it," I said. And I had asked a Presbyterian Labour man to close the meeting. "And in between we will have a Ratana Labour man - a Mana Motuhake man now Mat Rata, to say grace at our meal." "Why should everyone get a fair hearing?" I said, "because Mana Motuhake has been born from Labour. Now there's a lot of you anti-Labour fellows here, and a lot of you anti-Mana Motuhake fellows here who belong to the Labour movement, and there's a lot of you National fellows who are both anti-Mana Motuhake and anti-Labour". I said, "Now Mat, your job is to sell your message to this hui. If you can't sell it, well, I must say to this hui, as a travelling salesman, you will be rated 'D'. And if you sell it", I said, "Well, I'll help organise, run anything you want to do. I'm just as keen as the next person to know what Mana Motuhake is all about" ... Therein lies the difference between Maori politics and New Zealand politics. It goes deeper than politics. It goes into the religious life of the people. (Maanu Paul, interview 15 March 1981)

In order to reorient Maori alliances towards the Mana Motuhake Party Rata needed to subdue the differences which segregated Maori interests. He did this, initially, by promoting a message of Maori unity, and later by developing party policy on issues of general concern. At the expense of his own seat he launched a widely focused recruitment campaign to ensure the establishment of Mana Motuhake in all four electorates. To help overcome its novice image, and to forestall perceptions of the new organisation as the creature of radicals outside the mainstream of Maori politics, Mana Motuhake theoreticians set the party's foundations in the Labour/Ratana pact and provided a vision of its own history and source of authority by linking its philosophy with earlier resistance movements. Unlike Ratana before him, Rata did not profess to be a prophet. But as a thinker and as a highly principled member of the church, Rata was an apostle of Ratana's second mission in life - to build a political ark which would deliver his people from the battering storms of weakness and division.

In the midst of growing national and international uncertainties Mana Motuhake proposed a detailed program of social and political reform. Rata felt it was time for a 'new sense of morality in Maori leadership'. In turning his back on the financial security of a safe seat, five years before he was eligible for his parliamentary pension, he tried to illustrate to wider society that the Pakeha did not 'own the Maori'. Maori loyalty should not be interpreted as dependency, he pointed out. Neither should harmonious Maori/Pakeha relations be taken for granted. Maori people represented the largest group in the ranks of the unemployed, the underqualified, the underprivileged, and the imprisoned. Labour Party responsiveness to these grievances had declined since the death of Norman Kirk. Rata questioned whether affiliation with the Labour Party had brought any real share of power for the Maori. Maori offers of political partnership, he asserted, had been met with counter-offers of subordination, inequality, and silence. Sick at heart, Rata abandoned his position as a Labour backbencher, in an effort to break the cycle of Maori political subservience under the New Zealand party system.

Within a few short months Rata, his key advisers, officials, and supporters, had moulded a new vision of 'mana motuhake' - of Maori control over all things affecting the Maori people. Established national organisations like the NZMC, they reasoned, had failed to protect Maori interests or to effectively communicate Maori concerns to government. Equally, the protest movement had lacked the organisational coherence or credibility to spear-head their protests to political levels. The people needed the option of a real Maori political party - a party which would fearlessly represent Maori interests in Parliament. The movement, in turn, needed a political infrastructure which could direct national Maori action and which could mobilise sufficient political resources to be effective in 'bringing about a new deal for the Maori people', said Hohepa (interview 10 December 1980). Viewed from another perspective, the contemporary Maori network needed a political instrument.

The party was structured quite differently from the earlier Kingitanga, Kotahitanga, and Ratana movements. Mana Motuhake did not possess a distinct community base, and did not propose to assume responsibility for separate tribal regions or functions of self-government. Although the movement encouraged the strengthening of local and regional autonomy through the resurrection of Maori runanga, this was done in the context of party policy on the preservation of community life and the 'Maori way'. The administrative framework of Mana Motuhake, as outlined in its constitution, resembled the conventional party political structure of branches, area and electorate councils, special committees, and a secretariat. It was a framework with which the Maori voter was already familiar. Rata denied that the party in any way competed with existing Maori collective structures or tribal associations.

The objectives of the Mana Motuhake Party were straightforward. They aimed to develop an independent Maori people's party - that they might compete as equals in the national party political system; to make the Maori voice strong in Parliament and, if possible, to win the balance of power; to co-operate with other major or minor political parties on issues of common concern, but to resist co-option. Rata spoke of a reconstruction of New Zealand social thought and institutions which would incorporate the principles of biculturalism. In the society he envisaged, Maori practices of community ownership and shared responsibility might provide, in the light of failing national social and economic security, an alternative to the isolated support system of the nuclear family.

The genuine partnership to which Mana Motuhake supporters aspired in Maori/Pakeha relations was clearly enunciated in the party's campaign literature and in Walker's regular journalism. After the 1980 by-election Walker took pains to disarm the exponents of 'conservative reaction' who clung to the 'One People myth' by rejecting cultural distinctions or concepts of shared sovereignty. These responses reflected a lack of imagination and 'an abject failure to decode the messages of the decade'. The messages therefore had to be transmitted unencumbered by ambiguity. 'Maoris are not asking for sovereignty', asserted Walker in a 'Korero' column in 1980: 'They merely wish to control their own land, resources and cultural destiny. Surely that is an acceptable level of devolution in a society with two main cultural streams? It poses no threat to monarchy or government' (*New Zealand Listener* 6 September 1980; Walker 1987: 110).

The Maori 'code words' employed by Mana Motuhake during the 1981 election may have conveyed alarming possibilities to nervous Pakeha, but Walker was certain of their having a 'broad spectrum appeal' because they were 'central to Maori culture'. A campaign leaflet declared that Mana Motuhake stood for:

Te Tiriti Waitangi: that the Treaty of Waitangi be honoured by the government with respect to our lands, forests and fisheries;
Kotahitanga: unity of the Maori people to gain justice and honour in our own land;
Mana Maori: self determination in all things affecting us as Maoris;
Nga Koata E Wha: the four quarters, our representatives in Parliament. We vow to control them so our mana is recognised in the land;
Pupuri Whenua: retention of Maori land, safe-guarding our sacred places, building houses on our own land, and returning to our marae and papakainga;
Tikanga Maori: ancestors, our customs, traditions and culture;
Te Reo Maori: preservation of the Maori language and its inclusion in the education system from play-school to university;
Kaupapa Maori: transformation of all our social institutions (e.g. education, justice, local bodies, government etc.) to recognise and include Maori thinking and philosophy; recognition that we are bicultural, that we are two people in one nation;
Nga Runanga: the establishment of district tribal and urban runanga to administer tribal assets and take responsibility for community development from the Department of Maori Affairs. (*Te Kaupapa O Mana Motuhake*, undated canvassing circular, distributed 18 February, 1981, election campaign)

These concepts, resonating with historical allusions, were already embedded in Maori political consciousness. Irrespective of party differences a common language for the expression of Maori aspirations had emerged. Several decades of debate and action had removed some of the menace originally associated with what were once radical demands. While there could be disagreement over specific proposals, the legitimacy of a programme building on bicultural assumptions was now beyond dispute.

With the certainty that it could have only a minimal parliamentary presence there was some ambivalence about Mana Motuhake tactics. It behaved both as a political party and as a pressure group - making public comment upon a wide range of topics; distributing its own literature; educating public opinion through the media; communicating Maori concerns to government agencies; representing Maori interests in political arenas; and devising Maori affairs policies which were likely to be adopted by other political parties and, perhaps, inspire future governments.

Rata's strategic thinking and expectations placed considerable emphasis on the use of consumer power and union boycott techniques:

> We have in this country, tied up through finance, industry and incorporations, millions of dollars. We will withdraw this money and put it elsewhere. To newspapers who don't give us a fair exposure we will withdraw Maori purchasing power. On the problem of unemployment we will take industry, by industry. We will take direct action against them. We will not fear anyone any more. (Rata, interview February 1981)

On a later occasion he said, 'We go by the principles of arbitration and conciliation. As long as employers have the right to hire and fire, employees have the right to withhold their labour' (Rata, interview 4 March 1981). In relying on direct action, and indicating a willingness to see its policies espoused by the major parties, Mana Motuhake was implicitly recognising its own limitations as a political party. It could not aspire to govern. But it could aim to exercise influence. The theory of direct action was not, in fact, implemented in 1981. To have tried it would have been a severe test of rank and file unanimity and discipline. The risk of failure outweighed the likely benefits.

In private conversation Rata combined a gentle, unvindictive, spoken manner with a fearless expression of his point of view. His political style was never one of personal attack, though he certainly was not beyond using threats. Even his threats to an erring politician or newspaper were more readily couched in the form of a warning that Maori favours or support might be withdrawn, should a particular objectionable situation continue.

It was clear that he believed he could exert considerable influence in calling for the withdrawal of a large body of Maori support if he wished. Rata's persuasive manner was more likely to shame than to provoke retaliation. Appealing to fairness and logic, he appeared equally comfortable expressing disapproval to his people, to government, or to a senior police official - as the issue dictated. He won considerable respect among the European establishment as much for his smiling, reasoning, countenance as for his direct statements.

Although the new party had little time to prepare for its campaign, the 1981 general election provided an excellent vehicle for recruitment and mobilisation. The familiar face of Matiu Rata, now in a different guise; the earnestness and new-found conviction of his campaign; and the interest of the press, aroused public curiosity in Mana Motuhake candidates. There were many willing converts. In the environment of 'meaningless bureaucratic dialogue', observed one elder member, Mana Motuhake supporters were 'electrified' by the surge of new policy. While the majority of Maori people remained sceptical or strongly bound to the traditional parties it was understandable that some imaginations were ignited with the belief that Mana Motuhake was destined to unite the Maori people, and to herald their 'coming into their own'. 'I and the listeners feel that everything Matiu says is with perception and has meaning', related the elder. 'People are receptive to his words and trust him as a leader. Even I have flowered under the Mana Motuhake', he glowed (field notes, 28 March 1981).

Rata clothed his campaign with symbols and messages which offered comfort to the downtrodden. His simple philosophy of reinstating and giving greater security to family life was difficult to resist. His formidable bearing and radiant face, his confident and freely expressed views reflecting genuine beliefs and convictions were especially persuasive in personal contact and at public meetings. Generous and self-giving as he was, Rata's tireless initiative nevertheless was frequently interpreted as authoritarianism and a lack of humility. In a world which granted mana to lead but not to direct, he pushed on, planning and guiding with the passion of a man with little time to complete his task. It was a disarming intensity, one which even his opponents found difficult to deny. The seriousness with which Mana Motuhake members absorbed these convictions breathed a sincerity into the movement. The mutual concern of the members for each other provided a natural attraction to potential recruits. The sentiments and enthusiasm which bound Mana Motuhake members were a far cry from the procedural rigidities and factional deal-making of the older parties.

At the root of Rata's appeals for greater recognition of Maori rights was a very real fear that the tide of Maori grievance could not be stemmed much longer. Rata wanted, in particular, to help the younger generation of Maori. An incident at a marae public meeting illustrated the peculiarly personal nature of Rata's appeal. A young woman rose shyly and tentatively to address the president. In tears, she held up her thumb and fore-finger, showing the gathering that she was 'an inch away' from going into a mental hospital. She poured forth the tragic story of her life - first as an migrant child and later as an urban mother. She recounted a life of sleeping on floors, of violence and maladjustment, of confused identities, neglectful in-laws, and a deserting husband. She was uncertain of her rights to her three children, or her ability to raise them on her own. Her grief brought tears to the eyes of many listeners. But few failed to be moved by the compassion of Rata's reply:

Be strengthened by the collective wisdom and comfort of our group. We share your burdens. Our task is to help. Feel free to call on it if you feel you need help. Our hope is that we can help you look rationally at things and to offer you comfort ... to reinforce that family strength. Our task is to encourage families not to turn on one another, but to turn *to* one another. It's often said that the family is the basis of society. It has become a cliche, not a reality. Our task is to turn this into a reality. Our young people seem to be confronted by a conflict of values. When people have lost hope, we can not find solutions to our needless difficulties.

The Mana Motuhake does not provide a grandiose world. But it is a world where no-one is an outcast, where obligation exists, where one finds options, and where one finds the best course to take. When you look into the eyes of your children and grandchildren I am sure you become aware of the responsibilities you have. For years we thought the source of social and economic well-being was by becoming a brown version of a totally non-Maori way of life. Our task is to offer an option to that. Feel free to speak from the heart. Often people are so grieved they don't know where to turn. This courtyard is one of the unique institutions in this land, where one finds the freedom of speech. It is this which we must protect.

Two senior women stood at the side of the young mother, supporting her and holding her hands. Members rose spontaneously to their feet, some linking arms. Someone began a gentle, favoured Maori hymn. The atmosphere - warm, loving, comforting - was heavy with aroha. Soon all were singing (Mana Motuhake Secretariat Meeting, Tuwharetoa ite Aupouri Marae, Turangi, field notes, 28 February - 1 March 1981).

The charisma, the resurrection of communal values, the air of supernatural confirmation and spiritual significance which infused Mana Motuhake's activities provided a remarkably sweet nectar. It ensured the conversion of a sizeable proportion of the Maori vote to Mana Motuhake in a very short time. That it emerged in the strongly secular environment of modern party politics, and could be used in the establishment of the first Maori political party, again reflected the ingenuity of Maori political culture. It was also a renewed recognition of the indivisibility of the sacred and the profane in Maori social thought and action. Had Rata claimed a divine inspiration or purpose in the manner of Ratana he may well have alienated those for whom such a claim would have had little credibility. Without presuming to assert a spiritual mandate, which in a contemporary setting could be mocked or denied, he improvised appeals that would touch both believers and sceptics.

SUPPORT POOLS

Mana Motuhake rhetoric emphasised a shared history in Maori antiquity and later opposition to European exploitation, and a shared interest in contemporary 'Maori concerns'. Messages were sometimes composed for the ears of specific audiences during the campaign - particularly if that audience, like the Kingitanga people, represented a large voting pool. But the message, even in its specific garb, had a wider magnetism. It was designed to reinforce Maori ethnicity - in a way which would not offend the urban or rural, traditional or modern, youth or elders.

References to supernatural and ancestral confirmation; the use of conservative Maori committee procedure, voting, and election campaign practices; and the employment of pressure politics and moderate protest provided symbols and modes familiar to most Maori, even those who were not politically active. The interests of 'the Maori people' were articulated by Mana Motuhake neither through kinship, tribe, nor residence. Inter-tribal unity may well have been the high moral ground of the party, but not a pathway its members were required to tread in any practical sense, as this may have threatened the integrity of traditional or current alliances. Neither was it necessary to a party which was presented to the different Maori interests as merely their 'political arm', a party which took pains in its first year to establish representative branches in the four quarters of Maoridom. In 1981 the party did not achieve any formal coalition between the divided tribal groupings, but it clearly did pitch its appeal to these existing federations. It did not try to sell itself as a party of the 'brown proletariat', but its concern for the Maori working-class, unemployed, and underprivileged touched Maori people of all political persuasions who recognised an ethnic dimension to their people's misfortunes.

Just as Mana Motuhake's campaign was not exclusively focused, neither was its appeal. No Maori interest sector joined *en masse*. Recruitment depended more upon individual belief, conscience, and conviction. This was not just because the party had to compete with political habits in all these sectors. Support for Mana Motuhake came predominantly from the Labour membership, but some also came from the ranks of National and Social Credit. It attracted elders and youth, the passionate and the previously passive. In winning members from all interest sectors the party specialised in the interests of none. Internal tensions were unavoidable in the attempt to find common cause between disparate tribal and ideological factions. To realign and consolidate these divergent interests under a single banner was an ambitious task.

As a new venture in socio-political reform the party succeeded in providing considerable intellectual stimulus across the whole spectrum of Maori leadership. Understandably, however, some conservative leaders avoided joining a party which appeared to be dominated by liberals and ex-Labour supporters. But many conservatives supported the concept of 'mana motuhake' in principle. They looked with admiration on this effort to establish a Maori party, and consciously tried not to get in its way. Indeed, for the conservatives, there was something attractive about a movement that expressed their ethnic concerns while offering its principal challenge to their main political opponent, the Labour Party.

In the first hours of his resignation it was from the Labour cells of his own electorate that Matiu Rata built the foundation of his new party. For many years he had been 'their man in Parliament', and he was able to draw upon the personal loyalty of much of the Northern Labour branch network. Labour

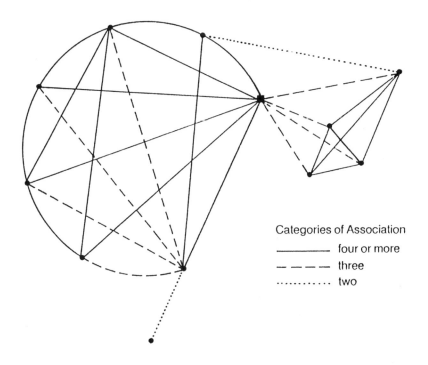

Categories of Association

———— four or more

– – – – three

············ two

**FIGURE 1: THE 'INNER CABINET' OF MANA MOTUHAKE -
STRENGTH OF TIES IN THE LEADERSHIP NET**

As all of the executive members held ties with the president, Rata was not included in this figure. The density of the grid depicting these ties would have obscured the nature of the ties between the members of his executive.

provided the founding membership for the first Mana Motuhake branches established in the Northern Maori electorate - giving an impression of an exodus of Labour support. Once the initial choice to follow Rata or to stay with the Labour Party had been made, however, the flood very quickly diminished into a trickle. Future support for the new party had to be won by hard work and expensive campaigning.

In addition to the Labour Party intellectuals and workers, Rata turned his attention to other reservoirs for support - the Ratana Church, the land rights activists, and the youthful discontented. He visited the more distant, autonomous, land-rich interests of the West Coast and East Coast and the Kingitanga people. He addressed the NZMC and other major Maori organisations and kept in close communication with the political developments and moods of the Social Credit party and trade unionists. In all these pockets there were friends and sympathisers - those who were willing to encourage the Mana Motuhake people to 'do their own thing'. Notwithstanding his years as an avowed socialist, Rata was also respected by conservatives for 'what he had done for Maoris' during his term in Parliament. Campaign overtures made by Mana Motuhake to conservative rural strongholds were graciously hosted. Political debate stimulated local imagination, particularly during an election year, and Mana Motuhake candidates generally commanded a good audience.

Mana Motuhake infrastructure was bolstered by an early recruitment of some of the Maori intelligentsia's most vocal and visionary members. Its executive consisted of a core of respected and hardworking leaders plucked from the local and regional political arenas. More importantly, the executive was steeled by pre-existing ties of solidarity between these individuals through earlier university or post-secondary education, compulsory military training, professional association, political and community work associations, and friendship. Much of the early success of the Mana Motuhake movement, and of Matiu Rata's success as party leader, must be attributed to the tight-knit nature of the organisation's 'inner cabinet'. These members shared either a common history of affiliation with the Labour Party, common liberal views, and/or personal friendships with each other. Six of the members also brought to the organisation powerful professional affiliations. Relationships between several of these colleagues had been formed 20 years earlier in their student days.

Only one of the 'intellectual' subset, however, shared territorial affiliation with the four other representatives of the Northern Maori sector first mobilised in the movement's infancy. This individual - Dr Patrick Hohepa - held the closest ties to all members of the executive and to the president himself and was therefore well positioned for his role as secretary-general of the executive. The remaining three had weak to middle-strength ties with the other members, two sharing territorial affiliation in the west. These observations would hardly be a revelation to a Maori participant as they reflect what has long been a reality in contemporary Maori social life. The Maori and non-Maori worlds have provided dual avenues of tribal/regional recognition and professional status, respectively, through which a Maori might rise in distinction.

CRITICISM AND OPPOSITION

Rata's roles as organisational administrator, political leader, and Northern candidate competed with each other. Many communities waited for Rata. They wished to be invited and convinced by the president himself to join Mana Motuhake. Because the president could not be in so many places at once ill-feeling persisted, particularly in the North. Some perceived that Rata had neither fully confided in his elders, nor consulted his electorate, before abandoning the Labour Party. Gradually his explanations for resigning were accepted, but the oversight in failing to visit some of these communities was not so easily forgiven. News of their disgruntled withholding of support soon reached head office. Quick tours were arranged, but Rata's pressing responsibilities as party leader and his efforts to establish the party in the other three electorates severely limited his own campaign for the Northern seat.

During the 1981 election campaign, senior Mana Motuhake officials became alarmed at the prospect that Rata might be jeopardising his own chances for re-election. He was the party's strongest candidate. Their efforts to convince him to delegate some of his administrative responsibilities to his officers were not entirely successful - not necessarily because the president was stubbornly committed to establishing the new electorates himself, but because those electorates pressed the president to come and speak to them on Mana Motuhake. The new branches and councils wanted the seal of the president upon their inaugural and candidate selection conferences. Consequently, he spent much of his time travelling throughout the country promoting the party. Rata had another important role as public spokesman for Mana Motuhake. By watching public and Maori issues closely he was able to regularly air Mana Motuhake views - obtaining much needed publicity for the campaign.

The 1980 by-election had alerted the Labour Party to the kind of damage Mana Motuhake could do to its constituencies. Although Labour's candidate Bruce Gregory held the seat with 52.41 percent of the votes (3580 votes), the 'defector' - then standing as an independent candidate - had retained or stimulated the adherence of 37.90 percent (2589) of the voters. Gregory's performance did not compare favourably with Rata's earlier popularity as the Labour candidate in the 1978 general election, in which Rata had been victor by 71.47 percent, or 6071 votes (Table 1).

The reaction against Matiu within some quarters of the Labour Party was ferocious. As leader of the Labour Party, Bill Rowling himself stood to lose much from a breach of the Maori/Labour alliance which, after 40 years, was deemed an institution. Those electorates most under threat received Rowling's personal attention. Rata also came under considerable personal attack from his former Labour colleagues. Press and platform reverberated with insinuations that Mana Motuhake recruits were being 'hoodwinked', 'blackmailed', and associated with 'violence'. Rata's criticisms of Labour Maori affairs policies were turned against him. He was blamed for its failures and treated as an impostor. His new party was characterised as, at best, a transient illusion and at worst a deceitful fabrication.

Contrary to the criticisms his new party was receiving from Labour quarters the president made it clear in many of his speeches that 'violence, radicalism and separatism were not part of the Mana Motuhake movement' (*Auckland Star* 17 November 1979). He did not pander to radical interests in his membership. The prominent activist Titewhai Harawira had been an early member of the party; other members of her family gave support at elections but did not join. 'They lost interest', Rata observed, 'once it was clear that they were not able to hijack or manipulate Mana Motuhake.' Syd Jackson, his own plan for a new party pre-empted, assisted in the first Mana Motuhake campaigns. But neither he nor his equally well-known wife, Hanna, became members (Rata to the author, 12 October 1991).

To the assertion of his enemies that Mana Motuhake would become powerless and cut adrift from the wider political system Rata replied:

> Raising the consciousness of our people will require hard work and dedication. There are no short cuts to those political, social and economic benefits we hope to make within our own people and within the political structure of the country. (Mana Motuhake Secretariat Meeting, Tuwhareatoa ite Aupori Marae, Turangi, 28 February 1981)

While its attacks did not destroy Mana Motuhake in the 1981 election the Labour Party in Northern Maori, spurred by the challenge, slightly increased its vote over the 1978 general election with 6,368 votes. By contrast, Mana Motuhake made a substantially smaller impact with 2,703 votes.

But perhaps the most significant difference between the 1980 by-election and the 1981 election was the leap in turnout. Totals of 8,556 and 8,495 valid votes were recorded in Northern Maori in the 1975 and 1978 general elections respectively. But in the 1981 election there was an increase to 11,772 valid votes. Increases were also seen in the Maori turnout in the other three Maori seats, though none quite as significant as that in the Northern electorate (Table 1; see also Sorrenson 1986; Chapman 1986). In each seat Mana Motuhake secured between 12 and 23 percent of the vote. Superficially, it looked like it was the 'Labour loss which had fuelled Mana Motuhake's rise', wrote Chapman (1986: B-101-4). Mana Motuhake's average gain of over 15 points of the total valid vote and Labour's drop of over 13 points indicated 'the one seeming to draw upon the other'. But closer analysis, while still inconclusive, showed that the more likely major source of Mana Motuhake support was what Chapman called 'the detachment from non-voting' (Chapman 1986: B-104). Some at least of the silenced majority had found their voice.

Rata's opponent, Bruce Gregory, was thought to lack Rata's gift of oratory and his political flair. But Gregory faithfully pursued his community rounds. 'He visited the marae and humbled himself as a servant to the people', said one informant. 'So the people put him up'. Rata's years in Parliament, which had distanced him from his electorate, had had the effect of alienating many potential supporters in the rural areas. Particularly as a minister he had succumbed to the bind which has trapped many a politician between the people and the government. While he served the people in the corridors of power he was not visible among those he counted on at the ballot box. Gregory's physical presence, on the other hand, was interpreted as a show of concern.

That Pakeha society had some investment in the fortunes of Mana Motuhake was quite clear from the 1981 campaign - the Labour Party in its failure, and the National and Social Credit parties in its success. The momentum of the Mana Motuhake movement, and the speed at which the party infrastructure was erected, was attributable not merely to the mobilising strategies employed by the movement but to the pre-existing and receptive network of relationships in the Maori world.

But, as the fate of the Social Credit Party had proved before it, seats in New Zealand elections are not gained by winning a scattering of votes throughout the country. Marginal seats must be identified and votes consolidated around them. The Mana Motuhake Party did not establish coalitions with any tribal or other interest grouping which would have ensured for it a bloc vote in its first election. Mana Motuhake rhetoric carried the vague message of 'Maori' solidarity but it did not challenge existing coalitions or loyalties, with the exception of voting loyalties to the Labour Party. Political solidarity in the quest for a just distribution of resources was seen to be the central objective. 'We are all fighting for reform in our different ways', was the message. This common platform for action was designed to minimise competition with traditional or conservative associations of territory, tribe, religion, or ideological sentiment. In the context of the segmented structural and political realities of the Maori world, however, it may have been precisely this diffuse appeal to ethnicity which magnified the party's ill-fortune. Recruitment was partially successful in all interest sectors, but a decisive conversion was gained from none.

The Kingitanga people, and other relatively self-sufficient areas of the East and West Coast, were not in need of national solidarity. Dame Te Atairangikaahu left the decision up to individual conscience - as did leaders of the Ratana Church. Old habits and caution prevailed. To those secure in the rural enclaves, the adversities of the urban poor and the clamour of the distant urban youth and radical protesters were more frequently a source of embarrassment than an inducement to new allegiances. In these circumstances, support for Mana Motuhake might be regarded as an eccentricity to be tolerated, rather than a valid alternative. There were misgivings too, about Rata's allusions to the use of union-style boycotts, and his demands for public accountability and rectification of injustices. On the other hand, activists, feminists, and even liberals at times, questioned whether Mana Motuhake - in modifying its message for conservative Maori - could sustain its commitment to the under-privileged and detribalised.

Over an eighteen month period Mana Motuhake branches had mushroomed at a rate astonishing to its opponents. But the party suffered from slender resources in leadership and funds. Communicating the message of Mana Motuhake, when it had hardly been formed by its central figures and policy councils, was also a problem. Party candidates and branch leaders were uncertain of party philosophy and purpose, and to a significant extent had to chart a course from their own ambitions for the Maori people. Major party policy was still emerging from Mana Motuhake conferences, policy papers, and pamphlets during the period of the campaign.

Although the movement did not lack an elite cadre, the organisational skills of those in the higher levels were not fully engaged in the 1981 election campaign. Many already bore heavy professional commitments and official responsibilities in their own regions. With the tasks of drafting the constitution, establishing an electoral organisation, and structuring the party machinery so recently achieved, the 1981 election came upon Mana Motuhake too swiftly. The tide of conversion which Mana Motuhake enthusiasts anticipated did not occur. Deeply ingrained habits of loyalty to Labour proved substantially resistant to new appeals and blandishments.

Rata came under severe criticism from his own officials for losing support in the Northern electorate. While capable Mana Motuhake executives were being given insufficient incentive to maintain their interest in the organisation there was little sympathy for the president's problem of overwork, his 'parliamentary' manner, and *prima donna* tendencies. Rata relied too much, they felt, upon party philosophy to regain the Northern seat. His hopes were undermined by Gregory's warning that political isolation with an insignificant party, however 'Maori', would not advance the Maori cause. Some Maori, unpersuaded by the latest appeal for their endorsement, felt it was a case of 'better the devil you know', and cast their vote with established parties. The Maori vote confirmed the fate of all independents.

THE VIABILITY OF POLITICAL ETHNICITY

Matiu Rata and his supporters had a vision of 'mana Maori', of Maori self-determination in all things affecting Maori people. The party sought to position itself as the most recent manifestation of the historic yearnings for inter-tribal solidarity which had been developing in the breast of Maoridom for more than a century. This was a vision fated to be impeded by the jealousies and self-preserving disposition of Maori interest group politics. It was also destined to be hampered by a New Zealand democratic system which had traditionally been uncongenial to third parties.

In seeking to transcend existing organisations and loyalties, Mana Motuhake offered an alternative, a specifically Maori vehicle of political expression. This was not, in inspiration or intention, a separatist movement. But it was manifestly an ethnic party, avowedly mobilising support on an ethnic basis and attempting to give an institutional form and focus to a shared ethnic consciousness. It sought greater cultural autonomy and, like politically active Blacks and Puerto Ricans in

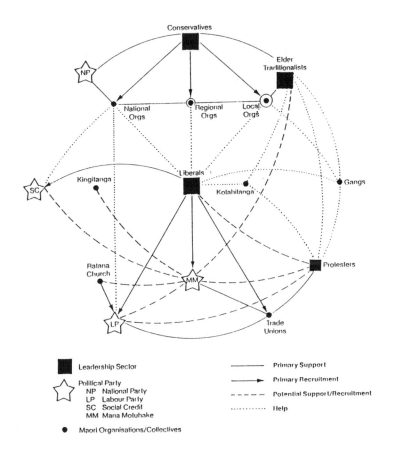

**FIGURE 2: THE 'MAORI WORLD' SYSTEM - ORGANISATIONAL
AND LEADERSHIP SUPPORT NETWORK 1981**

Only lines of primary support and primary recruitment are depicted. The stars on the edge of the Maori world sphere represent national political parties. As a Maori party, Mana Motuhake appears within the sphere itself. The squares represent the particular leadership styles/interest sectors, and the points represent a selection of significant Maori organisations, collectives, and groupings.

Where no lines of primary support and recruitment are shown, such as the Kingitanga movement, participating members of this grouping freely associated with the political party of their choice. To be a member of the Labour Party, the National Party, Social Credit, or Mana Motuhake did not affect one's standing as a Kingite.

So called 'conservative' modes of leadership did not necessarily imply a National Party affiliation, although support of and from this party was most likely. Formal organisations have been dominated by conservative elements in the past. While predominantly Labour, Social Credit or Mana Motuhake supporters, 'liberal' leaders also participated in formal national, regional, and local organisations like the New Zealand Maori Council, the Maori Women's Welfare League, the Maori Wardens Association. Liberal leaders, however, challenged the status quo, supporting less conventional sectors such as radical protest groups.

the U.S.A., 'a greater communal voice in the destiny of the overall nation-state' (Smith 1979:31).

By appealing to all sectors of the Maori world, Rata's movement not only took strength from many sources, it also became itself a new forum for old rivalries. Given the tribal, territorial, and interest group influences which dominate Maori political infrastructure and process, description of Maori society merely as an 'ethnic group' would be quite inadequate. As a dynamic interest net, with its own processes of recruitment and interaction, the Mana Motuhake experience exposed both the validity and the limitations of Cohen's observation that ethnicity is essentially a political construct (1974a: 15). In the 1981 general election, politically generated ethnicity failed to win Mana Motuhake a seat in Parliament. As an organising and recruiting principle, the concept of 'Maoriness' proved too weak to compete with other contemporary Maori allegiances or to overcome entrenched political indifference.

Through his pact with Labour in the 1930s Ratana had been the first to actively attempt to give Maori ethnicity prominence and form in the party political arena. During the 1970s the protest movement laid claim to continuity with primordial ethnicity in support of their causes.[1] Mana Motuhake went further with the development of an independent Maori party. But, with the New Zealand Maori Council and other national organisations already enjoying wide support as administrative and quasi-political bodies transcending party, Mana Motuhake could not hope to secure a political monopoly over Maori ethnicity - certainly not in a single election.

The fate of the Mana Motuhake Party in its early years was perhaps predictable. The party failed to secure the support of entrenched Maori interest sectors predominantly because the latter had a strong stake in maintaining society as it was. For many it was a tried and true arrangement. They chose between the parties most likely to be in power, the National Party or the Labour Party; and the parties never likely to be in power, Social Credit and Mana Motuhake. The majority of Maori voters - the workers and the unemployed - maintained the commitment of two generations to Labour.

Among many there was the very real fear that the mobilisation of ethnicity meant an unwelcome emphasis upon racial difference. For them, coalitions between Maori political groupings seemed an unwise invitation to defeat by weight of non-Maori numbers. The Maori were, in this view, better to maintain a strategy of permeation and influence in the dominant structures. What Mana Motuhake's limited impact in the 1981 election revealed was that a hastily conceived program of political ethnicity could not quickly forge a bond more pervasive or persuasive than party political preference and habitual affiliation. Political choices, whether deep-rooted party loyalties or temporary alignments on issues, had salience and resonance throughout Maori social life. They tempered friendship and association between Maori people at every level. Essentially the Maori had shown themselves to be a people deeply attuned to political issues and structural realities. But in the party political arena the majority of them remained firm in their conviction that their material interests lay with the working-class

(Sorrenson 1986: B-55). Of the 51.5 percent of the eligible Maori voting population who were registered on the Maori roll in 1981, 57.3 percent of these voted for Labour and only 13.3 percent voted for Mana Motuhake (Sorrenson 1986: B-76; B-82). The Labour Party's image as the party for the working-class or the disadvantaged was not fundamentally shaken by Mana Motuhake's ethnic appeal.

Rata's vision and hope for a unified Maori voice in government fell short of accomplishment, not merely because the dedication of his organisation's workers was ultimately frustrated by a lack of time and resources, or because the diversity of its membership created insurmountable tensions within, but rather because the 'Maori people', to whom he appealed, were neither sufficiently cohesive nor sufficiently alienated from New Zealand society to respond to his vision of a united Maori voice at the ballot box.

If Mana Motuhake's fate was a valid test, it seemed that the majority of the Maori people remained content with a regime that channelled political impulse into separate domains, bridged by institutions which articulated such ethnic demands as could not otherwise be satisfied. Whatever grievances or hopes may have been nursed or repressed, Mana Motuhake was not seen to be the answer in the 1981 election. For the majority, ethnic consciousness seemed untroubled by existing arrangements.

Perhaps because of the similarity of its rhetoric to that which Rata and his supporters had espoused in Labour garb, Mana Motuhake had failed to present a compellingly distinctive alternative. The dilemma of the new party was this: that if its program was simply what Labour policy would be if it was true to its promises, and Mana Motuhake's leaders were the same people who had failed to make Labour true to its word, why should voters believe against all the odds that a small clique of frustrated renegades could do what Labour could not or would not do? But it was a portent, not fully grasped at the time, that Rata's message had been at least as successful in mobilising the non-voter as in converting the politically engaged.

At a Taupo gathering Rata explained that Mana Motuhake had to compete with a 40-year habit of Maori Labour voting. The new party, he told his members, must strive to overcome the paranoia and 'suspicions of separatism among those Maoris who disagree with us, and the general public'. In his reflections after the election Rata acknowledged that his people had, for the time being, chosen to 'stay put'. Nevertheless, 'the Labour Party are on record as saying that we are still very much a political entity to deal with - and we propose to remain that way!'

When asked what he planned to do for the future of the party the president said that the Secretariat would have to carefully analyse the final election results and consider where it had failed. Rata admitted that it may be necessary for the organisation to undergo a change of personnel - in the administration and among the candidates. He reasoned further that future campaigns may have to aim at additional categories of membership. His message, he said, was not just for the

Maori people, not just for the younger New Zealander, but 'for the more thinking one':

> Without an ideology that is rooted in this country it's really just an academic exercise in politics ... We are beginning to think very deeply about our position as a people. We are saying that unless we begin to reflect more home grown ideas, as an independent sovereign state, as a Pacific country, we are really heading nowhere ... We are not saying that National or Labour won't be here with us for years to come but, who knows, there may evolve here, yet, a kind of Pacific Socialism ... It's natural evolution to move towards a more expressed independent viewpoint ... New Zealand's future lies in the wider Pacific Basin: we are not merely an extension of Europe and of England. If Mana Motuhake can somehow project that viewpoint, then ultimately it must attract some broader attention. (Rata, interview 4 December 1981)[2]

In reviewing the party's situation, Rata said he would be willing to stand down as president if the Secretariat felt this necessary. 'But', he said, 'you can't walk away from your first skirmish!' The team had emerged from battle 'in good heart'. But the party may need to take new directions in its campaign: 'I might recommend to Mana Motuhake members now to take on Maori committee posts around the country more; or to take a closer examination of one or two local government areas and secure appointments on these as well'. The party, he said, 'needed that kind of influence to maintain itself' (ibid.).

Premature notions of expansion, and the grand scheme of forming a New Zealand Republic, had not aided the capture of a single seat. But Rata's suggested strategy of taking Mana Motuhake leadership into the heart of Maori social and political arenas held promise. If Mana Motuhake was to have influence at a national parliamentary level it would need both to diversify and to consolidate its social appeal and its leadership base. So long as it was geared almost exclusively to election campaigning Mana Motuhake could not hope to command the intense partisanship enjoyed by the Labour Party, or to challenge the social cachet of the National Party. 'To establish itself successfully', wrote New Zealand political scientist, Barry Gustafson, a political party:

> must first win and must subsequently retain, a substantial electoral base in a particular socio-economic group or in a significantly large coalition of not too heterogeneous interests. Sometimes a party is able to appeal to a number of mutually reinforcing factors, such as class, and regional or national identification. (Gustafson 1976: 48)

In the case of Mana Motuhake it had not been enough to appeal broadly to Maori ethnicity. The Maori world was clearly not unified by identical perceptions and a single coherent interest. Distinct social and political groupings coexisted within the larger ideological framework of shared ethnicity. In the first instance, Mana Motuhake might try to refine and focus its recruitment campaign to win a more substantial base of support but there could be no guarantee of any massive shift of allegiance. In some communities the attitudes of large bodies of electors were likely to be strongly influenced by the attitudes of local leaders. It was hardly to be expected that there would be widespread, rapid, and substantial political defection. In the absence of some catastrophic discontinuity, or dramatic realignment - such as was attempted unsuccessfully by Rata with the Kingitanga and Ratana Church - an appropriate interval for consideration and consultation would be necessary before most leaders would feel able to repudiate long-defended allegiances.

Although separate Maori representation was established as a temporary arrangement in 1867 the abolition of the Maori electorates has never been seriously on the political agenda. Since 1975, when Maori voters were given the option of enrolling on either the Maori or the general roll, the majority have chosen to remain with the Maori electorates (McRobie 1978; Bean 1984; Sorrenson 1986). The inauguration of Mana Motuhake had not challenged this system. The party merely put up candidates for the Maori seats, declaring that it might eventually stand for general seats as well.

The New Zealand democratic ideal that the Maori minority should have guaranteed representation has not threatened powerful interests sufficiently to warrant a move for the elimination of the reserved seats. In a doctoral study of New Zealand electoral behaviour, Clive Bean (1984: 248-9) points out that, since 1935, there have only been two occasions, in the 1946 and the 1957 elections, when the Maori vote determined the governing party. But what if the Maori vote had been redistributed throughout the general electorate? Assuming that, with the removal of the Maori electorates, Maori voters would have cast their votes in favour of the same parties, Simpson (1985: 4) calculated that between 1972 and 1984 'the abolition of the Maori seats would have had little impact on the outcomes of the five general elections considered.' While the position of some marginal seats would have come under question the overall outcome would not have resulted in a change of government. 'If anything', Simpson wrote, 'the position of the National Party would have been strengthened by the loss of the few Maori seats with the failure of the Labour Party to gain more than they lost'.[3]

Mana Motuhake would have had least to gain by the abolition of the Maori seats. With only four main constituencies in which to compete, it could effectively concentrate its resources. Dispersed over many more seats, Mana Motuhake efforts would have been drastically diluted. Moreover, as the veteran political analyst Robert Chapman points out in his study for the Royal Commission on the Electoral System, Maori support for the Labour Party - which peaked to four-fifths of valid Maori votes in 1972 - still amounted to less than two-thirds of the vote in the 1981 election:

What this long succession of Labour members in Maori seats suggests, like the exceptionally high percentages of the valid votes cast in their favour, is that the separate Maori seats permitted their voters to choose and maintain a different course of political action from their fellow New Zealanders, one to which they have shown remarkable fidelity for over four decades. The Maori political system is part of and contributes to the general party system in that Labour continues to be one of New Zealand's two major parties from which Governments come. But the Maori course is removed from pakeha practice in that a very small portion indeed of Maori voters shift back and forth from one to the other major party. (Chapman 1986: B-87)

In observations which confirm the understanding with which I began my fieldwork in 1981, Chapman characterises Maori special representation as a 'unique and valuable sub-system' which is neither encapsulated nor dominated by the general system. Rather, it is partially integrated with the party political system of wider New Zealand society, and 'partially parallel' to it, in that it serves and is maintained by the separate interests of the Maori people:

the sub-system differs from the General system with which it interacts in many vital ways. The sub-system is distinct and different because it is supposed to do the different job of representing the other culture in our country in its Parliament. Maori electors and MPs see to it that it does. (Chapman 1986: B-l07)

This sub-system does not necessarily mirror trends in wider society. The National party may fare poorly in the Maori seats, but may win an election in the general seats. International and national economic and social conditions which affect Pakeha politics may impact quite differently, or even not at all, in Maori voting patterns.[4] The option which exists for the Maori to move their vote to the general roll emphasises the voluntary and independent nature of Maori participation in the Maori roll. As Chapman (ibid.) says, 'it is entirely free choice and, despite the accusation ... that it smacked of apartheid, it has been largely choice for decades'. It is therefore not surprising that the Maori people have made this system their own. The entry of a distinctly Maori party into that arena was simultaneously a development in Maori political autonomy, and in Maori and Pakeha relations. As the Labour alliance developed from Ratana initiatives, the Mana Motuhake Party developed from those of a Maori fragment detached from the Labour Party.

While there may have been some equivocation in the Mana Motuhake leadership about the desirability of drawing non-Maori recruits into their ranks, their essential strategic task after 1981 remained that of fostering Maori interest group support and in interpreting and expressing pan-Maori sentiment. The growing belief, based on demographic forecasts in the 1980s, that the Maori population would grow to a fifth of the New Zealand total in the next 25 years had the potential to become a significant factor in the growth of Maori political consciousness.

Rata's initiative was not preceded or accompanied by any blatant assault or freshly discovered scandal of such magnitude as to dislocate most Maori loyalties and commitments. He had been moved to act after many years of struggle and introspection, much of which was unknown to the public. The conclusions he and others like Hohepa and Walker might have reached, readily understandable though they might have been to those who had shared their experiences, could lack logic or persuasiveness to those on the fringes of the national Maori political network. In a short time it was also a difficult task to transform Rata's image. The admired achiever who had triumphed in the national political arena had somehow to be presented simultaneously as the victim of an unacceptable system and as the man best qualified to lead a movement which would reform it. It was a remarkable feat of political communication not only to maintain but to enhance Rata's credibility in these circumstances.

The unique achievement of the New Zealand polity has been to develop a parallel tradition of successful national, as well as ethnically exclusive, political forms and action. But party allegiances and voting habits of the last half century may well be eroded by the emergence of new voting cohorts and by an expanding realisation of Maori potency. With a more rapidly growing 'Maori' population, it may make decreasing sense to be identified as a Labour or National Maori. As late as 1988 Vasil was pessimistic. The Maori, he asserted, were afflicted by 'resignation', 'helplessness', and 'defeatism' '... so deep that they even had serious doubts about the usefulness of a Maori political party' (Vasil 1988: 16). However, for both the politically active, and for those who hitherto have chosen to opt out of the electoral system, there may be an increasing conviction that a vote for specifically Maori interests will not be wasted. The challenge for the New Zealand polity then will be to ensure that it is sufficiently responsive to the political demands of the expanding minority to sustain a commitment to peaceful cohabitation through power sharing.

NOTES

1. Primordial ethnicity: drawing on the natural, spiritual aspects of Maoriness (irrespective of tribal or other affiliations). As explained by Geertz: 'some attachments seem to flow more from a sense of natural - some would say spiritual - affinity than from social interaction' (1963: 110).

2. That Rata's radical call for a 'New Zealand Republic' entered the great mixing pot of ideas with little comment or retaliation is, at first sight, surprising in view of widespread respect and affection for the monarchy. But the explanation may lie in the New Zealand tradition of social and political experimentation, and of what Canadian writer Augie Fleras (1985a: 551) described as 'this nation's vaunted reputation as a global pacesetter in race relations'.

3. Simpson's analysis (1985: 8-9) suggested that an integrated roll probably would have been harmful to Maori interests. Where the Maori vote was insignificant, Simpson speculates, Maori interests would probably be ignored. 'Few political candidates, Maori

or non-Maori, could really afford to pay particular and continued attention to Maori matters under an integrated roll'. In those areas where the Maori vote was significant, the heightened lobbying of the major parties for their vote would most certainly serve to create added tension and division in the Maori community. 'Overall the effect would be to strengthen greatly the political impact of a few tribal areas, leaving the rest with no political electoral voice'. It was for this reason that Simpson concluded that the 'development of a Maori party based on separate representation' held most promise for increased Maori representation in Parliament (Simpson 1985: 9-11).

4. Illustrating this point Chapman (1986: B-88) wrote: 'The years from 1946 to 1951 saw National climb to its zenith in General voting, followed by the Korean War boom, soaring prices, industrial battle on the waterfront and Sidney Holland's successful snap election in 1951. Despite all these stirring developments on the general political stage, those same years were, by contrast, stable years in Maori politics. This would have been paradoxical if Maori politics had been simply a subdivision of pakeha politics. As a Maori political sub-system taking its own course, however, its independent results were clear enough'.

POSTSCRIPT

Maori protest over land and other grievances continued after 1981. Escalating violence in the Waitangi Day protests, the concerns of Maori people over Maori unemployment and underdevelopment, and the publicity which these attracted over the years were factors in drawing together broad support for a 'Hikoi', Great Peace March, from the royal marae at Ngaruawahia to Waitangi in 1984. After her successful crusade in winning back her tribal land from the Raglan Golf Club, Mrs Eva Rickard had accepted the presidency of the Kotahitanga movement. As a recently revived influence in the Maori world it was the Kotahitanga movement which led the Hikoi.

The royal pardon for Maori ancestors who had been denounced as 'rebels' in the early days of resistance to the European was not obtained from Queen Elizabeth II. But other ground was gained. In March 1985 the Labour Prime Minister, David Lange, recommended the appointment of the outspoken Maori Archbishop Paul Reeves as the country's next Governor-General. That same year a white paper, 'A Bill of Rights for New Zealand' (1985), was tabled in the House of Representatives by the Minister of Justice, and the government examined the completed Maori Affairs Bill and the Treaty of Waitangi Amendment Bill.

From the mid-1980s, the Treaty of Waitangi became increasingly the symbol and centre of debate for harmonious bicultural society, and the basis for a wide-ranging reassessment of race relations in New Zealand. A landmark 1987 Court of Appeal case (*New Zealand Maori Council v the Crown*) confirmed the special partnership between the Maori people and the Crown, inaugurated under the treaty, as an ongoing relationship.

In June 1987 the Minister of Maori Affairs announced the introduction of an improved system of service delivery and resource distribution to Maori communities. This initiative, developed in detail over the next eighteen months, entailed a devolution of decision-making to iwi (tribal) authorities. With the phasing down of the Department of Maori Affairs, and the increase of Maori participation in the political process, the Labour government sought to achieve greater social and economic equity between Maori and Pakeha.

From different perspectives, both Sir Graham Latimer and Matiu Rata found flaws in these developments. Latimer believed that the transfer of functions like housing, vocational training, land development, and Reo Kohanga to other departments was a return to assimilationist politics. If the Maori Affairs Department was to disappear Rata wanted a system of elected Maori Regional Authorities to replace it. The emphasis of Mana Motuhake was less on iwi restoration and self-management than on a comprehensive and efficient service delivery system (Jones 1990:66).

The defeat of the Labour government brought another change of direction in Maori affairs. Following the delivery of 'Ka Awatea: A Report of the Ministerial Planning Group', in March 1991 the National Party Cabinet endorsed a proposal to set up a specialist Maori Agency under the Minister of Maori Affairs. The Ministry of Maori Development, it recommended, should also have a regional presence in the form of Regional Development Agencies consisting of a small permanent staff and co-opted local expertise. The way in which these arrangements, or whatever superseded them, might be harmonised with the devolution of responsibility launched by the previous government, was a major item for the Maori political agenda of the 1990s.

By focusing attention on government responsibilities under the treaty, the 1987 Court of Appeal decision had also enhanced the powers of the Waitangi Tribunal. Under the Labour government, the Waitangi Tribunal was expanded from three to seven members - chaired by the Chief Judge of the Maori Land Court. The members, four of whom were to be Maori, were appointed by the Governor General.

By the mid-1980s the Waitangi Tribunal had grown the 'teeth' Rata, Latimer, and other Maori leaders had hoped for it. The Lange Labour government significantly increased the powers of the Tribunal when, under the Treaty of Waitangi Amendment Act (1985), it was empowered to hear claims retrospectively to 1840 - from the time of the signing of the Treaty. Although lacking the resources to cope with such a large backlog of claims, it began to address those Maori grievances which had played a central role in protest action in earlier years.

The Tribunal today may examine claims from any Maori individuals or groups who feel themselves or other Maori people 'prejudiced by any Act, policy or practice by or on behalf of the Crown which is inconsistent with the principles of the Treaty of Waitangi' (*New Zealand Official Yearbook 1988-1989*: 211). Large-scale Maori land and natural resource claims have become its primary area of deliberation.

In 1987, the Tribunal reported to government on the Orakei and Ngati Paoa claims. In both cases the re-establishment of the tribes on their ancestral land was recommended. In 1988 extensive claims were brought by the Ngai Tahu concerning land in the South Island, by the Waikato-Tainui people concerning land and coal resources in the central North Island, and by the Muriwhenua incorporation concerning fisheries in the Far North. The potential or actual loss of millions of dollars by government through these claims led to heated parliamentary debate over whether the courts or the government should have the supreme right to decide on treaty issues.

Over the next few years the Tribunal made recommendations on cases concerning Maori land and sea resources so favourable to Maori applicants, and so alarming to Pakeha opinion, that Lange's successor thought it necessary to affirm that the government itself, not courts or tribunals, would continue to determine policy bearing on interpretation of the Treaty. In January 1990 the new Labour Prime Minister, Geoffrey Palmer, announced the formation of a government task force which would negotiate the settlement of Maori claims once the Tribunal had made its recommendations. Some Maori applauded the direct access this would give them to their treaty partner; others were not so confident that land and resource issues would be decided by legal principles under this new arrangement.

During the 1980s concern continued to mount over the plight of the young. Gangs appeared to have an increasing attraction for the unemployed, bored, or socially disenchanted. Gangs provided identity for their members, observed their own code of ethics, provoked fights with rival gangs, and battered each other's headquarters. Public outrage over gang-related incidents provided 'good copy' for the press. Police warned that some gangs, mainly those dominated by Maori and Islander minorities, might become involved in drug trafficking and organised crime. There were fears that gangs may develop links with criminal groups overseas. On the other hand, some gangs were able to divert the attention of their members into government-assisted and private employment schemes, particularly in the demolition and construction business.

To address social problems a range of new programs designed to strengthen Maori family, community, and tribal structures was being developed. First set up in 1981, Kohanga Reo or 'language nest' programs for pre-school children spearheaded a resurgence of interest in Maori language and culture. They sought to provide a forum for the transmission of Maoritanga to the next generation. By 1987 522 Kohanga Reo centres throughout the country were catering for approximately 11,000 children (*New Zealand Official Yearbook 1988-1989*: 223). The government also provided some assistance to Matua Whangai schemes, directed to the care of young Maori people at risk of offending. Kokiri centres, and other marae-based programs designed to promote Maori culture, health, employment, training, and local resource management, were also increasing in strength through local participation and government funding.

In 1987 the Maori Language Act declared Maori an official language of New Zealand, creating a right for Maori to be used in court proceedings, and establishing a Maori Language Commission to assist in its official recognition in other areas of government and social policy. Today Maori continues to be the main language of communication on the marae, in celebration of Maori rites of passage, and in the performance of political and social processes which are essentially Maori. Since the time of this study a more generous allotment of media time for Maori programming has been granted on both radio and television. By 1988 national and regional radio and national television had quadrupled their airtime for Maori news and current affairs, providing daily programs in both the Maori and English language on Maori interests and events.

While one might have expected to see the social upheavals and political ambivalence of the five years leading up to the general election of 1981 having a more perceptible effect, the fact that they did not attests to the conservatism of the New Zealand voting public. The snap election announced on 14 June 1984, however, brought with it a decisive change. The National Party won only 39 seats under the leadership of Robert Muldoon, who was subsequently replaced as party leader by Jim McLay. Under the then popular David Lange, the Labour Party was firmly propelled into power with 56 seats. The fortunes of the Mana Motuhake Party also fluctuated in subsequent elections. Compared to the 1981 general election, when the party received 8,332 votes (15 percent of valid votes in the Maori electorates), in the 1984 election Mana Motuhake secured only 5,704 votes (9 percent).

A change had taken place in the administrative structure of Mana Motuhake. The presidency was divided into two: Rata, who was said to have maintained the 'political leadership' of the party, continued to act as public spokesperson on Mana Motuhake policy and concerns. He also continued to stand for the seat in Northern Maori. The 'administrative leadership' was handed over to its elected president and chairman of the Secretariat, Arapeta Tahana. Thus, to this extent, the determination of the Mana Motuhake executive to see a greater sharing of duties and power within the organisation had occurred. The thrust to 'reinvigorate the branches' of Mana Motuhake through a new administration, however, was undermined by the falling away of some feminist and radical support, including one of the party's generals, Dr Patrick Hohepa.

In August 1987 the Labour Party under David Lange maintained its 15 seat majority (56 seats) over the National Party (41 seats) in the general election. Votes for Mana Motuhake were the highest they had ever been (9,331, 17 percent of valid votes in the Maori electorates). There was a slight swing to National in the Maori seats in the 1987 election, 'but the swing to Mana Motuhake', observed Mackerras (1988: 61), 'was quite substantial (a swing of 8.4 percent)'. This was particularly apparent in Northern Maori. Matiu Rata's popularity in this election had clearly increased. From winning just under 23 percent of the valid vote for the Northern Maori seat in the 1981 election, and dropping to 18 percent in the 1984 election, his position had strengthened in the 1987 election to over 31 percent of the Northern vote. Nevertheless, in 1987 and throughout the 1980s Mana Motuhake was never able to win a seat.

As its leaders forecast in 1981, Mana Motuhake pursued its expansionist strategy by contesting marginal general seats. Mana Motuhake ran candidates in Otara, West Auckland, Whangarei, and Porirua in the 1984 general election, and in Gisborne, Mangere, and Porirua in 1987. These were electorates with a strong Maori base. All but Whangarei were retained by Labour, with the Maori party securing a total of only 285 valid votes in 1984, and 458 in 1987 from the general roll (Tables 2, 3).

In the public arena Mana Motuhake continued to be a force as a pressure group and leading commentator on all issues concerning the Maori people. Over the decade Mana Motuhake had become an established presence in the New

Zealand political setting, and a credible articulator of views more innovative than many Maori organisations might have been comfortable with asserting.

In addition to deriving benefits from the revision of the Town and Country Planning Act and other legislation infringing on Maori land rights, Maori entrepreneurs increasingly moved into new fields of cooperative economic activity. With greater freedom from the demands of the party, Matiu Rata become actively involved in, and was himself partly responsible for, a major economic resurgence in the North from the mid to late 1980s. Under the management of the Muriwhenua Incorporation, involving 64 affiliate owners and trusts, 7,290 hectares of land were being developed for forestry, tourism, produce farming, and fisheries. It was the largest single Maori development of its kind in the Northland.

Rata was able to play a key role in pushing forward the highly controversial Muriwhenua fisheries claim into the political arena and before the Waitangi Tribunal. He continued to act as entrepreneur, adviser, and broker on development projects in the North, occasionally being invited by government or Maori organisations to assist on major inquiries regarding economic issues. Rata's friends and followers frequently remarked upon the 'flowering' of the man following his defection from Labour. In every confrontation he gave his opponents a good run for their money. The more generous spirited found reason to express their admiration: 'my observations of Mat in more recent years', reflected Bill Rowling, 'suggest that he has acquired a skill to articulate the problems and aspirations of the Maori people in a way that he did not seem to enjoy back in the 1970s. All credit to him' (Sir Wallace Rowling to the author, 20 August 1991).

In a personal interview with the author in December 1987 Rata admitted that, because of their prior commitments to major parties, the older generation of voters had not been easy to convert to Mana Motuhake. The party, then seven years old, 'must look to the next generation of voters, the 18-20 year olds who were showing greatest promise'. The party's Youth Committee was strong and had already produced 'some outstanding leaders', he said. With a good election result in 1987 'the stage was set for younger people to come shining through'. Taking a long-term view, he contended, 'we expect to see the effect of this within the next nine years'. For a time Matiu Rata seriously contemplated stepping down as leader. But he was persuaded to again champion the cause in the Northern seat in 1990.

The 1990 election was catastrophic for Labour. In the landslide to the National Party there was a more than 10 percent drop in voting in the Maori seats. Nevertheless, Mana Motuhake increased its total votes to 10,869 in these electorates (Table 3). Mana Motuhake had needed a 14.8 percent swing to win the Northern Maori seat (Mackerras 1991). Rata himself won almost 41 percent (4,833 votes) of the Northern vote. But he was still eclipsed by 956 votes by the popular Northern Labour MP, Bruce Gregory. The Maori party, as a whole, gathered 22 percent of the votes in the Maori seats in the 1990 election. Rata now needed a tantalising 4.6 percent swing to win back his old seat - although in

Western, Eastern, and Southern Maori the gap between Labour and Mana Motuhake remained too wide to be bridged (Table 3).

Within a year Mana Motuhake was confronted with a fundamental strategic choice. The National government's popularity had plummeted once again, and it was riven by dissension. The resignation of two National backbenchers resulted in the formation of a 'Liberal Party' group. These events promoted discussion of a broad coalition of the Democratic Party (formally Social Credit), the independent 'New Labour' group, the newly formed Green Party, and Mana Motuhake. There had been friendly but inconclusive dialogues among these groups as early as May 1989, when Matiu Rata had been the first and only one of Jim Anderton's old colleagues to offer support when he left the Labour Party. At a hui in Auckland in February 1990 Rata and New Labour discussed policies and possible electoral arrangements. But each party fought the 1990 election separately. Under a new law denying free television advertising time to parties contesting fewer than ten seats Mana Motuhake was effectively silenced by the Labour government.

Sensitive to the various ambitions and aspirations which needed to be harmonised, Jim Anderton, the New Labour leader, proposed that all of the four smaller parties should retain their separate identity and structure but run one agreed candidate in each seat on a common policy platform. This arrangement, bringing Mana Motuhake into harness with other parties which shared some of its philosophy and purpose, seemed to Rata the most promising way forward. In June 1992 he wrote of his high hopes: 'Mana Motuhake is now part of the new Alliance - a new political force in New Zealand that may form part of a coalition government at the next election' (Rata to the author, 3 June 1992). In mid-February 1992 'The Alliance', officially formed on 1 December 1991, had come a close second in the Tamaki seat by-election, following Rob Muldoon's retirement from Parliament. Later in the year the Alliance was joined by the break-away Liberal Party. It contested the Labour held seat at Wellington Central by-election on 12 December 1992 but ran a disappointing third.

By the end of 1992 the promise of 'I shall return', made by Matiu Rata on the steps of Parliament House on the day of his resignation more than a decade earlier, had still to be fulfilled. Mana Motuhake had proved its capacity to endure throughout the vicissitudes of this period. In many ways, the project of ensuring that the New Zealand polity becomes a more genuine bicultural partnership had made substantial progress. But Mana Motuhake itself, respected as it was by many, could claim the right to speak directly for only a small minority of Maori. It had made gains at the ballot box without ever breaking through. In its first decade it had discovered the limits to the political expression of ethnicity in a polity more fundamentally united than its critics cared to admit.

Ironically, the most popular politician in the country in 1992 was a rebel National MP, recently expelled from the ministry. Winston Peters, of Maori/Scottish extraction himself, seemed to transcend a politics based on ethnic sentiment by advocating a 'restrained, responsible capitalism'.

APPENDICES

APPENDIX I

The Treaty of Waitangi Petition drafted by Dr Ranginui Walker for Mana Motuhake at the Waitangi Policy Hui, 29 March 1981 (first signed by Tawai Kawiti).

THE TREATY OF WAITANGI PETITION

Your Majesty Queen Elizabeth II, Queen of New Zealand and your other Realms and Territories, Head of the Commonwealth and Defender of the Faith.

We your Maori people whose ancestors signed the Treaty of Waitangi in 1840 as a sacred compact with your illustrious forebear Queen Victoria, look to the Treaty as the charter safeguarding our rights to the undisturbed possession and use of our lands, forests, fisheries, and all our cultural treasures.

That charter was betrayed by the Land Wars of the 1860's and our rights as British citizens denied by the predatory confiscation of millions of acres of land under the provisions of the New Zealand Settlements Act 1863. Subsequent laws passed to the advantage of colonial settlers broke the will of our people and separated them from their lands. This loss of our mana whenua debased us as a people. These laws prevent us even today from building houses freely on our remaining ancestral lands. Accordingly, we seek your Majesty's favour in the following matters:

1. We humbly request your Majesty to remind the Crown to live up to its obligations and honour the Treaty of Waitangi by its ratification.

2. We seek your Majesty's favour in the exercise of your Royal prerogative to grant a full pardon to our chiefly ancestors who fought to defend their homes, lands and families from colonial despoliation.

3. Finally, as a measure to restore faith and the confidence of our people in the future destiny of our bicultural nation, and to ensure that the foregoing matters are attended to, we seek your Majesty's favourable consideration for the appointment of a person of Maori ancestry to be your personal representative as the next Governor-General of New Zealand.

SIGNED:-

NAME	ADDRESS	TRIBE

Dr Ranginui Walker's notes on the circumstances surrounding the creation of the Treaty of Waitangi Petition for Mana Motuhake, 2 April 1981.

This document was prepared on Sunday 29.3.81 at the Waitangi meeting of Mana Motuhake. I met with Matiu Rata after breakfast in the dining hall, where he gave me a copy of his letter to the Prime Minister, Mr Muldoon, setting out the three main points he wanted submitted in an audience with Her Majesty Queen Elizabeth II. After receiving Rata's instructions I went across Te Tiriti O Waitangi Marae, intending to go to the hotel to search for a quiet place to prepare the petition.

As I crossed the marae an intuitive force drew me across the bridge and up the hill to the Treaty House. I paused for a short while in a wooded gully by a small stream to settle my spirit and seek inspiration from the Wao tu nui a Tane. I then proceeded to the Treaty House and settled on a park bench under a pohutukawa tree on the right side of the house facing the harbour. It was a bright sunny morning filled with bird song and made even more beautiful by the sparkling waters of the harbour.

After a while I began to write this document, the first draft of the petition. I then wrote the fair copy for presentation to the meeting. The task was completed in one and a half hours. As I returned down the hill towards the bridge another intuitive insight came to me. Instead of rejoining the meeting on the marae, I walked past the paepae almost in a state of automatism, and entered Te Tiriti O Waitangi Meeting House. I at first thought to place the document in the middle of the floor under the ridgepole, but instead I was drawn to the pakitara (back wall) where I placed the document to be sanctified and made tapu. It was only afterwards that I learned the centre of the back wall is where the Ngaa Puhi place their dead for a tangihanga. After a while I recovered the petition and delivered it to the meeting where it was read by Mr Rata and signed by Kawiti.

Prior to Rata reading the petition I explained to the meeting the circumstances surrounding its preparation. In Maori spiritual beliefs, the dining hall (kauta) is noa (common) - that is where the initial discussion on what to enter on the petition was held. The Treaty ground where the original Treaty was signed was the appropriate place for the preparation and writing of the petition about the Treaty and the redress of Maori grievances. Placing it in the meeting house to make it tapu completed the process. So the petition began its realisation in the realm of the profane and was transformed into the realm of the sacred.

Ranginui Walker
2 April 1981

GLOSSARY

Aotearoa 'the land of the long white cloud', Maori name for the land now encompassed by the New Zealand nation-state, originally attributed to the sightings of land at the time of the first migrations.

ariki paramount chief, first-born in the noble families.

aroha affection, love, pity, sympathy. The embracing of the individual by a community.

haka Maori action song. A postured war dance, symbolising the strength of the tribe.

hakari a celebratory feast.

hangi earth oven, used to cook for large gatherings.

hapu pregnant, clan or section of the tribe, sub-tribe, the extended family which traces its blood ties to a common ancestor. The most active co-operative unit in defence and economic production in traditional times.

hoko whenua land-sellers (pupuri whenua - non land-sellers).

hongi to smell, pressed noses in greeting, a ritual of official greeting onto a marae between hosts and visitors, still used as a common greeting between older Maoris.

hui a gathering, social occasion, meeting for discussion and social exchange, usually held on a marae.

iwi bone, nation. A Maori tribe consisting of several hapu villages, which recognise a common founding ancestor and territory and which unite in order to defend common tribal interests.

kai to eat, food.

karanga to call, hail, welcome. Women's call of welcome to visitors upon the marae.

kaumatua adult male or female elder.

kaupapa the main issue or idea being presented. Fleet of canoes, level surface, platform, stage.

kawa custom of the area or tribe, tribal lore, etiquette.

Kingitanga A land-sales resistance movement initially established in the nineteenth century, unifying several Waikato tribes under a powerful paramount chief - the Maori king.

koha respect, gift, donation, parting message.

kokiri throw, thrust. Today Kokiri Units are working groups for community development.

komiti committee. A modern adoption of the European word 'committee'.

korero conversation, news, talk, speak.

Kotahitanga Unity movement, initially established in the nineteenth century for the purpose of promoting large inter-tribal gatherings to discuss means of redressing the imbalance of power and resources between Maori and Pakeha.

makutu bewitch, magic, spell, curse, witchcraft, sorcery. Fears of the powers of makutu are still common.

mana secular and supernatural power, status, authority, standing, influence, prestige.

mana motuhake 'power cut away', permanent power, self-reliance, self-determination.

mangai 'the mouthpiece of God'.

manuhiri guests, visitors, strangers.

Maoritanga 'the Maori way', Maoriness, Maori culture, first used in the early 20th century to signify pride in being Maori.

marae enclosed grounds used as a meeting place, including meeting hall and other buildings within the grounds. Place of community debate and speeches. A meeting place for both secular and sacred activity.

mauri inner being, life force, talisman.

mihimihi (mihi) to acknowledge, greet, lament, admire, formal speech of welcome or farewell by an elder (particularly onto a marae), or in reply to a welcome or farewell. Ritual of encounter.

mokopuna descendant, grandchild, great niece, great nephew of either gender.

mokopuna (tane) grandson, great nephew.

mokopuna (wahine) granddaughter, great niece.

noa profane, common, free from tapu, safe (as opposed to sacred or tapu).

pa village, fortified village, stockade. A village located upon a hilltop in a strategic fighting position.

paepae bar or beam. Upright beam at the entrance of the meeting house.

Pakeha a Maori name for a person of European extraction, a European New Zealander. Sometimes loosely used to refer to all non-Maori residents in New Zealand.

papakainga marae zone. The land immediately surrounding a marae for which a marae committee, or Maori committee is responsible. Home ground. A place where one comes from or belongs.

patere 'flow freely', traditional chant.

poroporoaki farewell to the dead, ritual chant or speech.

pupuri whenua non land-sellers (hoko whenua - land-sellers).

rangatira chief, noble, high birth, senior line, aristocratic class, chieftainship, leadership.

rangatiratanga Chieftainship, sovereignty. Leadership selection on the basis of social rank and nobility.

Ratana Church Founded in 1918 by Wiremu Tahupotiki Ratana along Wesleyan lines, the church and later movement, sought to incorporate Maori culture into Christian worship, improve the lot of the poor and humble, fulfil the promises of the Treaty of Waitangi, and run Ratana candidates for the four Maori seats.

runanga assembly, group of learned people, discussion group, school of learning. A local council, administering land and whenua government of the area. A Maori land council.

take cause, origin, reason, subject of discussion.

Tane God of Nature and of trees.

tangata (whenua) 'people of the land'. Commonly recognised association of people with a rural homeland or tribal region, bringing with it specific rights and obligations of 'belonging' in both political and social terms. It is also contrasted with 'strangers'. Hosts at a welcoming ceremony. This term can also be broadly used to refer to the indigenous population in relation to more recent immigrant populations.

tangi to weep, wail, lament.

tangihanga funeral wake, frequently shortened to 'tangi'.

tapu sacred, spiritually potent or dangerous (sometimes 'unclean'), prohibited from defilement, under religious restriction. To be set apart from that which is noa or common.

teina junior, younger sibling of same sex, cousin of same sex and generation, in a junior line.

tipuna grandparent, ancestor, great uncle, great aunt.

tohunga traditional priest, healer, artist, an expert in a particular field.

tokotoko walking staff, talking stick, carried by elders particularly during public speeches.

tutua (ware) commoner, person of a low birth, of the junior lines, careless, ignorant, thoughtless.

utu price, return, payment, revenge, reward.

wahine female, woman, wife, girl.

waiata song, chant expressing a particular sentiment, a lament.

waka 'the ancestral canoe', descendants from the pioneers who, according to tradition, arrived in Aotearoa in a fleet of seven canoes in about the fourteenth century. A federation of tribes believed to have descended from ancestors from a common canoe in the first migrations.

wananga small gathering for discussion, knowledge, learning.

whaikorero formal speeches in reply by visitors during a marae greeting.

whakahihi too high, proud, vain.

whakaiti humble. Whakahihi and whakaiti are dual concepts of drive and virtue, which clash in the leadership personality. Too much drive can be criticised as a show of insufficient humility. Too much humility can be seen as having insufficient drive or authority.

whakama shame, shyness, psychological withdrawal, bewilderment, grief and sense of inadequacy.

whakapapa genealogy, ancestry frequently recited upon a marae to demonstrate one's esteemed lineage and status in the community. Knowing one's hapu, iwi and waka are essential aspects of knowing one's whakapapa.

whanau 'to give birth', the biological or extended family, also used loosely to refer to one's community - one's 'Maori family'.

whanaunga kinsmen.

whanaungatanga kinship.

whare a single roomed hut, house.

whare wananga 'house of learning', traditional school of higher learning in the arts, politics and religion.

wharenui large meeting house.

whenua land, country, ground.

Young Maori Party An outstanding group of Maori leaders who, for three decades from the turn of the twentieth century, combined European education with Maori knowledge and mixed race ethnicity to effect major change for Maori people at political and governmental levels. The high level conciliatory form of brokerage which they pioneered typifies the 'conservative' Maori leadership style.

BIBLIOGRAPHY

BOOKS, MONOGRAPHS

Alley, Roderic. (ed.) 1984. *New Zealand and the Pacific*. Boulder: Westview Press.

Ash, R. 1972. *Social movements in America*. Chicago: Markham Yves-Marie Berce.

Awatere, Donna. 1984. *Maori sovereignty*. Auckland: Broadsheet Magazine.

Bailey, F.G. 1977. *Stratagems and spoils: A social anthropology of politics*. Oxford: Basil Blackwell (1st ed. 1969).

Baker, Donald G. 1983. *Race, ethnicity and power: A comparative study*. London: Routledge and Kegan Paul.

Ballara, Angela. 1986. *Proud to be white?: A survey of Pakeha prejudice in New Zealand*. Auckland: Heinemann.

Banton, Michael. 1957. *West African city*. London: Oxford University Press for the International African Institute.

Banton, Michael. (ed.) 1966. *The social anthropology of complex societies*. London: Tavistock Publications (1st ed. 1954).

Barth, Fredrick. 1966. *Models of social organisation*. Royal Anthropological Institute of Great Britain and Ireland, Occasional Papers, No. 23, Glasgow: Robert MacLehose/ The University Press.

Barth, Fredrick. (ed.) 1969. *Ethnic groups and boundaries: The social organization of culture difference*. Boston: Little, Brown.

Bedggood, David. 1980. *Rich and poor in New Zealand: A critique of class, politics and ideology*. Auckland: George Allen and Unwin.

Belich, James. 1986. *The New Zealand wars and the Victorian interpretation of racial conflict*. Auckland: Oxford University Press/ Auckland University Press.

Best, E. 1924. *The Maori*, Vol. 1 and Vol. 2. Wellington: Board of Maori Ethnological Research.

Binney, J., Chaplin, G. and Wallace G. 1979. *Mihaia: The prophet Rua Kenana and his community at Maungapohatu*. Wellington: Oxford University Press.

Blau, Peter M. 1964. *Exchange and power in social life*. New York: John Wiley and Son.

Blondel, Jean. 1987. *Political leadership: Towards a general analysis*. London: Sage.

Boissevain, J.F. 1974. *Friends of friends: Networks, manipulators and coalitions*. Oxford: Basil Blackwell.

Boissevain, J.F. and Mitchell, J. Clyde. (eds.) 1973. *Network analysis: Studies in human interaction*. The Hague: Mouton.

Bott, E. 1957. *Family and social network*. London: Tavistock.

Bottomley, Gill. 1979. *After the odyssey: A study of Greek Australians*. St. Lucia: University of Queensland Press.

Brookes, R.H. and Kawharu, I.H. (eds.) 1967. *Administration in New Zealand's multi-racial society*. Oxford: Oxford University Press, Wellington: New Zealand Institute of Public Administration.

Buck, Peter. 1977. *The coming of the Maori*. Wellington: Maori Purposes Fund Board (1st ed. 1949).

Buddle, T.L. 1979. *The Maori King Movement in New Zealand: With a full report of the Native meetings held at Waikato*. Auckland: The New Zealander Office (1st ed. 1860).

Buick, T.L. 1976. *The Treaty of Waitangi*. Christchurch: Capper Press (1st ed. 1914).

Buick, T.L. 1934. *Waitangi ninety-four years after*. New Plymouth: Thomas Avery and Sons.

Bush, G.W.A. 1980. *Local government and politics in New Zealand*. Auckland: Allen and Unwin.

Butterworth, G.V. 1974. *The Maori people in the New Zealand economy*. Palmerston North: Department of Anthropology and Maori Studies, Massey University.

Caselberg, J. (ed.) 1975. *Maori is my name: Historical Maori writings in translation*. Dublin: John McIndoe.

Castile, George Pierre and Kushner, Gilbert. (eds.) 1981. *Persistent peoples: Cultural enclaves in perspective*. Tucson, Ariz.: University of Arizona Press.

Chapman, R.M. (ed.) 1975. *Ends and means in New Zealand politics*. Auckland: Auckland University Press (lst ed. 1961).

Chapman, R.M., Jackson, W.K. and Mitchell, A.V. 1962. *New Zealand politics in action: The general election*. London: Oxford University Press.

Chapple, Geoff. 1984. *1981: The tour*. Wellington: A.H and A.W Reed.

Cleave, Peter. 1989. *The sovereignty game: Power, knowledge and reading the Treaty*. Wellington: Institute of Policy Studies for Victoria University Press.

Cohen, Abner. 1969. *Custom and politics in urban Africa: A study of Hausa migrants in Yoruba towns*. London: Routledge and Kegan Paul.

Cohen, Abner. 1974a. *Two-dimensional man: An essay on the anthropology of power and symbolism in complex society*. London: Routledge and Kegan Paul.

Cohen, Abner. (ed.) 1974b. *Urban ethnicity*. London: Tavistock.

de Vos, George and Romanucci-Ross, Lola. (eds.) 1975. *Ethnic identity: Cultural continuities and change*. Palo Alto: Mayfield.

Easton, B. 1980. *Social policy and the welfare state in New Zealand*. Auckland: George Allen and Unwin.

Easton, D. 1965a. *A framework for political analysis*. Englewood Cliffs, N.J.: Prentice-Hall.

Easton, D. 1965b. *A systems analysis of political life*. New York: Wiley.

Firth, Raymond. 1951. *Elements of social organisation*. New York: Philosophical Library.

Firth, Raymond. 1959. *Economics of the New Zealand Maori*. Wellington: Government Printer (1st ed. 1929).

Fitzgerald, Thomas K. 1977. *Education and identity: A study of the New Zealand Maori graduate*. Wellington: New Zealand Council for Educational Research.

Forster, J. (ed.) 1969. *Social process in New Zealand: Readings in sociology*. Auckland: Longman Paul.

Franklin, S. Harvey. 1978. *Trade, growth and anxiety: New Zealand beyond the welfare state*. Wellington: Methuen.

Garnier, Tony and Levine, Stephen. 1981. *Election '81: An end to Muldoonism?* Auckland: Methuen.

Geertz, Clifford. 1973. *The interpretation of cultures: Selected essays*. New York: Basic Books.

Gluckman, M. 1958. *Analysis of a social situation in modern Zululand*. Manchester: Rhodes Livingstone Institute.

Gluckman, M. 1970. *Custom and conflict in Africa*. Oxford: Oxford University Press (1st ed. 1955).

Gold, H. (ed.) 1985. *New Zealand politics in perspective*. Auckland: Longman Paul.

Gorst, John. 1959. *The Maori King*. Hamilton: Paul's Book Arcade (1st ed. 1864).

Gould, John. 1982. *The Rake's progress: The New Zealand economy since 1945*. Auckland: Hodder and Stoughton.

Green, R.C. 1977. *Adaptation and change in Maori culture*. New Zealand: Stockton House (1st ed. 1975).

Gustafson, Barry. 1976. *Social change and party organisation: The New Zealand Labour Party since 1945*. London: Sage Publications.

Hancock, K. 1946. *New Zealand at war*. Wellington: A.H. and A.W. Reed.

Hanson, F.A. and Hanson, L. 1983. *Counterpoint in Maori culture*. London: Routledge and Kegan Paul.

Harmel, Robert. (ed.) 1985. *International political science review*. Special issue on 'New Political Parties', **6:4**, London: Sage Publications.

Harre, J. 1966. *Maori and Pakeha: A study of mixed marriages in New Zealand*. Wellington: A.H. and A.W. Reed.

Hayward, M. 1981. *Diary of the Kirk years*. Wellington/ Queen Charlotte Sound: A.H. and A.W. Reed Ltd/ Cape Catley.

Hazlehurst, Kayleen M. 1988b. *Racial conflict and resolution in New Zealand: The Haka Party incident and its aftermath 1979-1980*. Canberra: Peace Research Centre, Research School of Pacific Studies, Australian National University.

Heberle, R. 1951. *Social movements: An introduction to political sociology*. New York: Appleton-Century-Crofts.

Henderson, J.M. 1972. *Ratana: The man, the church and political movement*. Wellington: A.H. and A.W. Reed in association with the Polynesian Society (1st ed. 1963).

Hohepa, P.W. 1970. *A Maori community in Northland*. Wellington: A.H. and A.W. Reed (1st ed. 1964).

Horowitz, D.L. 1985. *Ethnic groups in conflict*. Los Angeles: University of California Press.

Jackson, Keith. 1973. *New Zealand politics of change*. Wellington: A.H. and A.W. Reed.

James, Colin. 1986. *The quiet revolution: Turbulence and transition in contemporary New Zealand*. Wellington: Allen and Unwin/ Port Nicholson Press.

Johnston, R.J. (ed.) 1977. *People, places and votes: Essays on the electoral geography of Australia and New Zealand*. Armidale: Department of Geography, New England University.

Kawharu, I.H. (ed.) 1975a. *Conflict and compromise*. Wellington: A.H. and A.W. Reed.

Kawharu, I.H. 1977. *Maori land tenure: Studies in a changing institution*. Oxford: Oxford University Press.

Kawharu, I.H. (ed.) 1989. *Waitangi: Maori and Pakeha perspectives of the Treaty of Waitangi*. Auckland: Oxford University Press.

Keyes, Charles F. (ed.) 1981. *Ethnic change*. Seattle: University of Washington Press.

King, M. 1977a. *Te Puea: A biography*. Auckland: Hodder and Stoughton.

King, M. (ed.) 1977b. *Te Ao Hurihuri the world moves on: Aspects of Maoritanga*. New Zealand: Hicks Smith, Methuen (1st ed. 1975).

King, M. (ed.) 1978. *Tihe Mauri Ora: Aspects of Maoritanga*. New Zealand: Methuen.

King, M. 1983. *Whina: A biography of Whina Cooper*. Auckland: Hodder and Stoughton.

King, M. 1986. *Being Pakeha: An encounter with New Zealand and the Maori renaissance*. Auckland: Hodder and Stoughton (1st ed. 1985).

Koopman-Boyden, Peggy G. and Scott, Claudia D. 1984. *The family and government policy in New Zealand*. Sydney: George Allen and Unwin.

Lane, Peter A. and Hamer, Paul. (eds.) 1973. *Decade of change: Economic growth and prospects in New Zealand 1960-1970*. Wellington: Reed Education.

Laumann, E.O. and Pappi, F.U. 1976. *Networks of collective action*. New York: Academic Press.

Leinhardt, Samuel. (ed.) 1977. *Social networks: A developing paradigm*. New York: Academic Press.

Levine, Stephen. (ed.) 1975. *New Zealand politics: A reader*. Melbourne: Cheshire.

Levine, Stephen. 1979. *The New Zealand political system*. Sydney: George Allen and Unwin.

Levine, Stephen. (ed.) 1978. *Politics in New Zealand: A reader*. Sydney: George Allen and Unwin.

Levine, Stephen and Vasil, Raj. 1985. *Maori political perspectives: He Whakaaro Maori Mo Nga Ti Kanga Kawanatanga*. Auckland: Hutchinson.

Levine, Stephen and Robinson, Alan. 1976. *The New Zealand voter: A survey of public opinion and electoral behaviour*. Wellington: Price Milburn for New Zealand University Press.

Manuel, G. and Posluns, M. 1974. *The fourth world: An Indian reality*. Canada: Collier Macmillan.

Mauss, M. 1974. *The gift: Forms and functions of exchange in archaic societies*. London: Routledge and Kegan Paul (1st ed. 1961).

Mayer, Philip and Mayer, Iona. 1974. *Townsmen or tribesmen: Conservatism and the process of urbanisation in a South African city*. Cape Town: Oxford University Press (1st ed. 1961).

McKenzie, D.F. 1985. *Oral culture, literacy and print in early New Zealand: The Treaty of Waitangi*. Wellington: Victoria University Press/Alexander Turnbull Library Endowment Trust.

McKinlay, Peter. (ed.) 1990. *Redistribution of power? Devolution in New Zealand*. Wellington: Victoria University Press for the Institute of Policy Studies.

McRobie, Alan. 1989. *New Zealand Electoral Atlas*. Wellington: GP Books.

Metge, Joan. 1964. *A new Maori migration: Rural and urban relations in northern New Zealand*. London/ Melbourne: London School of Economics, Monographs on Social Anthropology No. 27, The Athlone Press/ Melbourne University Press.

Metge, Joan. 1976. *The Maoris of New Zealand: Rautahi*. London: Routledge and Kegan Paul (1st ed. 1967).

Metge, Joan. 1986. *In and out of touch: Whakamaa in cross-cultural context*. Wellington: Victoria University Press.

Metge, Joan and Kinloch, Patricia. 1987. *Talking past each other: Problems of cross-cultural communication*. Wellington: Victoria University Press (1st ed. 1978).

Miller, J. 1973. *Early Victorian New Zealand: A study of racial tension and social attitudes 1839-1852*. Wellington: Oxford University Press (1st ed. 1958).

Mitcalfe, B. 1972. *Maori and Pakeha, 1900 until today*. Wellington: Price Milburn.

Mitcalfe, B. 1981. *Maori: The origin, art and culture of the Maori people of New Zealand*. Coromandel, New Zealand: Coromandel Press.

Mitchell, J. Clyde. (ed.) 1969. *Social networks in urban situations: Analyses of personal relationships in Central African towns*. Manchester: Manchester University Press.

Mitchell, J. Clyde. 1971. *The Kalela Dance*. The Rhodes-Livingstone papers No. 27. Manchester: Manchester University Press (1st ed. 1956).

Mitchell, J. Clyde. 1979. *Perspectives on social network research*. Center for Advanced Study in the Behavioral Sciences. New York: Academic Press.

Mitchell, J. Clyde. 1987. *Cities, society, and social perception: a Central African perspective*. Oxford: Clarendon Press.

Nash, Manning. 1989. *The cauldron of ethnicity in the modern world*. Chicago/ London: University of Chicago Press.

Oberschall, A. 1973. *Social conflict and social movements*. Englewood Cliffs, N.J.: Prentice-Hall.

Oliver, W.H. 1960. *The Story of New Zealand*. London: Faber and Faber.

Oliver, W.H. and Williams, B.R. (eds.) 1981. *The Oxford history of New Zealand*. Wellington: Oxford University Press.

Orange, Claudia. 1987. *The Treaty of Waitangi*. Wellington: Allen and Unwin.

Oxley, H.G. 1973. *Mateship in local organisation*. St. Lucia: University of Queensland Press.

Pearce, G.L. 1980. *The story of the Maori people*. Auckland: Collins (1st ed. 1968).

Pearson, David G. and Thorns, David C. 1983. *Eclipse of equality: Social stratification in New Zealand*. Sydney: George Allen and Unwin.

Penniman, H.R. (ed.) 1980. *New Zealand at the polls: The general election in 1978*. Washington, D.C.: American Enterprise Institute for Public Policy Research.

Phillips, Jock. 1987. *A man's country? The image of the Pakeha male - a history*. Auckland: Penguin Books.

Pitt, D. (ed.) 1977. *Social class in New Zealand*. Auckland: Longman Paul.

Pocock, J.G.A. (ed.) 1965. *The Maori and New Zealand politics*. Auckland: Blackwood and Janet Paul (1st ed. 1962).

Pomare, Eru W. 1980. *Maori standards of health: A study of the 20 year period 1955-1975*. Medical Research Council of New Zealand special report series, 7, December.

Pool, D. Ian. 1977. *The Maori population of New Zealand 1769-1971*. Auckland: Auckland University Press/ Oxford University Press.

Radcliffe-Brown, Alfred R. 1968. *Structure and function in primitive society: Essays and addresses*. London: Cohen and West (1st ed. 1952).

Rejai, Mostofa and Phillips, Kay. 1983. *World revolutionary leaders*. New Brunswick, N.J.: Rutgers University Press.

Ritchie, James E. (ed.) 1964. *Race relations: Six New Zealand studies*. Wellington: Victoria University of Wellington.

Rothschild, Joseph. 1981. *Ethnopolitics: A conceptual framework*. New York: Columbia University Press.

Sahlins, M.D. 1974. *Stone age economics*. Chicago: Aldine (1st ed. 1972).

Salmond, Ann. 1980. *Eruera: The teachings of a Maori elder*. Wellington: Oxford University Press.

Salmond, Ann. 1985. *Hui: A study of Maori ceremonial gatherings*. Wellington: A.H. and A.W. Reed (1st ed. 1975).

Schwimmer, E.G. (ed.) 1975. *The Maori people in the nineteen-sixties: A symposium*. Auckland: Longman Paul (1st ed. 1968).

Schwimmer, E.G. 1977. *The world of the Maori*. Wellington: A.H. and A.W. Reed (1st ed. 1966).

Simmons, D.R. 1979. *The great New Zealand myth*. Wellington: A.H. and A.W. Reed.

Simpson, T. 1979. *Riri Pakeha: The white man's anger*. Waiura, Martinborough: Alister Taylor.

Sinclair, Keith. 1980. *A history of New Zealand*. Harmondsworth: Penguin Books (1st ed. 1959).

Sinclair, Keith. 1986. *A destiny apart: New Zealand's search for national identity*. Wellington: Allen and Unwin in association with Port Nicholson Press.

Smith, N. 1962. *Maori land corporations*. Wellington: A.H. and A.W. Reed.

Spicer, Edward. H. 1980. *The Yaquis: A cultural history*. Tucson, Ariz.: University of Arizona Press.

Spoonley, Paul. 1987. *The politics of nostalgia: Racism and the extreme right in New Zealand*. Palmerston North: Dunmore Press.

Spoonley, P. 1988. *Racism and ethnicity. Critical issues in New Zealand society series*. Auckland: Oxford University Press.

Spoonley, P., Macpherson, C., Pearson, D. and Sedgwick, C. (eds.) 1984. *Tauiwi. Racism and ethnicity in New Zealand*. Palmerston North: Dunmore Press.

Stokes, Evelyn. (ed.) 1981. *Maori representation in parliament*. Occasional paper No. 14. Hamilton: Centre for Maori Studies and Research, University of Waikato.

Sutherland, I.L.G. (ed.) 1940. *The Maori people today*. Auckland: Whitcombe and Tombs.

Tilly, Charles. 1978. *From mobilization to revolution*. Reading, Mass.: Addison-Wesley Publishing Company.

Trlin, A.D. (ed.) 1977. *Social welfare and New Zealand society*. Wellington: Methuen.

Turner, Victor. 1974. *Dramas, fields, and metaphors: Symbolic action in human society*. Ithaca: N.Y. Cornell University Press.

Vasil, Raj. 1988. *Biculturalism: reconciling Aotearoa with New Zealand*. Wellington: Victoria University Press for Institute of Policy Studies.

Vaughan, Graham. (ed.) 1972. *Racial issues in New Zealand*. Auckland: Akarana Press.

Walker, Ranginui. 1987. *Nga Tau Tohetohe: Years of anger*. Auckland: Penguin Books.

Walker, Ranginui. 1990. *Ka Whawhai Tonu Matou: Struggle without end*. Auckland: Penguin Books (NZ) Ltd.

Ward, Alan. 1978. *A show of justice*. Toronto: University of Toronto Press (1st ed. 1974).

Webb, S.D. and Collette, J. (eds.) 1973. *New Zealand society: Contemporary perspectives*. Sydney: John Wiley and Sons Australasia.

Webster, P. 1979. *Rua and the Maori millennium*. Wellington: Price Milburn, Victoria University Press.

Wellman, B and Berkowitz, S.D. 1990. *Social Structures: A Network Approach*. Cambridge/New York: Cambridge University Press.

Wild, R.A. Bradstow. 1974. *A study of status, class and power in a small Australian Town*. Sydney: Angus and Robertson.

Wilkinson, Paul. 1971. *Social movement. Key concepts in political science* series. London: Pall Mall.

Williams, J.A. 1977. *Politics of the New Zealand Maori: Protest and co-operation, 1891-1909*. Auckland: Auckland University Press (1st ed. 1969).

Winiata, Maharaia. 1967. *The changing role of the leader in Maori society: A study in social change and race relations*. Merran Fraenkel (ed.) Auckland: Blackwood and Janet Paul.

Wright, H.M. 1967. *New Zealand, 1769-1840: Early years of western contact*. Cambridge, Mass.: Harvard University Press.

ARTICLES, CHAPTERS, PAPERS, LECTURES

Archer, Dane and Archer, Mary. 1973. Race, identity and the Maori People. S.D. Webb and J. Collette. (eds.) *New Zealand society: Contemporary perspectives*. Sydney: John Wiley and Sons Australasia.

Armstrong, Warwick. 1978. New Zealand: Imperialism, class and uneven development. *Australia and New Zealand Journal of Sociology*. **14**:3 (part two), October, 297-303.

Awatere, Donna. 1982. On Maori sovereignty. *Broadsheet 100*. Auckland: June.

Bailey, F.G. 1968. Parapolitical systems. M. Swartz. (ed.) *Local level politics*. Chicago: Aldine.

Ballara, A. 1982. The pursuit of Mana? A re-evaluation of the process of land alienation by Maoris, 1840-1890. *The Journal of the Polynesian Society.* **91**:4, 519-41.

Barnes, J.A. 1969. Networks and political process. J. Clyde. Mitchell. (ed.) *Social networks in urban situations: Analyses of personal relationships in Central African towns.* Manchester: Manchester University Press.

Barnes, J.A. 1977. Class and committees in a Norwegian Island parish. S. Leinhardt. (ed.) *Social networks: A developing paradigm.* New York: Academic Press, 233-53 (also *Human Relations* 1954, **7**, 39-58).

Bean, C.S. 1980. Political leaders and voter perceptions: Images of Muldoon and Rowling at the 1975 and 1978 New Zealand general elections. *Political Science.* **32**:1, July, 55-75.

Bean, C.S. 1982. From confusion to confusion: The 1981 New Zealand general election. Paper presented at *Work-in-Progress Seminar.* Canberra: Dept. of Political Science, Research School of Social Sciences, Australian National University.

Bean, C.S. 1988. Class and party in the Anglo-American democracies: The case of New Zealand in perspective. *British Journal of Political Science.* **18**, July, 303-21.

Bentley, G. Carter. 1983. Theoretical perspectives on ethnicity and nationality. Parts 1 and 2. *Sage Race Relations Abstracts.* **8**:2, May, 1-55; **8**:3, August, 1-26.

Bentley, G. Carter. 1987. Ethnicity and practice. *Comparative Studies in Society and History.* **29**:1, 24-55.

Bentley, G. Carter. 1991. Response to Yelvington. *Comparative Studies in Society and History.* **33**:1, January, 169-75.

Benton, Richard A. 1979. Who speaks Maori in New Zealand? Paper presented at *The symposium on New Zealand's language future,* 49th ANZAAS Congress. Wellington: New Zealand Council for Educational Research.

Berkowitz, S.D. 1980. Structural and non-structural models of elites: A critique. *Canadian Journal of Sociology.* **5**, 13-30.

Binney, Judith. 1986. Review of D.F. McKenzie. Oral culture, literacy and print in early New Zealand: The Treaty of Waitangi. Wellington: *Political Science.* **38**:2, December, 185-6.

Black, Tony. 1981a. The committee on gangs. *The New Zealand Law Journal.* 8, May, 238-9.

Black, Tony. 1981b. Protest - what protest. *The New Zealand Law Journal.* 12, September, 381-3.

Blank, Arapera. 1980. The role and status of Maori women. P. Bunkle and B. Hughes. (eds.) *Women in New Zealand society.* Auckland: George Allen and Unwin, 34-51.

Boissevain, J. 1979. Network analysis: A reappraisal. *Current Anthropology.* **20**:2, 392-4.

Boldt, Menno. 1981. Philosophy, politics and extralegal action: Native Indian leaders in Canada. *Ethnic and Racial Studies.* **4**:2, April, 205-21.

Boston, Jonathan. 1980. By-elections in New Zealand: An overview. *Political Science.* **32**:2, December, 103-27.

Boswell, D.M. 1969. Personal crisis and the mobilisation of the social network. J. Clyde. Mitchell. (ed.) *Social networks in urban situations: Analyses of personal relationships in Central African* towns. Manchester: Manchester University Press.

Bott, E. 1977. Urban families: Conjugal roles and social networks. S. Leinhardt. (ed.) *Social networks: A developing paradigm.* New York: Academic Press, 253-92 (also *Human Relations* 1955, **8**:4, 345-83).

Bowden, R. 1979. Tapu and mana: Ritual authority and political power in traditional Maori society. *The Journal of Pacific History.* **14**:1, 50-61.

Brosnan, Peter. 1984. Age, education and Maori-Pakeha income differences. *New Zealand Economic Papers.* **18**, 49-61.

Burgess, M. Elaine. 1978. The resurgence of ethnicity: Myth or reality. *Ethnic and Racial Studies.* **1**:3, 265-85.

Butterworth, G.V. 1972. A rural Maori renaissance? Maori society and politics 1920 to 1951. *The Journal of Polynesian Society.* **81**:2, June, 160-95.

Capshew, James H. 1986. Networks of leadership: A quantitative study of SPSSI presidents 1936-1986. *Journal of Social Issues.* **42**:1, 75-106.

Carmichael, Gordon A. 1979. The labour force. R.J. Warwick Neville and C. James O'Neill. (eds.) *The population of New Zealand: Interdisciplinary perspectives.* Auckland: Longman Paul, 213-58.

Carroll, W.K., Fox, J. and Ornstein, M.D. 1977. The networks of directorate interlocks among the largest Canadian firms. Canada: Institute of Behavioural Research, York University.

Chapman, Robert. 1986. Voting in the Maori political sub-system, 1935-1984. *Report of the Royal Commission on the electoral system: 'Towards a better democracy'.* Wellington: New Zealand Government Printer.

Chrisman, N.J. 1970. Situation and social network in cities. *The Canadian Review of Sociology and Anthropology.* **7**:4, 245-57.

Cleveland, Les 1978. Images of national identity in the New Zealand mass media. *Australia and New Zealand Journal of Sociology.* **14**:3 (part two), October, 304-8.

Coleman, James., Katz, Elihu and Menzel, Herbert 1977. The diffusion of an innovation among physicians. S. Leinhardt. (ed.) *Social Networks: A developing paradigm.* New York: Academic Press.

Collette, J. and O'Malley, P. 1974. Urban migration and selective acculturation: The case of the Maori. *Human Organization.* **33**:2, 147-54.

Craven, P. and Wellman, B. 1973. The network city. Research paper No. 59. Toronto, Canada: Centre for Urban and Community Studies, Department of Sociology.

Cross, Malcolm. 1978. Colonialism and ethnicity: A theory and comparative case study. *Ethnic and Racial Studies.* **1**:1, 35-59.

Dansey, Harry. 1977. A view of death. M. King. (ed.) *Te Ao Hurihui: The world moves on.* New Zealand: Hicks Smith/Methuen (lst ed. 1975).

Davis, King. E. 1982. The status of black leadership: implications for black followers in the 1980's. *Journal of the Applied Behavioural Sciences.* **18**:3, 309-22.

de Bres, Pieter H. 1985. The Maori contribution: Maori religious movements in Aotearoa. Brian Colless and Peter Donovan. (eds.), *Religion in New Zealand Society.* Palmerston North: Dunmore Press.

Deely, J.J and Trainor, Luke. 1981. Surveying voting behaviour in New Zealand: Papanui, 1978. *Political Science.* **33**:1, July, 20-32.

Douglas, Bronwen. 1979. Rank, power, authority: A reassessment of traditional leadership in South Pacific societies. *The Journal of Pacific History*. **14**:1, 2-27.

Easton, Brian. 1978. The class of New Zealand social science: A review of social class in New Zealand. *Australia and New Zealand Journal of Sociology*. **14**:2, June, 195-7.

Epstein, A.L. 1969. The network and urban social organisation. J. Clyde. Mitchell. (ed.) *Social networks in urban situations: Analyses of personal relationships in Central African towns*. Manchester: Manchester University Press.

Fleras, A. 1980b. From village runanga to the New Zealand Maori Wardens Association: A historical development of Maori Wardens. Wellington: Maori Studies Section, Department of Anthropology and Maori, Victoria University.

Fleras, A. 1985a. From social control toward political self-determination? Maori seats and the politics of separate Maori representation in New Zealand. *Canadian Journal of Political Science*. **18**:3, September.

Fleras, A. 1985b. Toward 'Tu Tangata': Historical development and current trends in Maori policy and administration. *Political Science*. **37**:1, 18-39.

Fleras, A. 1986. The politics of Maori lobbying: The case of the New Zealand Maori Council. *Political Science*. **38**:1, July, 27-43.

Forster, John. 1975. The social position of the Maori. E. Schwimmer. (ed.) *The Maori people in the nineteen-sixties: A symposium*. Auckland: Longman Paul, (lst ed. 1968).

Fox, Richard G., Aull, Charlotte, H. and Cimino, Louis F. 1981. Ethnic nationalism and the welfare state. Charles F. Keyes. (ed.) *Ethnic change*. Seattle: University of Washington Press.

Frame, Alex. 1981. Colonising attitudes towards Maori custom. *The New Zealand Law Journal*. **5**:17, March, 105-10.

Friedkin, Noah. 1980. A test of structural features of Granovetter's strength of weak ties theory. *Social Networks*. **2**, 411-22.

Geertz, Clifford. 1963. The integrated revolution. Clifford Geertz. (ed.) *Old societies and new societies*. Chicago: The Free Press.

Gough, Barry M. 1983. Maori and Pakeha in New Zealand historiography: Preoccupations and progressions. *Albion*. **14**:4, Winter, 337-41.

Gough, P.A. and Brunk, G.G. 1981a. Are economic conditions really important for New Zealand elections?. *Political Science*. **33**:1, July.

Gough, P.A. and Brunk, G.G. 1981b. A Re-examination of the relationships between economic conditions and elections. *Political Science*. **33**:2, December.

Graham, Jeanine. 1981. Settler society. W. H. Oliver with B. R. Williams. (eds.) *The Oxford history of New Zealand*. Oxford/ Wellington: The Clarendon Press/ Oxford University Press.

Granovetter, M. 1976. Network sampling: Some first steps. *American Journal of Sociology*. **81**:6, 1287-303.

Granovetter, M. 1977. The strength of weak ties. S. Leinhardt. (ed.) *Social networks: A developing paradigm*. New York: Academic Press, 347-70 (also *American Journal of Sociology*. 1973, **78**, 1360-80).

Green, Vera M. 1981. Blacks in the United States: The creation of an enduring people? G.P Castile and G. Kushner. (eds.) *Persistent peoples: Cultural enclaves in perspective*. Tucson, Ariz.: University of Arizona Press.

Greenland, H. 1984. Ethnicity as ideology: The critique of Pakeha society. P. Spoonley et al. (eds.) *Tauiwi. Racism and Ethnicity in New Zealand*. Palmerston North: Dunmore Press.

Harries-Jones, P. 1969. 'Home-boy' ties and political organisation in a Copperbelt township. J. Clyde. Mitchell. (ed.) *Social networks in urban situations: Analyses of personal relationships in Central African towns*. Manchester: Manchester University.

Haughey, E.J. 1979. The Maori Affairs Bill - its historical background. *New Zealand Law Journal*. 12, 246-50.

Hazlehurst, Kayleen M. 1985. Community care/ community responsibility: Community participation in criminal justice administration in New Zealand. K.M. Hazlehurst. (ed.) *Justice programs for Aboriginal and other indigenous communities*. Canberra: Australian Institute of Criminology.

Hazlehurst, Kayleen M. 1988a. Maori self-government 1945-1981: The New Zealand Maori Council and its antecedents. *British Review of New Zealand Studies*. 1, 64-98.

Hazlehurst, Kayleen M. [1993]. Ethnicity, ideology and social drama: The Waitangi Day incident 1981. A. Rogers and S. Vertovec. (eds.) *Urban context*. Oxford: Berg Publishers (in press).

Henderson, J.M. 1965. The Ratana movement. J.G.A. Pocock. (ed.) *The Maori and New Zealand politics*. Auckland: Blackwood and Janet Paul Ltd. (1st ed. 1962), 61-71.

Henderson, John. 1980. Muldoon and Rowling: A preliminary analysis of contrasting personalities. *Political Science*. 32:1, July, 26-46.

Hill, Craig and Brosnan, Peter. 1984. The occupational distribution of the major ethnic groups in New Zealand. *New Zealand Population Review*. 10:1, 33-42.

Hohepa, Pat. 1978. Maori and Pakeha: The one-people myth. Michael King (ed.) *Tihe Mauri Ora: Aspects of Maoritanga*. New Zealand: Methuen, 98-111.

Hunn, J.K. and Booth J.M. 1962. *The integration of Maori and Pakeha in New Zealand*. Study paper No. 1. Wellington: Department of Maori Affairs, New Zealand Government Printer.

Jackson, Michael D. 1975. Literacy, communications and social change. I.H. Kawharu. (ed.) *Conflict and compromise*. Wellington: A.H. and A.W. Reed.

Jackson, W.K. and Wood, G.A. 1964. The New Zealand parliament and Maori representation. *Historical studies: Australia and New Zealand*. 11.43, 383-96.

Jacobson, D. 1985. Boundary maintenance in support networks. *Social Networks*. 1:4, 341-51.

Jones, Pei Te Hurinui, 1975. Maori Kings. E. Schwimmer. (ed.) *The Maori people in the nineteen-sixties: A symposium*. Auckland: Longman Paul (1st ed. 1968).

Jones, Shane. 1990. Iwi and government. Peter McKinlay. (ed.) *Redistribution of power? Devolution in New Zealand*. Wellington: Victoria University Press for the Institute of Policy Studies, 64-78.

Kaai-Oldman, Tania. 1988. A history of New Zealand education from a Maori perspective. Walter Hirsh and Raymond Scott. (eds.) *Getting it right: Aspects of ethnicity and equity in New Zealand education*. Office of the Race Relations Conciliator. Auckland, 22-9.

Kapferer, B. 1969. Norms and the manipulation of relationships in a work context. J. Clyde. Mitchell. (ed.) *Social networks in urban situations: Analyses of personal relationships in Central African towns*. Manchester: Manchester University Press.

Karetu, Sam. 1977. Language and protocol of the marae. M. King. (ed.) *Te Ao Hurihui: The world moves on*. New Zealand: Hicks Smith/ Methuen (1st ed. 1975).

Kawharu, I.H. 1975b. Urban immigrants and Tangata Whenua. E. Schwimmer. (ed.) *The Maori people in the nineteen-sixties: A symposium*. Auckland: Longman Paul (1st ed. 1968), 174-86.

Kawharu, I.H. 1979. Land as Turangawaewae: Ngati Whatua's destiny at Orakei. K. Piddington. (ed.) *He Matapuna: Some Maori perspectives*. Wellington: New Zealand Planning Council, 53-8.

Kernot B. 1964. Maori - European relationships and the role of mediators. *Polynesian Society Journal*. Wellington: The Polynesian Society, **73**, 171-8.

Kernot, B. 1975. Maori strategies: Ethnic politics in New Zealand. S. Levine. (ed.) *New Zealand politics: A reader*. Melbourne: Chesire.

King, Michael. 1981. Between two worlds. W. H. Oliver with B. R. Williams. (eds.) *The Oxford history of New Zealand*. Oxford/ Wellington: The Clarendon Press/ Oxford University Press.

Lamare, James W. 1984. Party identification and voting behaviour in New Zealand. *Political Science*. **36**:1, July, 1-9.

Laumann, E.O. and Pappi, F.U. 1977. New directions in the study of community elites. S. Leinhardt. (ed.) *Social networks: A developing paradigm*. New York: Academic Press, 447-65 (also *American Sociological Review* 1973, **38**, 212-30).

Lebra, T.S. 1975. An alternative to reciprocity. *American Anthropologist*. **77**, 550-63.

Little, K.L. 1957. The role of voluntary associations in West African urbanization. *American Anthropologist*. **59**, 579-96.

Lopata, H.Z. 1967. The function of voluntary associations in an ethnic community: 'Polonia'. E. W. Burgess and D. J. Bogne. (eds.) *Urban Sociology*. Chicago, London: University of Chicago Press/ Phoenix Books (1st ed. 1964).

Lyons, Daniel. 1979. New Zealand. Alexander Mamak and Ahmed Ali. (eds.) *Race, class and rebellion in the South Pacific*. Sydney: George Allen and Unwin, 53-9.

Macpherson, Cluny. 1977. Polynesians in New Zealand: An emerging eth-class? David Pitt (ed.), *Social class in New Zealand*. Auckland: Longman Paul, 99-112.

Macpherson, Cluny. 1978. Reply to Easton. *Australia and New Zealand Journal of Sociology*. **14**:2, June, 199-200.

Macrae, John. 1978. Response to Easton. *Australia and New Zealand Journal of Sociology*. **14**:2, June, 198-9.

Mahuika, Api. 1977. Leadership: inherited and achieved. M. King. (ed.) *Te Ao Hurihui: The world moves on*. New Zealand: Hicks Smith/ Methuen (1st ed. 1975).

Mahuta, Robert. 1978. The Maori King Movement today. Michael King. (ed.) *Tihe Mauri Ora: Aspects of Maoritanga*. New Zealand: Methuen.

Mahuta, R.T. 1981a. Maori political representation: A case for change. E. Stokes (ed.) *Maori representation in Parliament*. Occasional paper No. 14. Hamilton: Centre for Maori Studies and Research, University of Waikato, 18-27.

Mahuta, R.T. 1981b. Talk to New Zealand Maori Council: Conference on future Maori development and legislation. University of Waikato, Centre for Maori Studies and Research.

Marsden, Maori. 1977. God, man and universe: A Maori view. M. King. (ed.) *Te Ao Hurihui: The world moves on*. New Zealand: Hicks Smith/ Methuen (1st ed. 1975).

Mayer, A.C. 1977. The significance of quasi-groups in the study of complex societies. S. Leinhardt. (ed.) *Social networks: A developing paradigm*. New York: Academic Press, (also in M. Banton (ed.) 1966 *The Social anthropology of complex societies*. London: A.S.A. Monographs 4, Tavistock Publications, 97-122).

McCraw, D., 1979. Social credit's role in the New Zealand Party System. *Political Science*. **31**:1, 54-60.

McCraw, D., 1983. Classifying the 1981 general election. *Political Science*. **35**:2, December, 190-7.

McEwen, J.M. 1967. Urbanisation and the multiracial society. R.H. Brookes and I.H. Kawharu. (eds.) *Administration in New Zealand's multiracial society*. Wellington: New Zealand Institute of Public Administration, 75-84.

McFerson, Hazel M. 1979. 'Racial tradition' and comparative political analysis: Notes toward a theoretical framework. *Ethnic and Racial Studies*. **2**:4, 477-97.

McKay, James. 1982. An exploratory synthesis of primordial and mobilizationist approaches to ethnic phenomena. *Ethnic and Racial Studies*. **5**:4, 395-420.

McKay, James and Lewins, Frank. 1978. Ethnicity and the ethnic group: A conceptual analysis and reformulation. *Ethnic and Racial Studies*. **1**:4, 412-27.

Mackerras, Malcolm. 1988. Lange builds on his margin for defeat. *The Bulletin*, January 26.

Mackerras, Malcolm. [1991]. New Zealand Election. (unpublished paper)

McLeay, E.M. 1980. Political argument about representation: The case of the Maori seats. *Political Studies*. **28**:1, 43-62.

McRobie, Alan D. 1978. Ethnic representation: The New Zealand experience. Stephen Levine. (ed.) *Politics in New Zealand*. Sydney: George Allen and Unwin.

McRobie, Alan. 1981. Ethnic representation: The New Zealand experience. E. Stokes. (ed.) *Maori representation in Parliament*. Occasional paper No. 14. Hamilton: Centre for Maori Studies and Research, University of Waikato.

Metge, J. 1970. The Maori family. Stewart Houston. (ed.) *Marriage and the family in New Zealand*. Wellington: Sweet and Maxwell, 111-41.

Miles, R. and Spoonley, P. 1985. The political economy of labour migration: An alternative to the sociology of 'race' and 'ethnic relations' in New Zealand. *The Australia and New Zealand Journal of Sociology*. **21**:1, March, 3-26.

Mitchell, J. Clyde. 1951. A note on the urbanization of Africans on the Copperbelt. *Rhodes-Livingstone Journal*. **12**.

Mitchell, J. Clyde. 1970. Tribe and social change in South Central Africa: A situational approach. *Journal of Asian and African Studies*. Canada: York University, **5**, 1-2.

Nagata, Judith. 1981. In defense of ethnic boundaries: The changing myths of charters of Malay identity. Charles F. Keyes. (ed.) *Ethnic change*. Seattle: University of Washington Press.

Ngata, Apirana T. 1940. Tribal organisation. 'I.L.G. Sutherland. (ed.) *The Maori people today.* Auckland: Whitcombe and Tombs.

Okamura, Jonathan Y. 1981. Situational ethnicity. *Ethnic and Racial Studies.* 4:4, 452-65.

Orbell, Margaret. 1978. The traditional Maori family. P.G. Koopman-Boyden. (ed.) *Families in New Zealand society.* Wellington: Methuen, 104-19.

Paine, Robert. 1974. Second thoughts about Barth's Models, Occasional paper No. 32. London: Royal Anthropological Institute of Great Britain and Ireland.

Paul, Maanu. 1981. Lecture on Maori politics. Delivered at Auckland University, 30 June, (unpublished).

Pearce, Neil E., Davis, Peter B., Smith, Allan H. and Foster, Frank H. 1984. Mortality and social class in New Zealand III: Male mortality by ethnic group. *The New Zealand Medical Journal.* 97:748, 25 January, 31-5.

Pearson, David. 1976. Directions in ethnic relations research: Britain and New Zealand in comparative perspective. *Australia and New Zealand Journal of Sociology.* 12:2, June, 107-11.

Pearson, David. 1984. The ethnic revival in New Zealand: A theoretical agenda. *Political Science.* 36:2, December, 96-111.

Pearson, David. 1985. The political economy of labour migration in New Zealand: A reply to Miles and Spoonley. *Australia and New Zealand Journal of Sociology.* 21:2, July, 269-74.

Pitt, David. 1978. Reply to Brian Easton's review. *Australia and New Zealand Journal of Sociology.* 14:2, June, 197-8.

Puketapu, I.P. 1982. Reform from within? C. Burns. (ed.) *The Path to Reform.* Wellington: New Zealand Institute of Public Administration, 40-61.

Rangihau, John 1977. Being Maori. Michael King. (ed.) *Te Ao Hurihuri. The world moves on: Aspects of Maoritanga.* Auckland: Hicks Smith/ Methuen (1st ed. 1975), 165-75.

Raureti, Moana. 1978. The origins of the Ratana movement. Michael King. (ed.) *Tihe Mauri Ora: Aspects of Maoritanga.* New Zealand: Methuen.

Ritchie, James E. 1965. The grass roots of Maori politics. J.G.A. Pocock. (ed.) *The Maori and New Zealand politics.* Auckland: Blackwood and Janet Paul (1st ed. 1962), 80-86.

Ritchie, Jane. 1961. Together or apart: A note on Maori residential preferences. *Journal of the Polynesian Society.* 70, 194-9.

Roberts, Nigel S., Walsh, Pat, and Sullivan, John. 1985. Political tolerance in New Zealand. *Australia and New Zealand Journal of Sociology.* 21:1, March, 82-99.

Rosenberg, W. 1977. Full employment: The fulcrum of social welfare. A.D. Trlin. (ed.) *Social welfare and New Zealand society.* Wellington: Methuen, 45-60.

Ross, Jeffrey A. 1982. Urban development and the politics of ethnicity: A conceptual approach. *Ethnic and Racial Studies.* 5:4, 440-56.

Ross, R.M. 1972. Te Tiriti O Waitangi: Texts and translations. *New Zealand Journal of History.* 6:2, October, 129-59.

Rowland, D.T. 1971. Maori migration to Auckland. *New Zealand Geographer.* 27, 21-37.

Rowland, D.T. 1972. Processes of Maori urbanisation. *New Zealand Geographer.* **28**, 1-22.

Rowland, D.T. 1974. The family status of Maoris in Auckland. *Australian Geographical Studies.* **12**, 27-37.

Sharples, Peter R. 1980. Our people today. Unpublished paper, Auckland.

Simpson, Alan C. 1981. Redistributing the Maori vote. E. Stokes. (ed.) *Maori representation in Parliament.* Occasional paper No. 14. Hamilton: Centre for Maori Studies and Research, University of Waikato, 28-52.

Simpson, Alan C. 1985. Redistributing the Maori vote: 1972-1984. Paper presented at the New Zealand Political Studies Association conference, University of Auckland, May.

Smith, Allan H. and Pearce, Neil E. 1984. Determinants of differences in mortality between New Zealand Maoris and non-Maoris aged 15-64. *The New Zealand Medical Journal.* **97**:749, February, 101-8.

Smith, Anthony D. 1979. Toward a theory of ethnic separatism. *Ethnic and Racial Studies.* **2**:1, 21-37.

Smith, J. 1970. Tapu removal in Maori religion. *Polynesian Society Memoir.* **40**, Wellington.

Smith, Susan J. 1984. Negotiating ethnicity in an uncertain environment. *Ethnic and Racial Studies.* **7**:3, 360-73.

Smolicz, J.J. 1983. Cultural alternatives in plural societies: Separatism or multiculturalism? *Journal of Intercultural Studies.* **3**, 47-68.

Sorrenson, M.P.K. 1986. A history of Maori representation in Parliament. *Report of the Royal Commission on the electoral system: 'Towards a better democracy'.* Wellington: New Zealand Government Printer.

Sorrenson, M.P.K. 1989. Towards a radical reinterpretation of New Zealand history: The role of the Waitangi Tribunal. I.H. Kawharu. (ed.) *Waitangi: Maori and Pakeha perspectives on the Treaty of Waitangi.* Auckland: Oxford University Press, 158-78.

Spicer, Edward H. 1971. Persistent cultural systems: A comparative study of identity systems that can adapt to contrasting environments. *Science.* **174**, 795-800.

Spoonley, P. 1982. Race relations. P. Spoonley et al. (eds.) *New Zealand: Sociological perspectives.* Palmerston North: Dunmore Press.

Spoonley, P. 1984. The politics of racism. P. Spoonley et al. (eds.) *Tauiwi: Racism and ethnicity in New Zealand.* Palmerston North: Dunmore Press.

Spread, Patrick. 1982. Blau's exchange theory, support and macrostructure. *The British Journal of Sociology.* **35**:2, June, 157-73.

Steven, Rob. 1978. Towards a class analysis of New Zealand. *Australia and New Zealand Journal of Sociology.* **14**:2, June, 113-48.

St George, Ross. 1980. The language skills of New Zealand Polynesian children: From deficiency to diversity. *Ethnic and Racial Studies.* **3**:1, January, 89-98.

Tarei, Wi. 1978. A church called Ringatu. Michael King. (ed.) *Tihe Mauri Ora: Aspects of Maoritanga.* Auckland: Methuen, 60-66.

Thompson, John L.P. 1983. The plural society approach to class and ethnic political mobilization. *Ethnic and racial studies.* **6**:2, April, 127-53.

Thompson, R.H.T. 1959. European attitudes to Maori: A projective approach. *Journal of the Polynesian Society*. **68**, 205-10.

Thompson, R.H.T. 1977. Race relations, social welfare and social justice. A.D. Trlin. (ed.) *Social welfare and New Zealand society*. Wellington: Methuen 154-65.

Tilly, Charles. 1979. Social movements and national politics. Working Paper No. 197. Ann Arbor, Center for Research on Social Organization, University of Michigan.

Trlin, A.D. 1979. Race, ethnicity, and society. R.J. Warwick and C. James O'Neill. (eds.) *The population of New Zealand. Interdisciplinary perspectives*. Auckland: Longman Paul, 185-212.

Trlin, A.D. 1982. The New Zealand Race Relations Act: Conciliators, conciliation and complaints (1972-1981). *Political Science*. **34**:2, December, 170-93.

Trosper, Ronald L. 1981. American Indian nationalism and frontier expansion. Charles F. Keyes. (ed.) *Ethnic change*. Seattle: University of Washington Press.

Tucker, Robert L. 1968. Theory of charismatic leadership. *Daedalus*. Summer, 731-56.

Van den Berghe, Pierre L. 1973. Pluralism. John J. Honigmann. (ed.) *Handbook of social and cultural anthropology*. Chicago: Rand McNally and Co., 959-77.

Vaughan, Graham M. 1978. Social change and intergroup preferences in New Zealand. *European Journal of Social Psychology*. **8**:3, July-September, 297-314.

Vaughan, G.M. and Thompson, R.H.T. 1961. New Zealand children's attitudes to Maoris. *Journal of Abnormal and Social Psychology*. **62**, 701-4.

Walker, Ranginui J. 1972a. Assimilation or cultural continuity. G. Vaughan. (ed.) *Racial issues in New Zealand*. Auckland: Akarana Press.

Walker, Ranginui J. 1972b. Urbanism and the cultural continuity of an ethnic minority: The Maori case. P. Baxter and B. Sansom. (eds.) *Race and social difference. Modern sociology readings*. Harmondsworth, England: Penguin, 399-410.

Walker, Ranginui J. 1975. The politics of voluntary association. I.H. Kawharu. (ed.) *Conflict and compromise*. Wellington: A.H. and A.W. Reed.

Walker, Ranginui J. 1979a. The urban Maori. K. Piddington. (ed.) *He Matapuna: Some Maori perspectives*. Wellington: New Zealand Planning Council, 31-42.

Walker, Ranginui J. (ed.) 1979b. Maori minority and the democratic process. J. Stephen Hoadley. (ed.) *Improving New Zealand's democracy*. Foundation for Peace Studies, Commission for the Future, Department of Political Studies, University of Auckland, 115-25.

Walker, Ranginui J. [ca 1979c]. Contemporary Maori society. Unpublished lecture. Auckland: Centre for Continuing Education, University of Auckland.

Walker, Ranginui J. [ca 1979d]. Matakite and the Maori Land March. Unpublished lecture, Auckland: Centre for Continuing Education, University of Auckland.

Walker, Ranginui J. [ca 1979e]. A summary of the history of Bastion Point. Unpublished lecture. Auckland: Centre for Continuing Education, Auckland University.

Walker, Ranginui J. 1980. Mana Motuhake, its origins and future. Auckland: Unpublished paper for Mana Motuhake, June.

Walker, Ranginui J. 1981a. Introduction to Maori society. unpublished lecture series. Auckland: Centre for Continuing Education, University of Auckland.

Walker, Ranginui J. 1981b. Perceptions and attitudes of the new generation of Maoris to Pakeha domination. unpublished lecture, Auckland: Centre for Continuing Education, University of Auckland.

Walker, Ranginui J. 1984a. The genesis of Maori activism. *Journal of Polynesian Society*. 1984. **93**:3, 267-281), Paper presented to the 15th Pacific Science Congress, Dunedin: 1-11 February 1983.

Walker Ranginui J. 1984b. The political development of the Maori people of New Zealand. paper presented to the Conference on Comparative Models of Political Development and Aboriginal Self-determination, Calgary, 16-17 March.

Walker, Ranginui. J. 1985. The Maori people: Their political development. Hyam Gold. (ed.) *New Zealand politics in perspective*. Auckland: Longman Paul.

Walker, Ranginui. J. 1989. The Treaty of Waitangi as the focus of Maori protest. I.H. Kawharu. (ed.) *Waitangi: Maori and Pakeha perspectives on the Treaty of Waitangi*. Auckland: Oxford University Press, 263-79.

Webber, Douglas C. 1978. Political leadership and succession in the National Party. S. Levine. (ed.) *Politics in New Zealand*. Sydney: George Allen and Unwin.

Webster, A.C. and Williams, L.Y. 1977. Family and community: Social welfare cults. A.D. Trlin. (ed.) *Social welfare and New Zealand society*. Wellington: Methuen, 78-105.

Weinrich, Peter. 1985. Rationality and irrationality in racial and ethnic relations: A metatheoretical framework. *Ethnic and Racial Studies*. **8**:4, October, 500-15.

Wellman, B. 1979. The community question: The intimate networks of East Yorkers. *American Journal of Sociology*. **84**:5, 1201-31.

Wellman, B. 1980. A guide to network analysis. Working paper No. 1A, Structural Analysis Programme. Toronto: Department of Sociology, University of Toronto, September.

Wellman, B. and Leighton, B. 1978. Networks, neighbourhoods and communities: Approaches to the study of the community question. Research Paper No. 97. Toronto: Centre for Urban and Community Studies, Dept of Sociology, University of Toronto, August (also in *Urban Affairs Quarterly* 1979, **14**, 363-90).

Wheeldon, P.D. 1969. The operation of voluntary associations and personal networks in the political process of an inter-ethnic community. J. Clyde. Mitchell. (ed.) *Social networks in urban situations: Analyses of personal relationships in Central African towns*. Manchester: Manchester University Press.

White, J.C., Boorman, S.A., and Breiger, R. 1976. Social structure from multiple networks: Blockmodels of roles and positions. *American Journal of Sociology*. **81**, 730-80.

Whitelaw, J.S. 1971. Migration patterns and residential selection in Auckland, New Zealand. *Australian Geographical Studies*. **9**, 61-76.

Williams, Brackette F. 1989. A class act: Anthropology and the race to nation across ethnic terrain. *Annual Review of Anthropology*. **18**, 401-44.

Williams, David V. 1989. Te Tiriti O Waitangi - unique relationship between Crown and Tangata Whenau? I.H. Kawharu. (ed.) *Waitangi: Maori and Pakeha perspectives on the Treaty of Waitangi*. Auckland: Oxford University Press, 64-91.

Winiata, Maharaia. 1956-57. Leadership in pre-European Maori society. *Polynesian Society Journal.* **65-66**, 212-31.

Wood, G.A. 1978. Race and politics in New Zealand. S. Levine. (ed.) *Politics in New Zealand.* London: George Allen and Unwin.

Yelvington, Kelvin A. 1991. Ethnicity as a practice? A comment on Bentley. *Comparative Studies in Society and History.* **33**:1, January, 158-68.

Yinger, J. Milton. 1981. Toward a theory of assimilation and dissimilation. *Ethnic and Racial Studies.* **4**:3, 249-64.

Yinger, J. Milton. 1983. Ethnicity and social change: The interaction of structural, cultural, and personality factors. *Ethnic and Racial Studies.* **6**:4, 395-409.

THESES, UNPUBLISHED MANUSCRIPTS AND PAPERS

Bean, Clive S. 1984. *A comparative study of electoral behaviour in Australia and New Zealand.* Canberra: Research School of Social Sciences, Australian National University. Doctoral thesis, Department of Political Science.

Bhagabati, A.C. 1967. *Social relations in a northland Maori community.* Auckland: University of Auckland, Doctoral thesis, Department of Anthropology.

Fleras, A.J. 1980a. *A descriptive analysis of Maori wardens in the historical and contemporary context of New Zealand society.* Wellington: Victoria University, Doctoral thesis, Department of Maori Studies.

Graham, J.S. 1972. *Social networks in Waiuku.* Auckland: University of Auckland, Master's thesis, Department of Anthropology.

Jackson, S.K. 1977. *Politics in the Eastern Maori electorate, 1928-69: An enquiry into Maori politics as a unique system.* Auckland: University of Auckland, Master's thesis, Department of Political Studies.

James, B.L. 1977. *The Maori Women's Welfare League: From social movement to voluntary association.* Hamilton: University of Waikato, Master's thesis, Department of Sociology.

Kernot, C.B.J. 1963. *Leadership amongst migrant Maoris.* Auckland: University of Auckland, Master's thesis, Department of Anthropology.

Orange, C.J. 1977. *A kind of equality: Labour and the Maori people 1935-1949.* Auckland: University of Auckland. Master's thesis, Department of History.

Tabacoff, D. 1972. *The role of the Maori M.P. in contemporary New Zealand politics.* Madison: University of Wisconsin. B.A. thesis.

Walker, R.J. 1970. *The social adjustment of the Maori to urban living in Auckland.* Auckland: University of Auckland. Doctoral thesis, Department of Anthropology.

Wayne, J., 1971. *Networks of informal participation in a suburban context.* University of Toronto. Doctoral thesis, Department of Sociology.

GOVERNMENT PUBLICATIONS

Community administration: Department of Maori Affairs paper on the Tu Tangata and Kokiri concepts. 1981. Wellington: Department of Maori Affairs.

Farming of Maori leasehold land: Report of the committee appointed to investigate problems associated with farming Maori leasehold. 1978. Wellington: Department of Maori Affairs, May.

Hansards. New Zealand Parliamentary Debates. 1968-1982. Wellington: Government Printer.

He Matapuna: Some Maori perspectives. Planning paper No. 14. 1979. Wellington: New Zealand Planning Council, December.

Hunn, J.K. 1961. *Report on the Department of Maori Affairs.* Wellington: Government Printer.

Ka Awatea: A Report of the Ministerial Planning Group. 1991. Wellington: Ministerial Planning Group, March.

Mead, S.M. (ed.) 1979. *He Ara Ki te Aomaarama: Finding a pathway to the future.* Planning paper No. 3, Wellington: New Zealand Planning Council, December.

New Zealand Census of Population and Dwellings 1960-1981. Auckland/ Wellington: Department of Statistics.

New Zealand Census of Population and Dwellings Personal Questionnaire Guide. 1981. Auckland/ Wellington: Department of Statistics, March.

New Zealand general elections and by-elections. 1949-1990. *Journals of the House of Representatives of New Zealand.* Wellington: Government Printer.

New Zealand Official Yearbooks. 1974-1989. Wellington: Department of Statistics.

1980 Parliamentary electoral roll revision. 1981. Wellington: Department of Justice.

Prichard, Ivor and Waetford, H.T. 1965. *Report of the Committee of Enquiry into the Laws Affecting Maori Land and the jurisdiction and powers of the Maori Land Court.* Wellington: Department of Maori Affairs.

Report and recommendations to the Prime Minister on representations regarding the proposed Springbok Rugby tour of New Zealand. 1981. Auckland: Human Rights Commission, 25 June.

Report of the Committee on Gangs. Report submitted to the Prime Minister by the Special Cabinet Committee for the Study of the Gang Situation in New Zealand. 1981. Wellington: April.

Rata, Hon. Matiu. 1975. *White Paper on Maori Affairs.* Wellington: Department of Maori Affairs (also reported in *Te Maori*, 1973, 6:1, December).

ARCHIVES, PRIVATE PAPERS
Auckland District Maori Council records and archives, Auckland:
Auckland District Maori Council minutes and correspondence, 1962-1981.

Mana Motuhake records and archives, Central Office, Auckland:
He Kaupapa Whakamaori I Nga Tari A Te Kawanatanga Na Te Mana Motuhake ('Institutional transformation of governing bodies to include Maoritanga from Mana Motuhake'). The Mana Motuhake Party's first official policy document, presented by Ranginiu Walker, to the Policy Hui, 27-28 March 1980, Te Tiriti O Waitangi Marae, adopted and released by the organisation, Waitangi: May 1980.

Mana Motuhake employment policy. Delivered at Tirahou Marae, Panmure: 17 June 1981.

Mana Motuhake, He Kaupapa Mo O Tatou Whenua, Land Policies. Report presented to the Whangarei Policy Hui, 3-4 May 1982.

Mana Motuhake Judicial Committee. Report presented to the Whangarei Policy Hui, 3-4 May 1980.

Mana Motuhake O Aotearoa (Inc.) Constitution and Rules. Adopted at a conference held at Waitahanui Marae, Taupo: 21-23 November 1980.

Mana Motuhake submission on the 1981 Electoral Amendment Bill. 11 September 1981.

Minutes and correspondence of the Mana Motuhake Party. Auckland: 1979-1981.

Nga Kaupapa O Mana Motuhake, Mana Motuhake Party Manifesto (first draft). Edited by Dr Ranginui Walker from policy documents of Mana Motuhake, October 1981.

Te Kaupapa O Mana Motuhake. Undated canvassing circular, 1981 election campaign.

Treaty of Waitangi Petition, to [Her] Majesty Queen Elizabeth II, Queen of New Zealand, Head of the Commonwealth, and Defender of the Faith from the Maori people whose ancestors signed the Treaty of Waitangi in 1840. Composed by Ranginui Walker, at the Mana Motuhake Policy Hui, 29 March 1981, Te Tiriti O Waitangi Marae, Waitangi (original document and notes dated 2 April 1981).

New Zealand and Pacific Department, Auckland Public Library, Auckland:

Governor Grey Collection. *Maori Parliament of New Zealand, First sitting at Waipatu 14 June 1892*. Te Waipatu Marae, Heretaunga.

New Zealand Maori Council records and archives, Wellington, and records of its chairman, Sir Graham Latimer, Paparoa:

A discussion paper on future Maori development and legislation. Legislative Review Committee of the New Zealand Maori Council. December 1980.

Looking towards the 1980s - submissions on the Maori Affairs Bill. New Zealand Maori Council submission to the Parliamentary Select Committee on Maori Affairs. Gisborne: May 1980.

Maori Land-Use National Conference, agenda and data papers. New Zealand Maori Council, Land-Use Advisory Council, Department of Maori Affairs, Centre for Continuing Education, Auckland University. Auckland: January 1981.

Maori representation in parliament. New Zealand Maori Council. Wellington: 9 June 1981.

Minutes and correspondence of the New Zealand Maori Council. Wellington: 1962-1981.

Nga Tumanako: National Conference of Maori Committees, New Zealand Maori Council. Evelyn Stokes. (ed.) University of Waikato, Centre for Maori Studies and Research. Hamilton: November 1978.

Policy statement on All Black tours to South Africa. New Zealand Maori Council. Wellington: 1969.

Report on the Treaty of Waitangi and Fisheries. New Zealand Maori Council government submission. October 1971.

The Treaty of Waitangi and parts of the current statutory law in contravention thereof. New Zealand Maori Council Report. Presented to the Minister of Maori Affairs, Hon. D. MacIntyre, and the Minister of Justice, Hon. D. Riddliford. Wellington: 4 October 1971.

New Zealand Police, Auckland Central Station, Auckland:
Policing of gangs. Report of the New Zealand Police, Jenkinson. Auckland: June 1981.

Ngata, Henry, private papers, Gisborne:
Murihiku choices for the land - Choices for the people. Proposals for the future of Maori lands in Murihiku Ngai Tahu Maori Trust Board. October 1980.
Submissions to the Parliamentary Select Committee on Maori Affairs. Proprietors of Mangatu Blocks. Gisborne: May 1980.

Rata, Matiu, private papers, Auckland:
Maori Policy Committee Report to the 56th Annual Labour Party Conference. Presented by Hon. Matiu Rata, 11 May 1972.
Submission to the Attorney-General, The Hon. J. McLay, on the pending charges and related issues arising from the Waitangi Day incident. By the Hon. Matiu Rata, president, Mana Motuhake O Aotearoa. Auckland: 29 May 1981.

University of Auckland Library newspaper files and Maori Organisations Newsletters files:
Maori Organisation on Human Rights (MOOHR) Manifesto. [ca. 1971].

Walker, Ranginui, private papers, Auckland:
An assessment of the New Zealand Maori Council and proposals for structural changes for the 1980s and beyond. Unpublished submission to the New Zealand Maori Council, by R.J. Walker, chairman, Auckland District Council, Auckland: June 1979.
'Korero' drafts, public issues column prepared for the *New Zealand Listener*, 1973-1981.
Memorial of Rights. Drafted and presented by Te Matakite to Prime Minister W. Rowling on 14 October, following the Te Roopu ote Matakite Land March on Parliament, September-October 1975.
Report of the Seminar on Fisheries for Maori Leaders. Centre for Continuing Education, University of Auckland, Auckland: August 1976.
Report of the Young Maori Leaders' Conference (four reports). Auckland University College, May 1939; Council of Adult Education, August 1959; Department of University Extension, August 1970; Centre for Continuing Education, September 1977, Auckland University, Auckland.
Submission on Maori representation. C.A.R.E. and A.C.O.R.D. (unpublished).
Submission to: Penal Policy Review Committee. Report by the Hoani Waititi Marae Committee. Auckland: June 1981.
Te Matakite Manifesto. Distributed September/ October 1975.
Te Roopu Ote Matakite land march on Parliament. September/ October 1975.
Waitangi Action/ Defence Committee Newsletter. Statements and leaflets, February-July 1981.

NEWSPAPERS, NEWSLETTERS, MAGAZINES AND EDITORIALS

'Korero', *New Zealand Listener,* Public issues column by Dr Ranginui J. Walker. Wellington 1973-1981.

Mana Motuhake Ki Tamaki. Newsletter, 1980.

Mana Motuhake O Aotearoa. Newsletter, September 1980-November 1981.

Maori Wardens News. Maori Wardens Association, Papatotoe: 1980-1981.

Nga Tamatoa. News bulletin, Nga Tamatoa Council. Ponsonby: 1971.

Takaparawha. News bulletin, Orakei Maori Committee Action Group. Bastion Point: 1977-1978.

Te Hokioi Maori Iwi. News bulletin. Wellington: 1968-1969.

Te Kaea. Department of Maori Affairs. Wellington: 1979-1982.

Te Kaunihera Maori. New Zealand Maori Council Magazine. Wellington: 1967-1969.

Te Manu Korero. Northern Maori Labour Party Newsletter. Auckland: 1981.

Te Maori. New Zealand Maori Council Magazine. Wellington: 1969-1981.

Te Matakite O Aotearoa. News bulletin, Te Matakite. Auckland/Wellington: 1975-1980.

Tu Tangata. New Zealand Maori Council magazine, Maori Women's Welfare League and Department of Maori Affairs. Wellington: 1981.

Auckland Star; Bay of Plenty Times; Canberra Times; The Dominion; Evening Post; National Business Review; New Zealand Herald; New Zealand Listener; New Zealand Peoples' Voice; New Zealand Times; Northern Advocate; Sunday News; Sun-Herald (Sydney); *Time Magazine; Waikato Times; Wanganui Chronicle; Western Leader.*

INDEX

About the Author

KAYLEEN M. HAZLEHURST is a Senior Lecturer in Cross-Cultural Studies in the Faculty of Arts, Queensland University of Technology, Australia. She is a fifth generation New Zealander, and has conducted extensive research on the Maori. Hazlehurst was employed for eight years as a Criminologist and Senior Criminologist at the Australian Institute of Criminology, Canberra, and has held policy and research positions with the National Aboriginal Conference and the Aboriginal Development Commission.